C/C++

PROGRAMMER'S REFERENCE
Second Edition

Herbert Schildt

D1316887

Osborne **McGraw-Hill**

Berkeley ▪ New York ▪ St. Louis ▪ San Francisco
Auckland ▪ Bogotá ▪ Hamburg ▪ London
Madrid ▪ Mexico City ▪ Milan ▪ Montreal
New Delhi ▪ Panama City ▪ Paris ▪ São Paulo
Singapore ▪ Sydney ▪ Tokyo ▪ Toronto

Osborne/**McGraw-Hill**
2600 Tenth Street
Berkeley, California 94710
U.S.A.

For information on translations or book distributors outside the U.S.A., or to
arrange bulk purchase discounts for sales promotions, premiums, or
fund-raisers, please contact Osborne/**McGraw-Hill** at the above address.

C/C++ Programmer's Reference, Second Edition

1234567890 DOC DOC 019876543210

ISBN 0-07-212706-6

Publisher   Brandon A. Nordin
Vice President and Associate Publisher   Scott Rogers
Acquisitions Editor   Megg Bonar
Project Editor   Lisa Theobald
Acquisitions Coordinators   Stephane Thomas, Cindy Wathen
Technical Editor   Greg Guntle
Copy Editor   Dennis Weaver
Proofreaders   Linda Medoff, Paul Medoff
Indexer   Sheryl Schildt
Computer Designers   Jani Beckwith, E. A. Pauw
Illustrator   Michael Mueller
Series Design   Peter Hancik

This book was composed with Corel VENTURA™ Publisher.

About the Author

Herbert Schildt is a leading authority on C and C++ and was a member of the ANSI/ISO committees that standardized C and C++. His books have sold more that 2.5 million copies worldwide and have been translated into all major foreign languages. He is the author of *C: The Complete Reference*, *C++: The Complete Reference*, *C++ from the Ground Up*, and many other best-sellers, including *Windows 2000 Programming from the Ground Up* and *MFC Programming from the Ground Up*. He is also the co-author of *Java 2: The Complete Reference*.

CONTENTS

3   Operators 39

4   The Preprocessor and Comments 55

---

5   Keyword Summary 67

---

8 The C Mathematical Functions 155

---

16 The C++ Standard Template Library 293

C and C++ are the world's most important programming languages. Indeed, to be a professional programmer today implies proficiency in these two languages. They are the foundation upon which modern programming is built.

C was invented by Dennis Ritchie in the 1970s. C is a middle-level language. It combines the control structures of a high-level language with the ability to manipulate bits, bytes, and pointers (addresses). Thus, C gives the programmer nearly complete control over the machine. C was first standardized late in 1989 when the American National Standards Institute (ANSI) standard for C was adopted. This version of C is commonly referred to as C89. This standard was also adopted by ISO (International Standards Organization). C89 was amended slightly in 1995.

C++ was created by Bjarne Stroustrup, beginning in 1979. The development and refinement of C++ was a major effort, spanning the 1980s and most of the 1990s. Finally, in 1998 an ANSI/ISO standard for C++ was adopted. In general terms, C++ is the object-oriented version of C. C++ is built upon the foundation of C89, including its 1995 amendments. In fact, the version of C defined by C89 is commonly referred to as the "C subset of C++." Although C++ began as a set of object-oriented extensions to C, it soon expanded into being a programming language in its own right. Today, C++ is nearly twice the size of the C language. Needless to say, C++ is one of the most powerful computer languages ever devised.

In 1999, a new ANSI/ISO standard for C was adopted. This version is called C99. It includes a number of refinements and several new features. Some of these "new" features were borrowed from C++, but some are entirely new innovations. Thus, several of the elements added by C99 are incompatible with C++. This means that with the advent of C99, Standard C is no longer a pure subset of C++. Fortunately, many of the incompatibilities relate to special-use features that are readily avoided. Thus, it is still easy to write code that is compatible with both C and C++. At the time of this writing, no major compiler currently accepts all of the C99 additions, but this is sure to change.

The following table synopsizes the relationships between C89, C99, and C++.

C89   The original ANSI/ISO standard for C. C89 is what most
             programmers today think of as C.
C++   The object-oriented version of C. The current ANSI/ISO
             standard for C++ is built upon C89. Thus, C89 forms a
             subset of C++.
C99   The latest standard for C. Includes all of C89, but adds
             several new features. Some of the new features are not
             supported by the current standard for C++.

The material in this book describes C89, C99, and C++. When a
feature is unique to one of these, it will be so flagged. Otherwise,
you can assume that the feature applies to all three.

As you are undoubtedly aware, C and C++ are large topics. It is, of
course, not possible to cover every aspect of these important
languages here. Instead, this quick reference distills their most
salient features into a convenient and easy to use form.

Chapter 1
Data Types, Variables, and Constants

C and C++ offer the programmer a rich assortment of built-in data types. Programmer-defined data types can be created to fit virtually any need. Variables can be created for any valid data type. Also, it is possible to specify constants of C/C++'s built-in types. In this section, various features relating to data types, variables, and constants are discussed.

The Basic Types

C89 defines the following elemental data types:

Type	Keyword
Character	char
Integer	int
Floating point	float
Double floating point	double
Valueless	void

To these, C99 adds the following:

Type	Keyword
Boolean (true/false)	_Bool
Complex	_Complex
Imaginary	_Imaginary

C++ defines the following basic types:

Type	Keyword
Boolean (true/false)	bool
Character	char
Integer	int
Floating point	float

Type	Keyword
Double floating point	double
Valueless	void
Wide character	wchar_t

As you can see, all versions of C and C++ provide the following five basic types: **char**, **int**, **float**, **double**, and **void**. Also notice that the keyword for the Boolean type is **bool** in C++ and **_Bool** in C99. No Boolean type is included in C89.

Several of the basic types can be modified using one or more of these type modifiers:

- signed
- unsigned
- short
- long

The type modifiers precede the type name that they modify. The basic arithmetic types, including modifiers, allowed by C and C++ are shown in the following table along with their guaranteed minimum ranges. Most compilers will exceed the minimums for one or more types. Also, if your computer uses two's complement arithmetic (as most do), then the smallest negative value that can be stored by a signed integer will be one more than the minimums shown. For example, the range of an **int** for most computers is −32,768 to 32,767. Whether type **char** is signed or unsigned is implementation dependent.

Type	Minimum Range
char	−127 to 127 or 0 to 255
unsigned char	0 to 255
signed char	−127 to 127
int	−32,767 to 32,767
unsigned int	0 to 65,535
signed int	same as int
short int	same as int
unsigned short int	0 to 65,535
signed short int	same as short int

Type	Minimum Range
long int	−2,147,483,647 to 2,147,483,647
signed long int	same as long int
unsigned long int	0 to 4,294,967,295
long long int	$-(2^{63}-1)$ to $2^{63}-1$ (C99 only)
signed long long int	same as long long int (C99 only)
unsigned long long int	0 to $2^{64}-1$ (C99 only)
float	6 digits of precision
double	10 digits of precision
long double	10 digits of precision
wchar_t	same as unsigned int

When a type modifier is used by itself, **int** is assumed. For example, you can specify an unsigned integer by simply using the keyword **unsigned**. Thus, these declarations are equivalent.

```
unsigned int i; // here, int is specified
unsigned i; // here, int is implied
```

Declaring Variables

All variables must be declared prior to use. Here is the general form of a declaration:

> *type variable_name*;

For example, to declare **x** to be a **float**, **y** to be an integer, and **ch** to be a character, you would write

```
float x;
int y;
char ch;
```

You can declare more than one variable of a type by using a comma-separated list. For example, the following statement declares three integers:

```
int a, b, c;
```

Initializing Variables

A variable can be initialized by following its name with an equal sign and an initial value. For example, this declaration assigns **count** an initial value of 100:

```
int count = 100;
```

An initializer can be any expression that is valid when the variable is declared. This includes other variables and function calls. However, in C, global variables and **static** local variables must be initialized using only constant expressions.

Identifiers

Variable, function, and user-defined type names are all examples of *identifiers*. In C/C++, identifiers are sequences of letters, digits, and underscores from one to several characters in length. (A digit cannot begin a name, however.)

Identifiers may be of any length. However, not all characters will necessarily be significant. There are two types of identifiers: external and internal. An external identifier will be involved in an external link process. These identifiers, called *external names*, include function names and global variable names that are shared between files. If the identifier is not used in an external link process, it is internal. This type of identifier is called an *internal name* and includes the names of local variables, for example. In C89, at least the first 6 characters of an external identifier and at least the first 31 characters of an internal identifier will be significant. C99 has increased these values. In C99, an external identifier has at least 31 significant characters and an internal identifier has at least 63 significant characters. In C++, at least the first 1,024 characters of an identifier are significant.

The underscore is often used for clarity, such as **first_time**, or to begin a name, such as **_count**. Uppercase and lowercase are different. For example, **test** and **TEST** are two different variables. C/C++ reserves all identifiers that begin with two underscores, or an underscore followed by an uppercase letter.

Classes

The *class* is C++'s basic unit of encapsulation. A class is defined
using the **class** keyword. Classes are not part of the C language.
A class is essentially a collection of variables and functions that
manipulate those variables. The variables and functions that form a
class are called *members*. The general form of **class** is shown here:

```
class class-name : inheritance-list {
  // private members by default
protected:
  // private members that can be inherited
public:
  // public members
} object-list;
```

Here, *class-name* is the name of the class type. Once the class
declaration has been compiled, the *class-name* becomes a new
type name that can be used to declare objects of the class. The
object-list is a comma-separated list of objects of type *class-name*.
This list is optional. Class objects can be declared later in your
program by simply using the class name. The *inheritance-list* is
also optional. When present, it specifies the base class or classes
that the new class inherits. (See the following section entitled
"Inheritance.")

A class can include a *constructor function* and a *destructor function*.
(Either or both are optional.) A constructor is called when an object
of the class is first created. The destructor is called when an object
is destroyed. A constructor has the same name as the class. A
destructor function has the same name as the class, but is preceded
by a ~ (tilde). Neither constructors nor destructors have return
types. In a class hierarchy, constructors are executed in order of
derivation and destructors are executed in reverse order.

By default, all elements of a class are private to that class and
can be accessed only by other members of that class. To allow
an element of the class to be accessed by functions that are not

members of the class, you must declare them after the keyword **public**, for example:

```
class myclass {
  int a, b; // private to myclass
public:
  // class members accessible by nonmembers
  void setab(int i, int j) { a = i; b = j; }
  void showab() { cout << a << ' ' << b << endl; }
} ;


myclass ob1, ob2;
```

This declaration creates a class type, called **myclass**, that contains two private variables, **a** and **b**. It also contains two public functions called **setab( )** and **showab( )**. The fragment also declares two objects of type **myclass** called **ob1** and **ob2**.

To allow a member of a class to be inherited, but to otherwise be private, specify it as **protected**. A protected member is available to derived classes, but is unavailable outside its class hierarchy.

When operating on an object of a class, use the dot (.) operator to reference individual members. The arrow operator (–>) is used when accessing an object through a pointer. For example, the following accesses the **putinfo( )** function of **ob** using the dot operator and the **show( )** function using the arrow operator:

```
struct cl_type {
  int x;
  float f;
public:
  void putinfo(int a, float t) { x = a; f = t; }
  void show() { cout << a << ' ' << f << endl; }
} ;


cl_type ob, *p;

// ...

ob.putinfo(10, 0.23);

p = &ob; // put ob's address in p

p->show(); // displays ob's data
```

It is possible to create generic classes by using the **template** keyword. (See **template** in the keyword summary in Chapter 5.)

Inheritance

In C++, one class can inherit the characteristics of another. The inherited class is usually called the *base class*. The inheriting class is referred to as a *derived class*. When one class inherits another, a *class hierarchy* is formed. The general form for inheriting a class is

```
class class-name : access base-class-name {
  // . . .
} ;
```

Here, *access* determines how the base class is inherited and it must be either **private, public,** or **protected**. (It can also be omitted, in which case **public** is assumed if the derived class is a **struct,** or **private** if the derived class is a **class**.) To inherit more than one class, use a comma-separated list.

If *access* is **public**, all **public** and **protected** members of the base class become **public** and **protected** members of the derived class, respectively. If *access* is **private**, all **public** and **protected** members of the base class become **private** members of the derived class. If *access* is **protected**, all **public** and **protected** members of the base class become **protected** members of the derived class.

In the following class hierarchy, **derived** inherits **base** as private. This means that **i** becomes a private member of **derived**.

```
class base {
public:
  int i;
};

class derived : private base {
  int j;
public:
  derived(int a) { j = i = a; }
  int getj() { return j; }
  int geti() { return i; } // OK, derived has access to i
};
```

```
derived ob(9); // create a derived object

cout << ob.geti() << " " << ob.getj(); // OK

// ob.i = 10; // ERROR, i is private to derived!
```

Structures

A structure is created using the keyword **struct**. In C++, a *structure* also defines a class. The only difference between **class** and **struct** is that, by default, all members of a structure are public. To make a member private, you must use the **private** keyword. The general form of a structure declaration is like this:

```
struct struct-name : inheritance-list {
  // public members by default
protected:
  // private members that can be inherited
private:
  // private members
} object-list;
```

In C, several restrictions apply to structures. First, they may contain only data members; member functions are not allowed. C structures do not support inheritance. Also, all members are public and the keywords **public**, **protected**, and **private** are not allowed.

Unions

A *union* is a class type in which all data members share the same memory location. In C++, a union may include both member functions and data. In a union, all of its members are public by default. To create private elements, you must use the **private** keyword. The general form for declaration of a **union** is

```
union class-name {
  // public members by default
private:
```

```
    // private members
    } object-list;
```

In C, unions may contain only data members and the **private** keyword is not supported.

The elements of a union overlay each other. For example,

```
union tom {
    char ch;
    int x;
} t;
```

declares union **tom**, which looks like this in memory (assuming 2-byte integers):

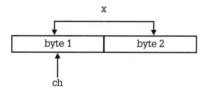

Like a class, the individual variables that comprise the union are referenced using the dot operator. The arrow operator is used with a pointer to a union.

There are several restrictions that apply to unions. First, a union cannot inherit any other class of any type. A union cannot be a base class. A union cannot have virtual member functions. No members may be declared as static. A union cannot have as a member any object that overloads the = operator. Finally, no object can be a member of a union if the object's class explicitly defines a constructor or destructor function. (Objects that have only the default constructors and destructors are acceptable.)

There is a special type of union in C++ called an *anonymous union*. An anonymous union declaration does not contain a class name and no objects of that union are declared. Instead, an anonymous union simply tells the compiler that its member variables are to share the same memory location. However, the variables themselves are referred to directly, without using the normal dot or arrow operator syntax. The variables that make up an anonymous union are at the same scope level as any other variable declared within

> ➤ **Programming Tip**

In C++, it is common practice to use **struct** when creating
C-style structures that include only data members. A **class**
is usually reserved for creating classes that contain function
members. Sometimes the acronym POD is used to describe a
C-style structure. POD stands for Plain Old Data.

the same block. This implies that the union variable names must
not conflict with any other names valid within their scope. For
example, here is an anonymous union:

```
union { // anonymous union
  int a;   // a and f share
  float f; // the same memory location
};

// ...

a = 10; // access a
cout << f; // access f
```

Here, **a** and **f** both share the same memory location. As you can
see, the names of the union variables are referred to directly
without the use of the dot or arrow operator.

All restrictions that apply to unions in general apply to anonymous
unions. In addition, anonymous unions must contain only data—no
member functions are allowed. Anonymous unions may not contain
the **private** or **protected** keywords. Finally, an anonymous union
with namespace scope must be declared as **static**.

Enumerations

Another type of variable that can be created is called an
enumeration. An enumeration is a list of named integer constants.
Thus, an enumeration type is simply a specification of the list of
names that belong to the enumeration.

1

To create an enumeration requires the use of the keyword **enum**. The general form of an enumeration type is

enum *enum-name* { *list of names* } *var-list*;

The *enum-name* is the enumeration's type name. The list of names is comma separated.

For example, the following fragment defines an enumeration of cities called **cities** and the variable **c** of type **cities**. Finally, **c** is assigned the value "Houston".

```
enum cities { Houston, Austin, Amarillo} c;
c = Houston;
```

In an enumeration, the value of the first (leftmost) name is, by default, 0; the second name has the value 1; the third has the value 2; and so on. In general, each name is given a value one greater than the name that precedes it. You can give a name a specific value by adding an initializer. For example, in the following enumeration, **Austin** will have the value 10:

```
enum cities { Houston, Austin=10, Amarillo };
```

In this example, **Amarillo** will have the value 11 because each name will be one greater than the one that precedes it.

C Tags

In C, the name of a structure, union, or enumeration does not define a complete type name. In C++, it does. For example, the following fragment is valid for C++, but not for C:

```
struct s_type {
  int i;
  double d;
};
// ...
s_type x; // OK for C++, but not for C
```

In C++, **s_type** defines a complete type name and can be used, by itself, to declare objects. In C, **s_type** defines a *tag*, which is not a complete type specifier. In C, you need to precede a tag name with either **struct**, **union**, or **enum** when declaring objects. For example,

```
struct s_type x; // now OK for C
```

The preceding syntax is also permissible in C++, but seldom used.

The Storage Class Specifiers

The type modifiers **extern**, **auto**, **register**, **static**, and **mutable** are used to alter the way C/C++ creates storage for variables. These specifiers precede the type that they modify.

extern

If the **extern** modifier is placed before a variable name, the compiler will know that the variable has external linkage. External linkage means that an object is visible outside its own file. In essence, **extern** tells the compiler the type of a variable without actually allocating storage for it. The **extern** modifier is most commonly used when there are two or more files sharing the same global variables.

auto

auto tells the compiler that the local variable it precedes is created upon entry into a block and destroyed upon exit from a block. Since all variables defined inside a function are **auto** by default, the **auto** keyword is seldom (if ever) used.

register

When C was first invented, the **register** modifier could be used only on local integer, character, or pointer variables because it caused the compiler to attempt to keep that variable in a register of the CPU instead of placing it in memory. This made all references to that variable extremely fast. The definition of **register** has since been expanded. Now, any variable may be specified as **register** and it is the compiler's job to optimize accesses to it. For characters, integers, and pointers, this still means putting them into a register in the CPU, but for other types of data, it may mean using cache memory, for example. Keep in mind that **register** is only a request. The compiler is free to ignore it. The reason for this is that only so many variables can be optimized for speed. When this limit is exceeded, the compiler will simply ignore further **register** requests.

static

The **static** modifier instructs the compiler to keep a local variable in existence during the lifetime of the program instead of creating and destroying it each time it comes into and goes out of scope. Therefore, making local variables **static** allows them to maintain their values between function calls.

The **static** modifier may also be applied to global variables. When this is done, it causes that variable's scope to be restricted to the file in which it is declared. This means that it will have internal linkage. Internal linkage means that an identifier is known only within its own file.

In C++, when **static** is used on a class data member, it causes only one copy of that member to be shared by all objects of its class.

mutable

The **mutable** specifier applies to C++ only. It allows a member of an object to override **const**ness. That is, a **mutable** member can be modified by a **const** member function.

Type Qualifiers

The type qualifiers provide additional information about the variables they precede.

const

Objects of type **const** cannot be changed by your program during execution. Also, an object pointed to by a **const** pointer cannot be modified. The compiler is free to place variables of this type into

> ## ➤ Programming Tip

If a class member function is modified by **const**, it cannot alter the object that invokes the function. To declare a **const** member function, put **const** after its parameter list. For example,

```
class MyClass {
  int i;
public:
  // a const function
  void f1(int a) const {
    i = a; // Error! can't modify invoking object
  }
  void f2(int a) {
    i = a; // OK, not const function
  }
};
```

As the comments suggest, **f1( )** is a **const** function and it cannot modify the object that invokes it.

read-only memory (ROM). A **const** variable will receive its value either from an explicit initialization or by some hardware-dependent means. For example,

```
const int a = 10;
```

will create an integer called **a** with a value of 10 that may not be modified by your program. It can, however, be used in other types of expressions.

volatile

The modifier **volatile** tells the compiler that a variable's value may be changed in ways not explicitly specified by the program. For example, a global variable's address may be passed to the clock routine of the operating system and updated with each clock tick. In this situation, the contents of the variable are altered without any explicit assignment statements in the program. This is important because compilers will sometimes automatically optimize certain expressions by making the assumption that the contents of a variable are unchanging inside an expression. This is done to achieve higher performance. The **volatile** modifier will prevent this optimization in those rare situations where this assumption is not the case.

restrict

C99 adds a new type qualifier called **restrict**. This qualifier applies only to pointers. A pointer qualified by **restrict** is initially the only means by which the object it points to can be accessed. Access to the object by another pointer can occur only if the second pointer is based on the first. Thus, access to the object is restricted to expressions based on the **restrict**-qualified pointer. Pointers qualified by **restrict** are primarily used as function parameters, or to point to memory allocated via **malloc( )**. The **restrict** qualifier does not change the semantics of a program. **restrict** is not supported by C++.

Arrays

You may declare arrays of any data type, including classes. The general form of a singly dimensioned array is

   type var-name[size];

where *type* specifies the data type of each element in the array and *size* specifies the number of elements in the array. For example, to declare an integer array **x** of 100 elements, you would write

```
int x[100];
```

This will create an array that is 100 elements long with the first element being 0 and the last being 99. For example, the following loop will load the numbers 0 through 99 into array **x**:

```
for(t=0; t<100; t++) x[t] = t;
```

Multidimensional arrays are declared by placing the additional dimensions inside additional brackets. For example, to declare a 10 × 20 integer array you would write

```
int x[10][20];
```

Arrays can be initialized by using a bracketed list of initializers. For example,

```
int count[5] = { 1, 2, 3, 4, 5 };
```

Defining New Type Names Using typedef

You can create a new name for an existing type using **typedef.** Its general form is

typedef *type newname*;

For example, the following tells the compiler that **feet** is another name for **int**:

```
typedef int feet;
```

Now, the following declaration is perfectly legal and creates an integer variable called **distance**:

```
feet distance;
```

Constants

Constants, also called *literals*, refer to fixed values that cannot be altered by the program. Constants can be of any of the basic data types. The way each constant is represented depends upon its type. Character constants are enclosed between single quotes. For example 'a' and '+' are both character constants. Integer constants are specified as numbers without fractional components. For example, 10 and −100 are integer constants. Floating-point constants require the use of the decimal point followed by the number's fractional component. For example, 11.123 is a floating-point constant. You may also use scientific notation for floating-point numbers.

There are two floating-point types: **float** and **double**. Also, there are several flavors of the basic types that are generated using the type modifiers. By default, the compiler fits a numeric constant into the smallest compatible data type that will hold it. The only exceptions to the smallest-type rule are floating-point constants, which are assumed to be of type **double**. For many programs, the compiler defaults are perfectly adequate. However, it is possible to specify precisely the type of constant you want.

To specify the exact type of numeric constant, use a suffix. For floating-point types, if you follow the number with an **F**, the number is treated as a **float**. If you follow it with an **L**, the number becomes a **long double**. For integer types, the **U** suffix stands for **unsigned** and the **L** for **long**. Some examples are shown next:

Data Type	Constant Examples
int	1 123 21000 −234
long int	35000L −34L
unsigned int	10000U 987U
float	123.23F 4.34e−3F
double	123.23 12312333 −0.9876324
long double	1001.2L

C99 also allows you to specify a **long long** integer constant by specifying the suffix **LL** (or **ll**).

Hexadecimal and Octal Constants

It is sometimes easier to use a number system based on 8 or 16 instead of 10. The number system based on 8 is called *octal* and uses the digits 0 through 7. In octal, the number 10 is the same as 8 in decimal. The base 16 number system is called *hexadecimal* and uses the digits 0 through 9 plus the letters A through F, which stand for 10, 11, 12, 13, 14, and 15. For example, the hexadecimal number 10 is 16 in decimal. Because of the frequency with which these two number systems are used, C/C++ allows you to specify integer constants in hexadecimal or octal instead of decimal if you prefer. A hexadecimal constant must begin with a 0x (a zero followed by an x) or 0X, followed by the constant in hexadecimal form. An octal constant begins with a zero. Here are two examples:

```
int hex = 0x80;  // 128 in decimal
int oct = 012;   // 10 in decimal
```

String Constants

C/C++ supports one other type of constant in addition to those of the predefined data types: a *string*. A string is a set of characters enclosed by double quotes. For example, "this is a test" is a string. You must not confuse strings with characters. A single-character constant is enclosed by single quotes, such as 'a'. However, "a" is a string containing only one letter. String constants are automatically null terminated by the compiler. C++ also supports a **string** class, which is described later in this book.

Boolean Constants

C++ specifies two Boolean constants: **true** and **false**.

C99, which adds the **_Bool** type to C, does not specify any built-in Boolean constants. However, if your program includes the header **<stdbool.h>**, then the macros **true** and **false** are defined. Also, including **<stdbool.h>** causes the macro **bool** to be defined as another name for **_Bool**. Thus, it is possible to create code that is compatible with both C99 and C++. Remember, however, that C89 does not define a Boolean type.

Complex Constants

In C99, if you include the header **<complex.h>**, then the following complex and imaginary constants are defined.

_Complex_I	(const float _Complex) *i*
_Imaginary_I	(const float _Imaginary) *i*
I	_Imaginary_I (or _Complex_I if imaginary types are not supported)

Here, *i* represents the imaginary value, which is the square root of −1.

Backslash Character Constants

Enclosing character constants in single quotes works for most printing characters, but a few, such as the carriage return, are impossible to enter into your program's source code from the keyboard. For this reason, C/C++ recognizes several *backslash character constants*, also called *escape sequences*. These constants are listed here:

Code	Meaning
\b	Backspace
\f	Form feed
\n	Newline
\r	Carriage return
\t	Horizontal tab
\"	Double quote
\'	Single quote
\ \	Backslash
\v	Vertical tab
\a	Alert
\N	Octal constant (where N is an octal constant)
\xN	Hexadecimal constant (where N is a hexadecimal constant)
\?	Question mark

The backslash constants can be used anywhere a character can. For example, the following statement outputs a newline and a tab and then prints the string "This is a test".

```
cout << "\n\tThis is a test";
```

Chapter 2
Functions, Scopes, Namespaces, and Headers

Functions are the building blocks of a C/C++ program. The elements of a program, including functions, exist within one or more scopes. In C++, there is a special scope called a *namespace*. The prototypes for all standard functions are declared within various headers. These topics are examined here.

Functions

At the heart of a C/C++ program is the function. It is the place in which all program activity occurs. The general form of a function is

```
ret-type function_name (parameter list)
{
   body of function
}
```

The type of data returned by a function is specified by *ret-type*. The *parameter list* is a comma-separated list of variables that will receive any arguments passed to the function. For example, the following function has two integer parameters called **i** and **j** and a **double** parameter called **count**:

```
void f(int i, int j, double count)
{ ...
```

Notice that you must declare each parameter separately.

In C89, if a function's return type is not explicitly specified, it defaults to **int**. C++ and C99 do not support "default-to-int", although most compilers will still allow it.

Functions terminate and return automatically to the calling procedure when the last brace is encountered. You may force a return prior to that by using the **return** statement.

All functions, except those declared as **void**, return a value. The type of the return value must match the type declaration of the function. Values are returned via the **return** statement.

In C++, it is possible to create generic functions using the keyword **template**. (See **template** in Chapter 5.)

Recursion

In C/C++, functions can call themselves. This is called *recursion*, and a function that calls itself is said to be *recursive*. A simple example is the function **factr( )** shown here, which computes the factorial of an integer. The factorial of a number N is the product of all the whole numbers from 1 to N. For example, 3 factorial is $1 \times 2 \times 3$, or 6.

```
// Compute the factorial of a number using recursion.
int factr(int n)
{
  int answer;

  if(n==1) return 1;
  answer = factr(n-1)*n;
  return answer;
}
```

When **factr( )** is called with an argument of 1, the function returns 1; otherwise, it returns the product of **factr(n–1) * n**. To evaluate this expression, **factr( )** is called with **n–1**. This process continues until **n** equals 1 and the calls to the function begin returning. When **factr( )** finally returns to the original caller, the final return value will be the factorial of the original argument.

When a function calls itself, new local variables and parameters are allocated storage on the stack, and the function code is executed with these new variables from its beginning. A recursive call does not make a new copy of the function. Only the arguments and local variables are new. As each recursive call returns, the old local variables and parameters are removed from the stack and execution resumes at the point of the recursive call inside the function. Recursive functions could be said to "telescope" out and back.

2

➤ Programming Tip

Although powerful, recursive functions should be used with care. The recursive versions of many routines execute a bit more slowly than the iterative equivalent because of the added overhead of the repeated function calls. Many recursive calls to a function could cause a stack overrun. Because storage for function parameters and local variables is on the stack and each new call creates a new copy of these variables, the stack space could become exhausted. If this happens, a *stack overflow* occurs. If this happens in the normal use of a debugged recursive function, try increasing the stack space allocated to your program.

When writing recursive functions, you must include a conditional statement somewhere that causes the function to return without the recursive call being executed. If you don't, once you call the function, it will call itself until the stack is exhausted. This is a very common error when developing recursive functions. Use output statements liberally during development so that you can watch what is going on and abort execution if you see that you have made a mistake.

Function Overloading

In C++, functions can be *overloaded*. When a function is overloaded, two or more functions share the same name. However, each version of an overloaded function must have a different number and/or type of parameters. (The function return types may also differ, but this is not necessary.) When an overloaded function is called, the compiler decides which version of the function to use based upon the type and/or number of arguments, calling the function that has the closest match. For example, given these three overloaded functions,

```
void myfunc(int a) {
  cout << "a is " << a << endl;
}

// overload myfunc
```

```
void myfunc(int a, int b) {
  cout << "a is " << a << endl;
  cout << "b is " << b << endl;
}

// overload myfunc, again
void myfunc(int a, double b) {
  cout << "a is " << a << endl;
  cout << "b is " << b << endl;
}
```

the following calls are allowed:

```
myfunc(10); // calls myfunc(int)
myfunc(12, 24); // calls myfunc(int, int)
myfunc(99, 123.23); // calls myfunc(int, double)
```

In each case, the type and number of arguments determine which version of **myfunc( )** is actually executed.

Function overloading is not supported by C.

Default Arguments

In C++, you may assign a function parameter a default value, which will be used automatically when no corresponding argument is specified when the function is called. The default value is specified in a manner syntactically similar to a variable initialization. For example, this function assigns its two parameters default values:

```
void myfunc(int a = 0, int b = 10)
{ // ...
```

Given the default arguments, **myfunc( )** can be legally called in these three ways:

```
myfunc();        // a defaults to 0; b defaults to 10
myfunc(-1);      // a is passed -1; b defaults to 10
myfunc(-1, 99);  // a is passed -1; b is passed 99
```

When you create functions that have default arguments, you must specify the default values only once: either in the function prototype or in its definition. (You cannot specify them each place, even if you use the same values.) Generally, default values are specified in the prototype.

When giving a function default arguments, remember that you must specify all nondefaulting arguments first. Once you begin to specify default arguments, there may be no intervening nondefaulting ones.

Default arguments are not supported by C.

Prototypes

In C++, all functions must be prototyped. In C, prototypes are technically optional, but strongly recommended. The general form of a prototype is shown here:

ret-type name(*parameter list*);

In essence, a *prototype* is simply the return type, name, and parameter list of a function, followed by a semicolon.

The following example shows how the function **fn( )** is prototyped:

```
float fn(float x); // prototype

   .
   .
   .
// function definition
float fn(float x)
{
   // ...
}
```

To specify the prototype for a function that takes a variable number of arguments, use three periods at the point at which the variable number of parameters begin. For example, the **printf( )** function could be prototyped like this:

```
int printf(const char *format, ...);
```

When specifying the prototype to an overloaded function, each version of that function must have its own prototype. When a member function is declared within its class, this constitutes a prototype for the function.

In C, to specify the prototype for a function that has no parameters, use **void** in its parameter list. For example,

```
int f(void);
```

In C++, an empty parameter list in a prototype means that the function has no parameters; the **void** is optional. Thus, in C++, the preceding prototype can be written like this:

```
int f();
```

In C++, you can include **void** in the parameter list, but doing so is redundant.

➤ Programming Tip

Two terms are commonly confused in C/C++ programming: *declaration* and *definition*. Here is what they mean. A declaration specifies the name and type of an object. A definition allocates storage for it. These definitions apply to functions, too. A function declaration (prototype) specifies the return type, name, and parameters of a function. The function itself (that is, the function with its body) is its definition.

In many cases, a declaration is also a definition. For example, when a non-**extern** variable is declared, it is also defined. Or, when a function is defined prior to its first use, its definition also serves as its declaration.

> # Understanding Scopes
> # and Variable Lifetimes

C and C++ define *scope rules*, which govern the visibility and lifetime of objects. Although there are several subtleties, in the most general sense, there are two scopes: *global* and *local*.

The global scope exists outside all other scopes. A name declared in the global scope is known throughout the program. For example, a global variable is available for use by all functions in the program. Global variables stay in existence the entire duration of the program.

A local scope is defined by a block. That is, a local scope is begun by an opening brace and ends with its closing brace. A name declared within a local scope is known only within that scope. Because blocks can be nested, local scopes, too, can be nested. Of course, the most common local scope is the one defined by a function. Local variables are created when their block is entered, and destroyed when their block is exited. This means that local variables do not hold their values between function calls. You can use the **static** modifier, however, to preserve values between calls.

In C++ and C99, local variables can be declared nearly anywhere within a block. In C89, they must be declared at the start of a block, before any "action" statements occur. For example, the following code is valid for C++ and C99, but not for C89:

```
void f(int a)
{
   int a;

   a = 10;

   int b; // OK for C++ and C99, but not C89
```

A global variable must be declared outside of all functions, including outside the **main( )** function. Global variables are generally placed at the top of the file, prior to **main( )**, for ease of reading and because a variable must be declared before it is used.

The formal parameters to a function are also local variables and, aside from their job of receiving the value of the calling arguments, behave and can be used like any other local variable.

Namespaces

In C++, it is possible to create a local scope using the **namespace** keyword. A namespace defines a declarative region. Its purpose is to localize names. The general form of **namespace** is shown here:

```
namespace name {
  // ...
}
```

Here, *name* is the name of the namespace. For example,

```
namespace MyNameSpace {
  int count;
}
```

This creates a namespace called **MyNameSpace** and the variable **count** is declared inside it.

Names declared within a namespace can be referred to directly by other statements within the same namespace. Outside their namespace, names can be accessed two ways. First, you can use the scope resolution operator. For example, assuming **MyNameSpace** just shown, the following statement is valid:

```
MyNameSpace::count = 10;
```

You can also specify a **using** statement, which brings the specified name or namespace into the current scope. For example,

```
using namespace MyNameSpace;
count = 100;
```

In this case, **count** can be referred to directly because it has been brought into the current scope.

When C++ was originally invented, items declared in the C++ library were in the global (i.e., unnamed) namespace. However, Standard C++ puts all of these items into the **std** namespace.

The main( ) Function

In a C/C++ program, execution begins at **main( )**. (Windows programs call **WinMain( )**, but this is a special case.) You must not have more than one function called **main( )**. When **main( )** terminates, the program is over and control passes back to the operating system.

The **main( )** function is not prototyped. Thus, different forms of **main( )** may be used. For both C and C++, the following versions of **main( )** are valid:

```
int main()
int main(int argc, char *argv[])
```

As the second form shows, at least two parameters are supported by **main( )**. They are **argc** and **argv**. (Some compilers will allow additional parameters.) These two variables will hold the number of command-line arguments and a pointer to them, respectively. **argc** is an integer, and its value will always be at least 1 because the program name is the first argument as far as C/C++ is concerned. **argv** must be declared as an array of character pointers. Each pointer points to a command-line argument. Their usage is shown below in a short program that will print your name on the screen:

```
#include <iostream>
using namespace std;

int main(int argc, char *argv[])
{
  if(argc<2)
    cout << "Enter your name.\n";
  else
    cout << "hello " << argv[1];

  return 0;
}
```

Function Arguments

If a function is to use arguments, it must declare variables that accept the values of the arguments. These variables are called the *formal parameters* of the function. They behave like other local variables inside the function and are created upon entry into the function and destroyed upon exit. As with local variables, you can make assignments to a function's formal parameters or use them in any allowable C/C++ expression. Even though these variables perform the special task of receiving the value of the arguments passed to the function, they can be used like any other local variable.

In general, subroutines can be passed arguments in one of two ways. The first is called *call by value*. This method copies the value of an argument into the formal parameter of the subroutine. Changes made to the parameters of the subroutine have no effect on the variables used to call it. *Call by reference* is the second way a subroutine can have arguments passed to it. In this method, the *address* of an argument is copied into the parameter. Inside the subroutine, the argument is accessed through this address. This means that changes made to the parameter affect the variable used to call the routine.

By default, C and C++ use call by value to pass arguments. This means that you generally cannot alter the variables used to call the function. Consider the following function:

```
int sqr(int x)
{
  x = x*x;
  return x;
}
```

In this example, when the assignment **x = x * x** takes place, the only thing modified is the local variable **x**. The argument used to call **sqr( )** still has its original value.

Remember that only a copy of the value of the argument is passed to a function. What occurs inside the function has no effect on the variable used in the call.

Passing Pointers

Even though C and C++ use call-by-value parameter passing by
default, it is possible to manually construct a call by reference by
passing a pointer to the argument. Since this passes the address
of the argument to the function, it is then possible to change the
value of the argument outside the function.

Pointers are passed to functions just like any other value. Of
course, it is necessary to declare the parameters as pointer types.
For example, the function **swap( )**, which exchanges the value of
its two integer arguments, is shown here:

```
// Use pointer parameters.
void swap(int *x, int *y)
{
  int temp;

  temp = *x;   // save the value at address x
  *x = *y;     // put y into x
  *y = temp;   // put x into y
}
```

It is important to remember that **swap( )** (or any other function
that uses pointer parameters) must be called with the *addresses
of the arguments*. The following fragment shows the correct way
to call **swap( )**:

```
int a, b;

a = 10;
b = 20;
swap(&a, &b);
```

In this example, **swap( )** is called with the addresses of **a** and **b**.
The unary operator **&** is used to produce the addresses of the
variables. Therefore, the addresses of **a** and **b**, not their values,
are passed to the function **swap( )**. After the call, **a** will have the
value 20 and **b** will have the value 10.

Reference Parameters

In C++, it is possible to automatically pass the address of a variable
to a function. This is accomplished using a *reference parameter*.

When using a reference parameter, the address of an argument is passed to the function and the function operates on the argument, not a copy.

To create a reference parameter, precede its name with the **&** (ampersand). Inside the function, you can use the parameter normally, without any need to use the * (asterisk) operator. The compiler will automatically dereference the address for you. For example, the following creates a version of **swap( )** that uses two reference parameters to exchange the values of its two arguments:

```
// Use reference parameters.
void swap(int &x, int &y)
{
   int temp;

   temp = x;   // save the value at address x
   x = y;      // put y into x
   y = temp;   // put x into y
}
```

When invoking **swap( )**, you simply use the normal function-call syntax. For example,

```
int a, b;

a = 10;
b = 20;
swap(a, b);
```

Because **x** and **y** are now reference parameters, the addresses of **a** and **b** are automatically generated and passed to the function. Inside the function, the parameter names are used without any need for the * operator because the compiler automatically refers to the calling arguments each time **x** and **y** are used.

Reference parameters apply only to C++.

Constructors and Destructors

In C++, a class may contain a constructor function, a destructor function, or both. A constructor is called when an object of the class is first created and the destructor is called when an object of the class is destroyed. A constructor has the same name as the class of which it is a member and the destructor's name is the same as its class, except that it is preceded by a ~. Neither constructors nor destructors have return values.

Constructor functions may have parameters. You can use these parameters to pass values to a constructor function, which can be used to initialize an object. The arguments that are passed to the parameters are specified when an object is created. For example, this fragment illustrates how to pass a constructor an argument:

```
class myclass {
  int a;
public:
  myclass(int i) { a = i; } // constructor
  ~myclass() { cout << "Destructing..."; }
};

// ...

myclass ob(3); // pass 3 to i
```

When **ob** is declared, the value 3 is passed to the constructor's parameter **i**, which is then assigned to **a**.

Function Specifiers

C++ defines three function specifiers: **inline**, **virtual**, and **explicit**. The **inline** specifier is also supported by C99. **inline** is a request to the compiler to expand a function's code in-line rather than to call it. If the compiler cannot in-line the function, it is free to ignore the request. Both member and nonmember functions may be specified as **inline**.

A **virtual** function is defined in a base class and overridden by a derived class. Virtual functions are how C++ supports polymorphism.

The **explicit** specifier applies only to constructors. Any time that you have a constructor that requires only one argument, you can use either *ob(x)* or *ob* = *x* to initialize an object. The reason for this is that whenever you create a constructor that takes one argument, you are also implicitly creating a conversion from the type of that argument to the type of the class. A constructor specified as **explicit** will be used only when an initialization uses the normal constructor syntax, *ob(x)*. No automatic conversion will take place and *ob = x* will not be allowed. Thus, an **explicit** constructor creates a "nonconverting constructor."

Linkage Specification

Because it is common to link a C++ function with functions generated by another language (such as C), C++ allows you to specify a *linkage specification* that tells the compiler how to link a function. It has this general form:

    extern "*language*" function-prototype

As you can see, the linkage specification is an extension to the **extern** keyword. Here, *language* denotes the language to which you want the function to link. C and C++ linkages are guaranteed to be supported. Your compiler may support other linkages, too. To declare several functions using the same linkage specification, you can use this general form:

    extern "*language*" {
       function-prototypes
    }

The linkage specification applies only to C++. It is not supported by C.

The C and C++ Standard Libraries

Neither C nor C++ have keywords that perform I/O, manipulate strings, perform various mathematical computations, or a number of other useful procedures. These things are accomplished by using a set of predefined library functions that are supplied with the compiler. There are two basic styles of libraries: the C function library, which is supplied with all C and C++ compilers, and the C++ class library, which applies only to C++. Both libraries are summarized later in this guide.

2

Before your program can use a library function, it must include the appropriate *header*. In general, headers are usually files, but they are not necessarily files. It is permissible for a compiler to predefine the contents of a header internally. However, for all practical purposes, the standard C headers are contained in files that correspond to their names. The following table shows the standard headers defined by C89, along with those added by the 1995 Amendment 1.

Header	Supports
<assert.h>	The **assert( )** macro
<ctype.h>	Character handling
<errno.h>	Error reporting
<float.h>	Implementation-dependent floating-point limits
<iso646.h>	Macros that correspond to various operators, such as **&&** and ^; added in 1995 by Amendment 1
<limits.h>	Various implementation-dependent limits
<locale.h>	Localization
<math.h>	Various definitions used by the math library
<setjmp.h>	Nonlocal jumps
<signal.h>	Signal values
<stdarg.h>	Variable-length argument lists
<stddef.h>	Commonly used constants
<stdio.h>	File I/O
<stdlib.h>	Miscellaneous declarations
<string.h>	String functions
<time.h>	System time and date functions
<wchar.h>	Multibyte and wide-character functions; added in 1995 by Amendment 1
<wctype.h>	Multibyte and wide-character classification functions; added in 1995 by Amendment 1

The following table shows those headers added by C99.

Header	Supports
<complex.h>	Complex arithmetic.
<fenv.h>	The floating-point status flags and other aspects of the floating-point environment.
<inttypes.h>	Standard, portable set of integer type names; also supports functions that handle greatest-width integers.
<stdbool.h>	Boolean data types and defines the macro **bool**, which helps with C++ compatibility.
<stdint.h>	Standard, portable set of integer type names. This file is included by **<inttypes.h>**.
<tgmath.h>	Type-generic floating-point macros.

For C++, headers are specified using standard header names, which do not end with **.h**. Thus, the C++ headers do not specify filenames. Instead, they are simply standard identifiers that the compiler can handle as it sees fit. This means that a header may be mapped to a filename, but this is not required. The C++ headers are shown here. Those associated either directly or indirectly with the Standard Template Library (STL) are indicated.

C++ Header	Supports
<algorithm>	Various operations on containers (STL)
<bitset>	Bitsets (STL)
<complex>	Complex numbers
<deque>	Double-ended queues (STL)
<exception>	Exception handling
<fstream>	Stream-based file I/O
<functional>	Various function objects (STL)
<iomanip>	I/O manipulators
<ios>	Low-level I/O classes
<iosfwd>	Forward declarations for I/O system
<iostream>	Standard I/O classes
<istream>	Input streams
<iterator>	Access to contents of containers (STL)
<limits>	Various implementation limits
<list>	Linear lists (STL)
<locale>	Localization-specific information

C++ Header	Supports
<map>	Maps (keys with values) (STL)
<memory>	Memory allocation via allocators (STL)
<new>	Memory allocation using **new**
<numeric>	General-purpose numeric operations (STL)
<ostream>	Output streams
<queue>	Queues (STL)
<set>	Sets (STL)
<sstream>	String streams
<stack>	Stacks (STL)
<stdexcept>	Standard exceptions
<streambuf>	Buffered streams
<string>	Standard **string** class (STL)
<typeinfo>	Runtime type information
<utility>	General purpose templates (STL)
<valarray>	Operations on arrays containing values
<vector>	Vectors (dynamic arrays) (STL)

C++ also defines the following headers that correspond to the C
headers (except those added by C99).

<cassert>	<cctype>	<cerrno>
<cfloat>	<ciso646>	<climits>
<clocale>	<cmath>	<csetjmp>
<csignal>	<cstdarg>	<cstddef>
<cstdio>	<cstdlib>	<cstring>
<ctime>	<cwchar>	<cwctype>

In standard C++, all of the information relating to the standard
library is defined under the **std** namespace. Thus, to gain direct
access to these items, you will need to include the following **using**
statement after including the necessary headers:

```
using namespace std;
```

Alternatively, you can qualify each library identifier with **std::**,
such as **std::cout**, rather than bringing the entire library into
the global namespace. However, qualifying each name can get
to be tedious.

➤ Programming Tip

If you are using an older C++ compiler, then it may not support the modern-style C++ headers or the **namespace** command. If this is the case, then you will need to use the older, traditional-style headers. These use the same names as the modern headers but include the **.h** (thus, they resemble C headers). For example, the following includes **<iostream>** using the traditional approach:

```
#include <iostream.h>
```

When using the traditional-style header, all of the names defined by the header are placed in the global namespace, not the one defined by **std**. Thus, no **using** statement is required.

Chapter 3
Operators

C/C++ has a rich set of operators that can be divided into the following classes: arithmetic, relational and logical, bitwise, pointer, assignment, I/O, and miscellaneous.

Arithmetic Operators

C/C++ has the following seven arithmetic operators:

Operator	Action
−	Subtraction, unary minus
+	Addition
*	Multiplication
/	Division
%	Modulus
− −	Decrement
+ +	Increment

The **+**, **−**, *****, and **/** operators work in the expected fashion. The **%** operator returns the remainder of an integer division. The increment and decrement operators increase or decrease the operand by one.

These operators have the following order of precedence:

Precedence	Operators
Highest	++ − − − (unary minus)
	* / %
Lowest	+ −

Operators on the same precedence level are evaluated left to right.

Relational and Logical Operators

The relational and logical operators are used to produce Boolean (true/false) results and are often used together. In C/C++, *any* nonzero number evaluates as true. Zero is false. In C++, the outcome of the relational and logical operators is of type **bool**. In C, the outcome is a zero or nonzero integer. The relational operators are listed here:

Operator	Meaning
>	Greater than
>=	Greater than or equal
<	Less than
<=	Less than or equal
==	Equal
!=	Not equal

The logical operators are shown here:

Operator	Meaning
&&	AND
||	OR
!	NOT

The relational operators compare two values, producing a Boolean result. The logical operators connect two Boolean values or, in the case of !, reverse a value. The precedence of these operators is shown here:

Precedence	Operators
Highest	!
	> >= < <=
	== !=
	&&
Lowest	||

As an example, the following **if** statement evaluates to true and prints the line **x is less than 10**:

```
x = 9;
if(x < 10) cout << "x is less than 10";
```

However, in the following example, no message is displayed because both operands associated with **&&** must be true for the outcome to be true:

```
x = 9;
y = 9;
if(x < 10 && y > 10)
  cout << "This will not print.";
```

The Bitwise Operators

C and C++ provide operators that act upon the actual bits that comprise a value. The bitwise operators can be used only on integral types. The bitwise operators are as follows:

Operator	Meaning
&	AND
|	OR
^	XOR
~	One's complement
>>	Right shift
<<	Left shift

&, |, and ^

The truth tables for **&**, | , and ^ are as follows:

p	q	p & q	p | q	p ^ q
0	0	0	0	0
0	1	0	1	1
1	1	1	1	0
1	0	0	1	1

These rules are applied to each bit in each operand when the bitwise AND, OR, and XOR operations are performed.

For example, a sample bitwise AND operation is shown here:

```
      0 1 0 0  1 1 0 1
  &   0 0 1 1  1 0 1 1
      0 0 0 0  1 0 0 1
```

A bitwise OR operation looks like this:

```
      0 1 0 0  1 1 0 1
  |   0 0 1 1  1 0 1 1
      0 1 1 1  1 1 1 1
```

A bitwise XOR operation is shown here:

```
      0 1 0 0  1 1 0 1
  ^   0 0 1 1  1 0 1 1
      0 1 1 1  0 1 1 0
```

The One's Complement Operator

The one's complement operator, ~, will invert all the bits in its operand. For example, if a character variable, **ch**, has the bit pattern

```
0 0 1 1   1 0 0 1
```

then,

```
ch = ~ch;
```

places the bit pattern

```
1 1 0 0   0 1 1 0
```

into **ch**.

The Shift Operators

The right (>>) and left (<<) shift operators shift all bits in an integral value by the specified amount. As bits are shifted off one end, zeros are brought in the other end. (If the value being shifted is a negative, signed number and a right shift is performed, then ones are shifted in to preserve the sign.) The number on the right side of the shift operator specifies the number of positions to shift. The general form of each shift operator is

> *value* >> *number*
> *value* << *number*

Here, *number* specifies the number of positions to shift *value*.

Given this bit pattern (and assuming an unsigned value),

0 0 1 1   1 1 0 1

a shift right yields

0 0 0 1   1 1 1 0

while a shift left produces

0 1 1 1   1 0 1 0

➤ Programming Tip

A shift right is effectively a division by 2, and a shift left is a multiplication by 2. For many computers, a shift is faster than a multiply or a divide. Therefore, if you need a fast way to multiply or divide by 2, consider using the shift operators. For example, the following code fragment will first multiply and then divide the value in **x** by 2:

```
int x;

x = 10;
x = x << 1;
x = x >> 1;
```

Of course, when using the shift operators to perform multiplication, you must be careful not to shift bits off the end.

The precedence of the bitwise operators is shown here:

Precedence	Operators
Highest	~
	>> <<
	&
	∧
Lowest		

Pointer Operators

The two pointer operators are * and **&**. A *pointer* is an object that contains the address of another object. Or, put differently, an object that contains the address of another object is said to "point to" the other object.

The & Pointer Operator

The **&** operator returns the address of the object it precedes. For example, if the integer **x** is located at memory address 1000, then

```
p = &x;
```

places the value 1000 into **p**. The **&** can be thought of as "the address of". For example, the previous statement could be read as "place the address of x into p".

The * Pointer Operator

The * is the *indirection operator*. It uses the current value of the variable it precedes as the address at which data will be stored or obtained. For example, the following fragment

```
p = &x; /* put address of x into p */
*p = 100; /* use address contained in p */
```

places the value 100 into **x**. The * can be remembered as "at address". In this example, it could be read, "place the value 100 at address p". Since **p** contains the address of **x**, the value 100 is actually stored in **x**. In words, **p** is said to "point to" **x**. The * operator can also be used on the right-hand side of an assignment. For example,

```
p = &x;
*p = 100;
z = *p / 10;
```

places the value of 10 into **z**.

Assignment Operators

In C/C++, the assignment operator is the single equal sign. When assigning a common value to several values, you can "string together" several assignments. For example,

```
a = b = c = 10;
```

assigns **a**, **b**, and **c** the value 10.

There is a convenient "shorthand" for assignments that have this general form:

var = *var op expression*;

Assignments of this type can be shortened to

var op = *expression*;

For example, these two assignments

```
x = x+10;
y = y/z;
```

can be recoded as shown here:

```
x += 10;
y /= z;
```

The ? Operator

The **?** operator is a *ternary operator* (it works on three expressions). It has this general form:

expression1 ? *expression2* : *expression3*;

If *expression1* is true, then the outcome of the operation is *expression2*; otherwise, it is the value of *expression3*.

> ## ➤ Programming Tip

The **?** is often used to replace **if-else** statements of this general type:

> if(*expression1*) *var* = *expression2*;
> else *var* = *expression3*;

For example, the sequence

```
if(y < 10) x = 20;
else x = 40;
```

can be rewritten like this:

```
x = (y<10) ? 20 : 40;
```

Here, **x** is assigned the value of 20 if **y** is less than 10 and 40 if it is not.

One reason that the **?** operator exists, beyond saving typing on your part, is that the compiler can produce very fast code for this statement—much faster than for the similar **if-else** statements.

Member Operators

The . (dot) operator and the –> (arrow) operator are used to reference individual members of classes, structures, and unions. The dot operator is applied to the actual object. The arrow operator is used with a pointer to an object. For example, given the following structure:

```
struct date_time {
  char date[16];
  int time;
} tm;
```

to assign the value "3/12/2003" to the **date** member of object **tm**, you would write

```
strcpy(tm.date, "3/12/2003");
```

However, if **p_tm** is a pointer to an object of type **date_time**, the following statement is used:

```
strcpy(p_tm->date, "3/12/2003");
```

3

The Comma Operator

The comma operator causes a sequence of operations to be performed. The value of the entire comma expression is the value of the last expression of the comma-separated list. For example, after execution of the following fragment,

```
y = 15;
x = (y=y-5, 50/y);
```

x will have the value 5 because **y**'s original value of 15 is reduced by 5 and then that value is divided into 50, yielding 5 as the result. You can think of the comma operator as meaning "do this and this" and so on.

The comma operator is used most often in the **for** statement. For example,

```
for(z=10, b=20; z<b; z++, b--) { // ...
```

Here, **z** and **b** are initialized and modified using comma-separated expressions.

sizeof

Although **sizeof** is also a keyword, it is a compile-time operator that determines the size, in bytes, of a variable or data type, including classes, structures, and unions. If used with a type, the type name must be enclosed by parentheses.

For most 32-bit compilers, the following example prints the number 4:

```
int x;
cout << sizeof x;
```

For C99, **sizeof** is evaluated at runtime when it is applied to a variable-length array.

The Cast

A *cast* is a special operator that forces one data type to be converted into another. Both C and C++ support the form of cast shown here:

   (*type*) *expression*

where *type* is the desired data type.

For example, the following cast causes the outcome of the specified integer division to be of type **double**:

```
double d;
d = (double) 10/3;
```

C++ Casts

C++ supports additional casting operators. They are **const_cast**, **dynamic_cast**, **reinterpret_cast**, and **static_cast**. Their general forms are shown here:

   const_cast<*type*> (*object*)
   dynamic_cast<*type*> (*object*)
   reinterpret_cast<*type*> (*object*)
   static_cast<*type*> (*object*)

Here, *type* specifies the target type of the cast and *object* is the object being cast into the new type.

The **const_cast** operator is used to explicitly override **const** and/or **volatile** in a cast. The target type must be the same as the source type except for the alteration of its **const** or **volatile** attributes. The most common use of **const_cast** is to remove **const**ness.

dynamic_cast performs a runtime cast that verifies the validity
of the cast. If the cast cannot be made, the cast fails and the
expression evaluates to null. Its main use is for performing casts on
polymorphic types. For example, given two polymorphic classes B
and D, with D derived from B, a **dynamic_cast** can always cast a D*
pointer into a B* pointer. A **dynamic_cast** can cast a B* pointer
into a D* pointer only if the object being pointed to actually is a D
object. In general, **dynamic_cast** will succeed if the attempted
polymorphic cast is permitted (that is, if the target type can legally
apply to the type of object being cast). If the cast cannot be made,
then **dynamic_cast** evaluates to null.

The **static_cast** operator performs a nonpolymorphic cast. For
example, it can be used to cast a base class pointer into a derived
class pointer. It can also be used for any standard conversion. No
runtime checks are performed The **reinterpret_cast** operator
changes one type into a fundamentally different type. For
example, it can be used to change a pointer into an integer.
A **reinterpret_cast** should be used for casting inherently
incompatible pointer types.

Only **const_cast** can cast away **const**ness. That is, neither
dynamic_cast, static_cast, nor **reinterpret_cast** can alter the
constness of an object.

The I/O Operators

In C++, the << and the >> are overloaded to perform I/O
operations. When used in an expression in which the left operand
is a stream, the >> is an input operator and the << is an output
operator. In the language of C++, the >> is called an *extractor*
because it extracts data from the input stream. The << is called an
inserter because it inserts data into the output stream. The general
form of these operators is shown here:

> *input-stream* >> *variable*;
> *output-stream* << *expression*

For example, the following fragment inputs two integer variables:

```
int i, j;
cin >> i >> j;
```

The following statement displays "This is a test 10 20":

```
cout << "This is a test " << 10 << << ' ' << 4*5;
```

The I/O operators are not supported by C.

The .* and –>* Pointer-to-Member Operators

C++ allows you to generate a special type of pointer that "points" generically to a member of a class, not to a specific instance of that member in an object. This sort of pointer is called a *pointer to a member,* or *pointer-to-member,* for short. A pointer to a member is not the same as a normal C++ pointer. Instead, a pointer to a member provides only an offset into an object of the member's class at which that member can be found. Since member pointers are not true pointers, the . and –> operators cannot be applied to them. To access a member of a class given a pointer to it, you must use the special pointer-to-member operators .* and –>*. They allow you to access a member of a class given a pointer to that member.

When you are accessing a member of an object given an object or a reference to an object, use the .* operator. When accessing a member given a pointer to an object, use the –>* operator.

A pointer to a member is declared by using the general form shown here:

    type class-name::**ptr;*

Here, *type* is the base type of the member, *class-name* is the name of the class, and *ptr* is the name of the pointer-to-member variable being created. Once created, *ptr* can point to any member of its class that is of type *type*.

Here is a short example that demonstrates the .* operator. Pay special attention to the way the member pointers are declared.

```
#include <iostream>
using namespace std;

class cl {
public:
  cl(int i) { val=i; }
  int val;
  int double_val() { return val+val; }
};

int main()
{
  int cl::*data; // int data member pointer
  int (cl::*func)(); // func member pointer
  cl ob1(1), ob2(2); // create objects

  data = &cl::val; // get offset of val
  func = &cl::double_val;  // get offset

  cout << "Here are values: ";
  cout << ob1.*data << " " << ob2.*data << "\n";

  cout << "Here they are doubled: ";
  cout << (ob1.*func)() << " ";
  cout << (ob2.*func)() << "\n";

  return 0;
}
```

The pointer-to-member operators are not supported by C.

The :: Scope Resolution Operator

The :: *scope resolution operator* specifies the scope to which a member belongs. It has this general form:

   name::*member-name*

Here, *name* is the name of the class or namespace that contains the member specified by *member-name*. Put differently, *name* specifies the scope within which can be found the identifier specified by *member-name*.

To reference the global scope, you do not specify a scope name. For example, to refer to a global variable called **count** that is being hidden by a local variable called **count**, you can use this statement:

```
::count
```

The scope resolution operator is not supported by C.

new and delete

new and **delete** are C++'s dynamic allocation operators. They are also keywords. See Chapter 5 for details.

C does not support the **new** and **delete** operators.

typeid

In C++, the **typeid** operator returns a reference to a **type_info** object, which describes the type of the object to which **typeid** is being applied. **typeid** has this general form:

```
typeid(object)
```

typeid supports runtime type identification (RTTI) in C++. Your program must include the header **<typeinfo>** in order to use **typeid**.

The **type_info** class defines the following public members:

```
bool operator==(const type_info &ob) const;
bool operator!=(const type_info &ob) const;
bool before(const type_info &ob) const;
const char *name( ) const;
```

The overloaded **==** and **!=** provide for the comparison of types. The **before( )** function returns true if the invoking object is before the object used as a parameter in collation order. (This function is mostly for internal use only. Its return value has nothing to do with inheritance or class hierarchies.) The **name( )** function returns a pointer to the name of the type.

When **typeid** is applied to a base class pointer of a polymorphic class, it will automatically return the type of the object being pointed to. (A polymorphic class is one that contains at least one virtual function.) Thus, **typeid** can be used to determine the type of object pointed to by a base class pointer.

typeid is not supported by C.

Operator Overloading

In C++, operators can be overloaded by using the **operator** keyword. (See Chapter 5.) Operator overloading is not supported by C.

Operator Precedence Summary

The following table lists the precedence of all C and C++ operators. Please note that all operators, except the unary operators, the assignment operators, and **?**, associate from left to right.

Precedence	Operators
Highest	( ) [ ] -> :: .
	! ~ ++ -- - * & sizeof new delete typeid *type-casts*
	.* ->*
	* / %
	+ -
	<< >>
	< <= > >=
	== !=

Precedence	Operators
	&
	^
	|
	&&
	||
	?:
	= += _= *= /= %= >>= <<= &= ^= |=
Lowest	'

Chapter 4
The Preprocessor and Comments

C and C++ include several preprocessor directives, which are used to give instructions to the compiler. The preprocessor directives are listed here:

#define	#elif	#else	#endif
#error	#if	#ifdef	#ifndef
#include	#line	#pragma	#undef

Each is discussed briefly in this section.

#define

#define is used to perform macro substitutions of one piece of text for another. The general form of the directive is

> #define *macro-name character-sequence*

Here, each time *macro-name* is encountered, the specified *character-sequence* is substituted. Notice that there is no semicolon in this statement. Further, once the character sequence has started, it is terminated only by the end of the line.

For example, if you want to substitute the value 1 for the word "TRUE" and the value 0 for the word "FALSE", you would declare these two macro **#define** statements:

```
#define TRUE 1
#define FALSE 0
```

This will cause the compiler to substitute a 1 or a 0 each time the word TRUE or FALSE is encountered.

The **#define** directive has another feature: the macro can have arguments. A macro that takes arguments acts much like a function. In fact, this type of macro is often referred to as a *function-like macro*. Each time the macro is encountered, the

55

arguments associated with it are replaced by the actual arguments found in the program. For example,

```
#include <iostream>
using namespace std;

#define ABS(a) ((a)<0 ? -(a) : (a))

int main()
{
  cout << "abs of -1 and 1: " << ABS(-1)
       << ' ' << ABS(1);

  return 0;
}
```

When this program is compiled, **a** in the macro definition will be substituted with the values −1 and 1.

➤ Programming Tip

You must be sure to completely parenthesize function-like macros that you create. If you don't, they may not work in all situations. For example, the parentheses surrounding **a** in the preceding example are necessary to ensure proper substitution in all cases. If the parentheses around **a** were removed, the expression

```
ABS(10-20)
```

would be converted to

```
10-20<0 ? -10-20 : 10-20
```

thus yielding the wrong result. If you have a function-like macro that misbehaves, check your parentheses.

#error

The **#error** directive forces the compiler to stop compilation when it is encountered. It is used primarily for debugging. Its general form is

#error *message*

When **#error** is encountered, the message and the line number are displayed.

4

#if, #ifdef, #ifndef, #else, #elif, and #endif

The **#if**, **#ifdef**, **#ifndef**, **#else**, **#elif**, and **#endif** preprocessor directives selectively compile various portions of a program. The general idea is that if the expression after an **#if**, **#ifdef**, or **#ifndef** is true, the code that is between one of the preceding and an **#endif** will be compiled; otherwise, it will be skipped over. The **#endif** is used to mark the end of an **#if** block. The **#else** can be used with any of the above to provide an alternative.

The general form of **#if** is

#if *constant-expression*

If the constant expression is true, the code sequence that immediately follows will be compiled.

The general form of **#ifdef** is

#ifdef *macro-name*

If the *macro-name* has been defined in a **#define** statement, the following code sequence will be compiled.

The general form of **#ifndef** is

    #ifndef *macro-name*

If *macro-name* is currently undefined by a **#define** statement, the code sequence is compiled.

For example, here is the way some of these preprocessor directives work together. The code

```
#define ted 10

// ...

#ifdef ted
  cout << "Hi Ted\n";
#endif
  cout << "Hi Jon\n";
#if 10<9
  cout << "Hi George\n";
#endif
```

will print "Hi Ted" and "Hi Jon" on the screen, but not "Hi George".

The **#elif** directive is used to create an **if-else-if** statement. Its general form is

    #elif *constant-expression*

You can string together a series of **#elif**s to handle several alternatives.

You can also use **#if** or **#elif** to determine whether a macro name is defined using the **defined** preprocessing operator. It takes this general form:

    #if defined *macro-name*
    statement sequence
    #endif

If the *macro-name* is defined, the statement sequence will be compiled. Otherwise, it will be skipped. For example, the following fragment compiles the conditional code because **DEBUG** is defined by the program:

```
#define DEBUG
// ...
int i=100;
// ...
#if defined DEBUG
cout << "value of i is: " << i << endl;
#endif
```

You can also precede **defined** with the **!** operator to cause conditional compilation when the macro is not defined.

4

#include

The **#include** directive causes the compiler to read and compile another source file. It takes these general forms:

#include "*filename*"

#include <*filename*>

The source file to be read in must be enclosed between double quotes or angle brackets. For example,

```
#include "MyFuncs.h"
```

will instruct the compiler to read and compile the file **MyFuncs.h**.

If the filename is enclosed by angle brackets, the file is searched for in a manner defined by the creator of the compiler. Often, this means searching some special directory set aside for header files. If the filename is enclosed in quotes, the file is looked for in another implementation-defined manner. For many implementations, this means searching the current working directory. If the file is not found, the search is repeated as if the filename had been enclosed in angle brackets. You must check your compiler's user manual for details on the differences between angle brackets and double quotes. **#include** statements can be nested within other included files.

In addition to files, a C/C++ program uses the **#include** directive to include a *header*. C and C++ define a set of standard headers that provide the information necessary for the various libraries. A header might refer to a file, but need not. Thus, a header is simply an abstraction that guarantees that the appropriate information is included. As a practical matter, however, C headers are nearly always files and the names of the headers are valid filenames. However, for C++, the situation is different. All C++ header names are standard identifiers that the compiler may map to a filename, or handle in another manner. Since the C++ headers are not filenames, they do not have .**h** extensions. For example, to include the header information for the C++ I/O system, use

```
#include <iostream>
```

Here, **<iostream>** is the standard header for the I/O classes.

#line

The **#line** directive changes the contents of _ _**LINE**_ _ and _ _**FILE**_ _, which are predefined identifiers. The basic form of the command is

    #line *number* "*filename*"

where *number* is any positive integer and the *filename* is any valid file identifier. The value of *number* becomes the number of the current source line and *filename* becomes the name of the source file. The name of the file is optional. **#line** is primarily used for debugging purposes and special applications.

The _ _**LINE**_ _ identifier is an integer, and _ _**FILE**_ _ is a null-terminated string.

For example, the following sets the current line counter to 10 and the filename to "test":

```
#line 10 "test"
```

#pragma

The **#pragma** directive is an implementation-defined directive that allows various instructions to be given to the compiler. For example, a compiler may have an option to support the tracing of program execution. A trace option would then be specified by a **#pragma** statement. You must check your compiler's documentation for the pragmas it supports.

The C99 _Pragma Operator

C99 includes another way to specify a pragma in a program: the **_Pragma** operator. It has this general form:

4

 _Pragma ("*directive*")

Here, *directive* is the pragma being invoked. The **_Pragma** operator was added to allow pragmas to participate in macro replacement.

The C99 Built-In Pragmas

C99 defines the following built-in pragmas:

Pragma	Meaning
STDC FP_CONTRACT ON/OFF/DEFAULT	When on, floating-point expressions are treated as indivisible units that are handled by hardware-based methods. The default state is implementation defined.
STDC FENV_ACCESS ON/OFF/DEFAULT	Tells the compiler that the floating-point environment might be accessed. The default state is implementation defined.
STDC CX_LIMITED_RANGE ON/OFF/DEFAULT	When on, tells the compiler that certain formulas involving complex values are safe. The default state is off.

#undef

The **#undef** directive removes a previously defined macro name. The general form is

 #undef *macro-name*

For example, in the following code,

```
#define LEN 100
#define WIDTH 100

char array[LEN][WIDTH];

#undef LEN
#undef WIDTH
/* at this point both LEN and WIDTH are
   undefined */
```

both **LEN** and **WIDTH** are defined until the **#undef** statements are encountered.

The # and ## Preprocessor Operators

C/C++ provides two preprocessor operators: # and ##. These operators are used in a **#define** macro.

The # operator causes the argument it precedes to be turned into a quoted string. For example, consider this program:

```
#include <iostream>
using namespace std;

#define mkstr(s)  # s

int main()
{
  cout << mkstr(I like C++);

  return 0;
}
```

The preprocessor turns the line

```
cout << mkstr(I like C++);
```

into

```
cout << "I like C++";
```

The ## operator is used to concatenate two tokens. For example, in the following program,

```
#include <iostream>
using namespace std;

#define concat(a, b)   a ## b

int main()
{
  int xy = 10;

  cout << concat(x, y);

  return 0;
}
```

the preprocessor transforms

```
cout << concat(x, y);
```

into

```
cout << xy;
```

If these operators seem strange to you, keep in mind that they are not needed or used in most programs. They exist primarily to allow some special cases to be handled by the preprocessor.

Predefined Macro Names

C/C++ specifies several built-in predefined macro names. They are

  _ _LINE_ _
  _ _FILE_ _
  _ _DATE_ _
  _ _STDC_ _
  _ _TIME_ _
  _ _cplusplus

The _ _**LINE**_ _ and _ _**FILE**_ _ macros are described in the **#line** discussion. The others will be examined here.

The _ _**DATE**_ _ macro is a string, in the form *month*/*day*/*year*, that is the date of the translation of the source file into object code.

The time of the translation of the source code into object code is contained as a string in _ _**TIME**_ _. The form of the string is *hour*:*minute*:*second*.

The macro _ _**cplusplus** is defined when compiling a C++ program. This macro will not be defined by a C compiler. The macro _ _**STDC**_ _ is defined by a C program and may be defined by a C++ compiler. In both cases, check your compiler's documentation for details.

Most C/C++ compilers define several other built-in macros that relate to the specific environment and implementation.

Additional Built-In Macros Defined by C99

C99 adds the following macros to those just described. They are not supported by C++.

_ _**STDC_HOSTED**_ _	1 if an operating system is present
_ _**STDC_VERSION**_ _	199901L or greater; represents version of C
_ _**STDC_IEC_559**_ _	1 if IEC 60559 floating-point arithmetic is supported
_ _**STDC_IEC_599_COMPLEX**_ _	1 if IEC 60559 complex arithmetic is supported
_ _**STDC_ISO_10646**_ _	A value of the form *yyyymmL* that states the year and month of the ISO/IEC 10646 specification supported by the compiler

Comments

C++ and C99 define two styles of comments. The first is a multiline comment. It begins with a /* and is terminated with a */. Anything between the comment symbols is ignored by the compiler. A multiline comment can extend over several lines.

The second type of comment is the single-line comment. It begins with a // and ends at the end of the line.

Multiline comments are the only type of comment supported by C89. However, many C89 compilers will accept single-line comments even though they are nonstandard.

C99 Variable Argument Lists

4

C99 adds to the preprocessor the ability to create macros that take a variable number of arguments. This is indicated by an ellipsis (. . .) in the definition of the macro. The built-in preprocessing identifier **_ _VA_ARGS_ _** determines where the arguments will be substituted. For example, given this definition,

```
#define MyMax(...) max(_ _VA_ARGS_ _)
```

this statement

```
MyMax(a, b);
```

is transformed into

```
max(a, b);
```

There can be other arguments prior to the variable ones. For example, given

```
#define compare(compfunc, ...) compfunc(_ _VA_ARGS_ _)
```

this statement

```
compare(strcmp, "one", "two");
```

is transformed into

```
strcmp("one", "two");
```

As the example shows, _ _**VA_ARGS**_ _ is replaced by all of the remaining arguments.

Chapter 5
Keyword Summary

The C89 language defines the following 32 keywords.

auto	double	int	struct
break	else	long	switch
case	enum	register	typedef
char	extern	return	union
const	float	short	unsigned
continue	for	signed	void
default	goto	sizeof	volatile
do	if	static	while

C++ includes all keywords defined by C89 and adds the following:

asm	bool	catch	class
const_cast	delete	dynamic_cast	explicit
export	false	friend	inline
mutable	namespace	new	operator
private	protected	public	reinterpret_cast
static_cast	template	this	throw
true	try	typeid	typename
using	virtual	wchar_t	

Older versions of C++ also defined the **overload** keyword, but it is obsolete.

C99 includes all of the keywords defined by C89 and adds the following:

_Bool	_Complex	_Imaginary	inline	restrict

A brief synopsis of the keywords follows.

asm

asm is used to embed assembly language directly into your C++ program. The general form of the **asm** statement is shown here:

    asm ("*instruction*");

Here, *instruction* is an assembly language instruction, which is passed directly to the compiler for assembly in your program.

Many C++ compilers allow additional forms of the **asm** statement. For example,

    asm *instruction*;
    asm {
      instruction sequence
    }

Here, *instruction sequence* is a list of assembly language instructions.

auto

auto declares local variables. It is completely optional and seldom used.

bool

The type specifier **bool** is used to declare Boolean (i.e., true/false) values.

_Bool

C99 includes the **_Bool** data type, which is capable of storing the values 1 and 0 (i.e., true/false). **_Bool** is an integer type, and it differs from the C++ keyword **bool**. Thus, C99 and C++ are incompatible on this point. Also, C++ defines the built-in Boolean constants **true** and **false**, but C99 does not. However, C99 adds the header **<stdbool.h>**, which defines the macros **bool**, **true**, and **false**. Thus, C/C++-compatible code can be easily created.

The reason that **_Bool** rather than **bool** was specified as a keyword for C99 is that many existing C programs had already defined their own custom versions of **bool**. By defining the Boolean type as **_Bool,** C99 avoids breaking this preexisting code. However, for new C programs, it is best to include **<stdbool.h>** and then use the **bool** macro.

break

break is used to exit from a **do**, **for**, or **while** loop, bypassing the normal loop condition. It is also used to exit from a **switch** statement.

An example of **break** in a loop is shown here:

```
do {
  x = getx();
  if(x < 0) break; // terminate if negative
  process(x);
} while(!done);
```

Here, if **x** is negative, the loop is terminated.

In a **switch** statement, **break** keeps program execution from "falling through" to the next **case**. (Refer to the **switch** statement for details.)

A **break** terminates only the **for**, **do**, **while**, or **switch** that contains it. It will not break out of any nested loops or **switch** statements.

case

The **case** statement is used with a **switch** statement. See **switch**.

catch

The **catch** statement handles an exception generated by **throw**. See **throw**.

char

char is a data type used to declare character variables.

class

class is used to declare classes—C++'s basic unit of encapsulation. Its general form is shown here:

```
class class-name : inheritance-list {
    // private members by default
protected:
    // private members that can be inherited
public:
    // public members
} object-list;
```

Here, *class-name* is the name of the new data type being generated by the **class** declaration. The *inheritance-list*, which is optional, specifies any base classes inherited by the new class. By default, members of a **class** are private. They may be made protected or public through the use of the **protected** and **public** keywords, respectively.

The *object-list* is optional. If not present, a class declaration simply specifies the form of a class. It does not create any objects of the class.

NOTE: For additional information on **class**, see Chapter 1.

_Complex

C99 includes the keyword **_Complex**, which supports complex arithmetic. The following **_Complex** types are defined:

float _Complex

double _Complex

long double _Complex

The reason that **_Complex**, rather than **complex**, was specified as a keyword for C99 is that many existing C programs had already defined their own custom complex data types using the name **complex**. By using the keyword **_Complex**, C99 avoids breaking this preexisting code.

The header **<complex.h>** defines (among other things) the macro **complex**, which expands to **_Complex**. Thus, for new C programs, it is best to include **<complex.h>** and then use the **complex** macro.

const

The **const** modifier tells the compiler that a variable cannot be changed by your program. A **const** variable may, however, be given an initial value when it is declared.

const_cast

The **const_cast** operator is used to explicitly override **const** and/or **volatile** in a cast. It has this general form:

const_cast<*type*> (*object*)

The target type must be the same as the source type except for the alteration of its **const** or **volatile** attributes. The most common use of **const_cast** is to remove **const**ness.

continue

continue is used to bypass portions of code in a loop and forces the conditional expression to be evaluated. For example, the following **while** loop reads characters from the keyboard until an **s** is typed:

```
while(ch = getchar()) {
  if(ch != 's') continue;   // read another char
  process(ch);
}
```

The call to **process( )** will not occur until **ch** contains the character **s**.

default

default is used in the **switch** statement to signal a default block of code to be executed if no matches are found in the **switch**. See **switch**.

delete

The **delete** operator frees the memory pointed to by its argument. This memory must have previously been allocated using **new**. The general form of **delete** is

    delete p_var;

where *p_var* is a pointer to previously allocated memory.

To free an array that has been allocated using **new**, use this general form of **delete**:

    delete [ ] p_var;

5

do

The **do** loop is one of three loop constructs available in C++. The general form of the **do** loop is

    do {
        statement block
    } while(condition);

If only one statement is repeated, the braces are not necessary, but they add clarity to the statement.

The **do** loop is the only loop in C/C++ that will always have at least one iteration because the condition is tested at the bottom of the loop.

double

double is a data type specifier used to declare double-precision floating-point variables.

dynamic_cast

dynamic_cast performs a runtime cast that verifies the validity of the cast. It has this general form:

> dynamic_cast<*type*> (*object*)

The main use for **dynamic_cast** is to perform casts on polymorphic types. For example, given two polymorphic classes B and D, with D derived from B, a **dynamic_cast** can always cast a D* pointer into a B* pointer. A **dynamic_cast** can cast a B* pointer into a D* pointer only if the object being pointed to actually is a D object. In general, **dynamic_cast** will succeed if the attempted polymorphic cast is permitted (that is, if the target type can legally apply to the type of object being cast). If the cast cannot be made, then **dynamic_cast** evaluates to null. (If a bad cast occurs while casting a reference, a **bad_cast** exception is thrown.)

else

See **if**.

enum

The **enum** type specifier is used to create enumeration types. An enumeration is simply a list of named integer constants. The general form of an enumeration is shown here:

enum *name* {*name-list*} *var-list*;

The *name* is the type name of the enumeration. The *var-list* is optional, and enumeration variables can be declared separately from the type definition, as the following example shows. This code declares an enumeration called **color** and a variable of that type called **c**. It then performs an assignment and a conditional test.

```
enum color {red, green, yellow} c;

c = red;
if(c==red) cout << "is red\n";
```

NOTE: For more information on enumerations refer to **Enumerations** in Chapter 1.

5

explicit

The **explicit** specifier applies only to constructors. A constructor specified as **explicit** will be used only when an initialization exactly matches that specified by the constructor. No automatic conversion will take place. Thus, it creates a "non-converting constructor". (See "Function Specifiers" in Chapter 2.)

export

The **export** keyword can precede a **template** declaration. It allows other files to use a template declared in a different file by specifying only its declaration rather than duplicating its entire definition.

extern

extern is a data type modifier that tells the compiler about a variable that is defined elsewhere in the program. This is often used in conjunction with separately compiled files that share the same global data. In essence, it notifies the compiler about the type of a variable without redefining it. For example, if **first** were defined in another file as an integer, the following declaration would be used in subsequent files:

```
extern int first;
```

This declaration specifies **first**'s type, but storage for it has not been created.

For C++ only, **extern** is also used to create a linkage specification. It has this general form:

extern "*language*" *function-prototype*

Here, *language* denotes the language to which you want the function to link. C and C++ linkages are guaranteed to be supported. Your compiler may support other linkages, too. To declare several functions using the same linkage specification, you can use this general form:

extern "*language*" {
    function-prototypes
}

false

false is the Boolean constant for false.

float

float is a data type specifier used to declare floating-point variables.

for

The **for** loop allows automatic initialization and incrementation of a counter variable. The general form is

```
for(initialization; condition; increment) {
    statement block
}
```

If the *statement block* is only one statement, the braces are not necessary.

Although the **for** allows a number of variations, generally the *initialization* sets a loop control variable to its starting value. The *condition* is usually a relational statement that checks the loop control variable against a termination value, and *increment* increments (or decrements) it. If the *condition* is false to begin with, the body of the **for** loop will not execute even once.

The following statement will print the message "hello" ten times:

```
for(t=0; t<10; t++) cout << "hello\n";
```

friend

The keyword **friend** grants a nonmember function access to the private members of a class. To specify a friend function, include that function's prototype in the public section of a class declaration and precede the entire prototype with the keyword **friend**. For example, in the following class, **myfunc( )** is a friend, not a member, of **myclass**:

```
class myclass {
    // ...
public:
```

```
friend void myfunc(int a, float b);
// ...
};
```

Keep in mind that a **friend** function does not have a **this** pointer because it is not a member of the class.

goto

The **goto** keyword causes program execution to jump to the label specified in the **goto** statement. The general form of **goto** is

goto *label*;
.
.
.
label:

➤ Programming Tip

Although the **goto** fell out of favor decades ago as a method of program control, it does occasionally have its uses. One of them is as a means of exiting from a deeply nested routine. For example, consider this fragment:

```
int i, j, k;
int stop = 0;

for(i=0; i<100 && !stop; i++) {
  for(j=0; j<10 && !stop; j++) {
    for(k=0; k<20; k++) {
      // ...
      if(something()) {
        stop = 1;
        break;
      }
    }
  }
}
```

As you can see, the variable **stop** is used to cancel the two outer loops if some program event occurs. However, a better way to accomplish this is shown below, using a **goto**:

```
int i, j, k;

for(i=0; i<100; i++) {
  for(j=0; j<10; j++) {
    for(k=0; k<20; k++) {
      // ...
      if(k+4 == j + i) {
        goto done;
      }
    }
  }
}

done: // ...
```

As you can see, the use of the **goto** eliminates the extra overhead that was added by the repeated testing of **stop** in the previous version.

Although the **goto** as a general-purpose form of loop control should be avoided, it can occasionally be employed with great success.

All labels must end in a colon and must not conflict with keywords or function names. Furthermore, a **goto** can branch only within the current function—not from one function to another.

if

The **if** keyword allows a course of action to be based on the outcome of a condition. The general form of the **if** statement is

```
if(condition) {
    statement block 1
}
```

```
else {
    statement block 2
}
```

If single statements are used, the braces are not needed. The **else** is optional.

The *condition* may be any expression. If that expression evaluates to true (any value other than zero), then *statement block 1* will be executed; otherwise, if it exists, *statement block 2* will be executed.

The following fragment checks whether **x** is greater than 10:

```
if(x > 10)
  cout << "x is greater than 10.";
else
  cout << "x is less than or equal to 10.";
```

_Imaginary

C99 includes the keyword **_Imaginary**, which supports complex arithmetic. However, no implementation is required to implement imaginary types, and freestanding implementations (those without operating systems) do not have to support complex types. The following **_Imaginary** types are defined:

float _Imaginary

double _Imaginary

long double _Imaginary

The reason that **_Imaginary**, rather than **imaginary**, was specified as a keyword for C99 is that many existing C programs had already defined their own custom imaginary data types using the name **imaginary**. By using the keyword **_Imaginary**, C99 avoids breaking this preexisting code.

The header **<complex.h>** defines (among other things) the macro **imaginary**, which expands to **_Imaginary**. Thus, for new C programs, it is best to include **<complex.h>** and then use the **imaginary** macro.

---

inline

The **inline** specifier tells the compiler to expand a function's code inline rather than calling the function. The **inline** specifier is a request, not a command, because several factors may prevent a function's code from being expanded inline. Some common restrictions include recursive functions, functions that contain loops or **switch** statements, or functions that contain static data. The **inline** specifier precedes the rest of a function's declaration.

The following tells the compiler to generate inline code for **myfunc( )**:

```
inline void myfunc(int i)
{
   // ...
}
```

When a function's definition is included within a class declaration, that function's code is automatically inlined, if possible.

---

int

---

int is the type specifier used to declare integer variables.

---

long

---

long is a data type modifier used to declare long integer or floating-point variables.

mutable

The **mutable** specifier allows a member of an object to override **const**ness. That is, a **mutable** member can be modified by a **const** member function.

namespace

The **namespace** keyword allows you to partition the global namespace by creating a declarative region. In essence, a namespace defines a scope. The general form of **namespace** is shown here:

```
namespace name {
   // declarations
}
```

In addition, you can have unnamed namespaces as shown here:

```
namespace {
   // declarations
}
```

Unnamed namespaces allow you to establish unique identifiers that are known only within the scope of a single file.

Here is an example of a **namespace**:

```
namespace MyNameSpace {
   int i, k;
   void myfunc(int j) { cout << j; }
}
```

Here, **i**, **k**, and **myfunc( )** are part of the scope defined by the **MyNameSpace** namespace.

Since a namespace defines a scope, you need to use the scope resolution operator to refer to objects defined within one. For example, to assign the value 10 to **i**, you must use this statement:

```
MyNameSpace::i = 10;
```

If the members of a namespace will be frequently used, the **using** directive can simplify their access. The **using** statement has these two general forms:

> using namespace *name;*
> using *name::member;*

In the first form, *name* specifies the name of the namespace you want to access. All of the members defined within the specified namespace can be used without qualification. In the second form, only a specific member of the namespace is made visible. For example, assuming **MyNameSpace** as shown earlier, the following **using** statements and assignments are valid:

```
using MyNameSpace::k; // only k is made visible
k = 10; // OK because k is visible

using namespace MyNameSpace;
   // all members of MyNameSpace are visible
i = 10;
   // OK because all members of MyNameSpace are now visible
```

5

new

The **new** operator allocates dynamic memory and returns a pointer of the appropriate type to it. Its general form is shown here:

> *p_var* = new *type;*

Here, *p_var* is a pointer variable that will receive the address of the allocated memory, and *type* is the type of data that the memory will hold. The **new** operator automatically allocates sufficient memory to hold one item of data of the specified type. For example, this code fragment allocates sufficient memory to hold a **double**:

```
double *p;

p = new double;
```

If the allocation request fails, a **bad_alloc** exception is thrown.

NOTE: Older compilers may exhibit a different behavior on allocation failure than just described. For example, it is possible that no exception will be thrown and that a null pointer will be returned. Check your compiler's documentation for information that applies to your current working environment.

You can initialize the allocated memory by specifying an initializer, using this general form:

   p_var = new *type* (*initializer*);

Here, *initializer* is the value that will be assigned to the allocated memory.

To allocate a single-dimension array, use the following general form:

   p_var = new *type*[*size*];

Here, *size* specifies the length of the array. **new** will automatically allocate sufficient room to hold an array of the specified type and of the specified size. When allocating arrays, no initializations may be given.

If your C++ compiler fully complies with the ANSI/ISO standard, then it supports a "no-throw" form of **new**, which has this general form:

   p_var = new(nothrow) *type*;

The **nothrow** form of **new** returns a null if an allocation failure occurs, rather than throwing an exception. To use this form, your program must include the header **<new>**.

operator

The **operator** keyword is used to create overloaded operator functions. Operator functions come in two varieties: member and nonmember. The general form of a member operator function is shown here:

> *ret-type class-name*::operator#(*param-list*) {
>   // ...
> }

Here, *ret-type* is the return type of the function, *class-name* is the name of the class for which the operator is overloaded, and # is the operator to be overloaded. When overloading a unary operator, the *param-list* is empty. (The operand is passed implicitly in **this**.) When overloading a binary operator, the *param-list* specifies the operand on the right side of the operator. (The operand on the left is passed implicitly in **this**.)

For nonmember functions, an operator function has this general form:

> *ret-type* operator#(*param-list*) {
>   // ...
> }

Here, *param-list* contains one parameter when overloading a unary operator and two parameters when overloading a binary operator. When overloading a binary operator, the operand on the left is passed in the first parameter, and the operand on the right is passed in the second parameter.

Several restrictions apply to operator overloading. You cannot alter the precedence of the operator. You cannot change the number of operands required by an operator. You cannot change the meaning of an operator relative to C++'s built-in data types. You cannot create a new operator. The preprocessor operators # and ## cannot be overloaded. You cannot overload the following operators:

> . :: .* ?

5

private

The **private** access specifier declares private members of a class. It is also used to inherit a base class privately. When used to declare private members, it has this general form:

```
class class-name {
    // ...
private:
    // private members
};
```

Since members of a **class** are private by default, the access specifier **private** will only be used in a **class** declaration to begin another block of private declarations. For example, this is a valid **class** declaration:

```
class myclass {
    int a, b; // private by default
public: // begin public declarations
    int x, y; // these are public
private: // return to private declarations
    int c, d; // these are private
};
```

When used as an inheritance specifier, **private** has this general form:

```
class class-name : private base-class { // ...
```

By specifying a base class as **private**, all public and protected members of the base class become private members of the derived class. All private members of the base class remain private to it.

protected

The **protected** access specifier declares members that are private to a class but that can be inherited by a derived class. It has the following general form:

```
class class-name {
    // ...
protected: // make protected
    // protected members
};
```

For example,

```
class base {
  // ...
protected:
  int a;
  // ...
};

// Now, inherit base into derived class.
class derived : public base {
  // ...
public:
  // ...
  // derived has access to a
  void f() { cout << a; }
};
```

Here, **a** is private to **base** and cannot be accessed by any nonmember function. However, **derived** inherits access to **a**. If **a** were simply defined as **private**, **derived** would not have access to it.

When used as an inheritance specifier, **protected** has this general form:

```
class class-name : protected base-class { // ...
```

By specifying a base class as **protected**, all public and protected members of the base class become protected members of the derived class. In all cases, **private** members of the base class remain private to that base.

public

The **public** access specifier declares public members of a class. It is also used to publicly inherit a base class. When used to declare public members, it has this general form:

```
class class-name {
    // private members by default
public: // make public
    // public members
};
```

Members of a **class** are private by default. To declare public members of a **class**, you must specify them as **public**.

When used as an inheritance specifier, **public** has this general form:

```
class class-name : public base-class { // ...
```

By specifying a base class as **public**, all public members of the base class become public members of the derived class and all protected members of the base class become protected members of the derived class. In all cases, **private** members of the base class remain private to that base.

register

The **register** storage class modifier requests that access to a variable be optimized for speed. Traditionally, **register** applied only to integer, character, or pointer variables, causing them to be stored in a register of the CPU instead of being placed in memory.

However, the meaning of **register** has since been broadened to include all types of data. However, data other than integers, characters, and pointers cannot usually be stored in a CPU register. For other types of data, either cache memory (or some other sort of optimizing scheme) is used, or the **register** request is ignored.

register can be used only on local variables. In C, you cannot take the address of a **register** variable, but in C++ you can (although doing so may prevent the variable from being optimized).

reinterpret_cast

5

The **reinterpret_cast** operator changes one type into a fundamentally different type. For example, it can be used to change a pointer into an integer. It has this general form:

reinterpret_cast<*type*> (*object*)

A **reinterpret_cast** should be used for casting inherently incompatible pointer types.

restrict

C99 adds the **restrict** type qualifier, which applies only to pointers. A pointer qualified by **restrict** is initially the only means by which the object it points to can be accessed. Access to the object by another pointer can occur only if the second pointer is based on the first. Thus, access to the object is restricted to expressions based on the **restrict**-qualified pointer. Pointers qualified by **restrict** are primarily used as function parameters, or to point to memory allocated via **malloc( )**.

By qualifying a pointer with **restrict**, the compiler is better able to optimize certain types of routines by making the assumption that the **restrict**-qualified pointer is the sole means of access to the object. For example, if a function specifies two **restrict**-qualified pointer parameters, then the compiler can assume that the pointers point to different (that is, nonoverlapping) objects. Consider what has become the classic example of **restrict**: the **memcpy( )** function. In C89 and C++, it is prototyped as shown here:

void *memcpy(void *str1, const void *str2, size_t size);

In the description for **memcpy( )** it is stated that if the objects pointed to by str1 and str2 overlap, the behavior is undefined. Thus, **memcpy( )** is guaranteed to work for only nonoverlapping objects.

In C99, **restrict** can be used to explicitly state in **memcpy( )**'s prototype what C89 and C++ must explain with words. Here is the C99 prototype for **memcpy( )**:

void *memcpy(void * restrict str1, const void * restrict str2,
                size_t size);

By qualifying str1 and str2 with **restrict**, the prototype explicitly asserts that they point to nonoverlapping objects.

return

The **return** statement forces a return from a function and can be used to transfer a value back to the calling routine. It has these two forms:

return;
return value;

In C99 and C++, the form of **return** that does not specify a value must be used only in **void** functions.

The following function returns the product of its two integer arguments:

```
int mul(int a, int b)
{
  return a*b;
}
```

Keep in mind that as soon as a **return** is encountered, the function will return, skipping any other code that may be in the function.

Also, a function can contain more than one **return** statement.

short

short is a data type modifier used to declare short integers.

signed

The principal use of the **signed** type modifier is to specify a **signed char** data type. Its use on other integer types is redundant since integers are signed by default.

sizeof

The **sizeof** compile-time operator returns the length (in bytes) of the variable or type it precedes. If it precedes a type, that type must be enclosed in parentheses. If it precedes a variable, the parentheses are optional. For example, given

```
int i;
cout << sizeof(int);
cout << sizeof i;
```

both output statements will print 4 in most 32-bit environments.

static

static is a data type modifier that creates permanent storage for the local variable that it precedes. This enables the specified variable to maintain its value between function calls, for example.

static can also be used to declare global variables. In this case, it limits the scope of the variable that it modifies to the file in which it is declared.

In C++, when **static** is used on a class data member, it causes only one copy of that member to be shared by all objects of its class.

static_cast

The **static_cast** operator performs a nonpolymorphic cast. For example, it can be used to cast a base class pointer into a derived class pointer. It can also be used for any standard conversion. No runtime checks are performed. It has this general form:

```
static_cast<type> (object)
```

struct

The **struct** keyword is used to create an aggregate data type called a structure. In C++, a structure can contain both function and data members. It has the same capabilities as a class except that, by default, its members are public rather than private. The general form of a C++ structure is

```
struct class-name : inheritance-list {
    // public members by default
protected:
    // private members that can be inherited
private:
    // private members
} object-list;
```

The *class-name* is the type name of the structure, which is a class type. The individual members are referenced using the dot operator when acting on an object or by using the arrow operator when acting through a pointer to the object. The *object-list* and *inheritance-list* are optional.

In C, structures must contain only data members, the **private**, **public**, and **protected** specifiers are not allowed, and no inheritance list is allowed.

The following C-style structure contains a string called **name** and two integers called **high** and **low**. It also declares one variable called **my_var**.

```
struct my_struct {
  char name[80];
  int high;
  int low;
} my_var;
```

NOTE: Chapter 1 covers structures in more detail.

5

switch

The **switch** statement is C/C++'s multiway branch statement. It is used to route execution one of several different ways. The general form of the statement is

```
switch (expression) {
    case constant 1: statement sequence 1;
        break;
    case constant 2: statement sequence 2;
        break;

        .
        .
        .

    case constant N: statement sequence N;
        break;
    default: default statements;
}
```

Each statement sequence may be from one to several statements long. The **default** portion is optional. Both *expression* and the **case** constants must be integral types.

The **switch** works by checking the *expression* against the constants. If a match is found, that sequence of statements is executed. If the statement sequence associated with the matching **case** does not contain a **break**, execution will continue on into the next **case**. Put differently, from the point of the match, execution will continue until either a **break** statement is found or the **switch** ends. If no match is found and a **default** case is existent, its statement sequence is executed. Otherwise, no action takes place. The following example processes a menu selection:

```
switch(ch) {
  case 'e': enter();
    break;
  case 'l': list();
    break;
  case 's': sort();
    break;
  case 'q': exit(0);
    break;
  default:
    cout << "Unknown command!\n";
    cout << "Try Again.\n";
}
```

template

The **template** keyword is used to create generic functions and classes. The type of data operated upon by a generic function or class is specified as a parameter. Thus, one function or class definition can be used with several different types of data. The details concerning template functions and classes follow.

A generic function defines a general set of operations that can be applied to various types of data. A generic function has the type of data that it will operate upon passed to it as a parameter. Using this mechanism, the same general procedure can be applied to a wide range of data. As you know, many algorithms are logically the same no matter what type of data is being operated upon. For example, the Quicksort algorithm is the same whether it is applied to an array of integers or an array of floating-point numbers. It is just that the type of the data being sorted is different. By creating a generic function, you can define, independent of any data, the nature of the algorithm. Once this is done, the compiler automatically generates the correct code for the type of data that is actually used when you call the function. In essence, when you create a generic function you are creating a function that can automatically overload itself.

The general form of a **template** function definition is shown here:

```
template <class data-type> ret-type func-name(parameter list)
{
    // body of function
}
```

Here, *data-type* is a placeholder for the type of data upon which the function will actually operate. You can define more than one generic data type using the **template** statement, with a comma-separated list.

Here is an example. The following program creates a generic function that swaps the values of the two variables with which it is called. Because the general process of exchanging two values is independent of the type of the variables, it is a good candidate to be made into a generic function.

```cpp
// Function template example.
#include <iostream>
using namespace std;

// Here is a template function.
template <class X> void swapvals(X &a, X &b)
{
  X temp;

  temp = a;
  a = b;
  b = temp;
}

int main()
{
  int i=10, j=20;
  float x=10.1, y=23.3;

  cout << "Original i, j: " << i << ' ' << j
       << endl;
  cout << "Original x, y: " << x << ' ' << y
       << endl;

  swapvals(i, j); // swap integers
  swapvals(x, y); // swap floats
```

5

```
cout << "Swapped i, j: " << i << ' ' << j
     << endl;
cout << "Swapped x, y: " << x << ' ' << y
     << endl;

return 0;
}
```

In this program, the line,

```
template <class X> void swapvals(X &a, X &b)
```

tells the compiler two things: first, that a template function is being created; and second, that **X** is a generic type that is used as a placeholder. The body of **swapvals( )** is defined using **X** as the data type of the values that will be swapped. In **main( )**, the **swapvals( )** function is called using two different types of data: integers and floating-point numbers. Because **swapvals( )** is a generic function, the compiler automatically creates two versions of **swapvals( )**—one that will exchange integer values and one that will exchange floating-point values.

Generic functions are similar to overloaded functions except that they are more restrictive. When functions are overloaded, you can have different actions performed within the body of each function. A generic function must perform the same general action for all versions.

In addition to generic functions, you can also define a *generic class*. When you do this, you create a class that defines all algorithms used by that class, but the actual type of the data being manipulated will be specified as a parameter when objects of that class are created.

Generic classes are useful when a class contains generalizable logic. For example, the same algorithm that maintains a queue of integers will also work for a queue of characters. Also, the same mechanism that maintains a linked list of mailing addresses will also maintain a linked list of auto parts. By using a generic class, you can create a class that will maintain a queue, linked list, and so on, for any type of data. The compiler will automatically generate the correct type of object based upon the type you specify when the object is created.

Here is the general form of a generic class declaration:

```
template <class data_type> class class-name {
  // ...
};
```

In this case, *data_type* is a placeholder for a type of data upon
which the class will operate. When you declare an object of a
generic class, you specify the type of data between angle brackets,
using this general form:

   class-name<type> object;

The following is an example of a generic class. This program
creates a very simple generic singly linked list class. It then
demonstrates the class by creating a linked list that stores
characters.

```cpp
// A simple generic linked list.
#include <iostream>
using namespace std;

template <class data_t> class list {
  data_t data;
  list *next;
public:
  list(data_t d);
  void add(list *node) { node->next = this;
                         next = 0; }
  list *getnext() { return next; }
  data_t getdata() { return data; }
};

template <class data_t>
list<data_t>::list(data_t d)
{
  data = d;
  next = 0;
}

int main()
{
  list<char> start('a');
  list<char> *p, *last;
  int i;
```

```
// build a list
last = &start;
for(i=0; i<26; i++) {
  p = new list<char> ('a' + i);
  p->add(last);
  last = p;
}

// follow the list
p = &start;
while(p) {
  cout << p->getdata();
  p = p->getnext();
}

return 0;
}
```

As you can see, the declaration of a generic class is similar to that of a generic function. The actual type of data stored by the list is made generic in the class declaration. In **main( )**, objects and pointers are created that specify that the data type of the list will be **char**.

Pay special attention to this declaration:

```
list<char> start('a');
```

Notice how the desired data type is passed inside the angle brackets.

this

this is a pointer to the object that generated a call to a member function. All member functions are automatically passed a **this** pointer.

throw

throw is part of C++'s exception-handling subsystem. Exception handling is built upon three keywords: **try**, **catch**, and **throw**. In the most general terms, program statements that you want to monitor for exceptions are contained in a **try** block. If an exception (i.e., an error) occurs within the **try** block, it is thrown (using **throw**). The exception is caught, using **catch**, and processed. The following discussion elaborates upon this general description.

As stated, code that you want to monitor for exceptions must have been executed from within a **try** block. (Functions called from within a **try** block may also throw an exception.) Any exception must be caught by a **catch** statement that immediately follows the **try** statement that throws the exception. The general form of **try** and **catch** are shown here:

5

```
try {
    // try block
}
catch (type1 arg) {
    // catch block
}
catch (type2 arg) {
    // catch block
}
catch (type3 arg) {
    // catch block
}
// ...
catch (typeN arg) {
    // catch block
}
```

The **try** block must contain that portion of your program that you want to monitor for errors. This can be as short as a few statements within one function or as all-encompassing as enclosing the **main( )** function code within a **try** block (which effectively causes the entire program to be monitored).

When an exception is thrown, it is caught by its corresponding **catch** statement, which processes the exception. There can be more than one **catch** statement associated with a **try**. The **catch** statement to execute is determined by the type of the exception. That is, if the data type specified by a **catch** matches that of the exception, then that **catch** statement is executed (and all others are bypassed). When an exception is caught, *arg* will receive its value. Any type of data can be caught, including classes that you create. If no exception is thrown (that is, no error occurs within the **try** block), then no **catch** statement is executed.

The general form of the **throw** statement is shown here:

    throw *exception*;

throw must be executed either from within the **try** block proper, or from any function called (directly or indirectly) from within the **try** block. *exception* is the value thrown.

If you throw an exception for which there is no applicable **catch** statement, an abnormal program termination may occur. Throwing an unhandled exception causes the **terminate( )** function to be invoked. By default, **terminate( )** calls **abort( )** to stop your program. However, you may specify your own handlers if you like, using **set_terminate( )**.

Here is a simple example that shows the way C++ exception handling operates:

```
// A simple exception handling example.
#include <iostream>
using namespace std;

int main()
{
  cout << "Start\n";

  try { // start a try block
    cout << "Inside try block\n";
    throw 100; // throw an error
    cout << "This will not execute";
  }
  catch (int i) { // catch an error
    cout << "Caught an exception -- value is: ";
    cout << i << "\n";
```

```
  }

  cout << "End";

  return 0;
}
```

This program displays the following output:

```
Start
Inside try block
Caught an exception -- value is: 100
End
```

As you can see, there is a **try** block containing three statements and a **catch(int i)** statement that processes an integer exception. Within the **try** block, only two of the three statements will execute: the first **cout** statement and the **throw**. Once an exception has been thrown, control passes to the **catch** expression and the **try** block is terminated. That is, **catch** is *not* called. Rather, program execution is transferred to it. (The program's stack is automatically reset as needed to accomplish this.) Thus, the **cout** statement following the **throw** will never execute.

5

true

true is the Boolean constant for true.

try

try is part of C++'s exception-handling mechanism. See **throw**.

typedef

The **typedef** keyword allows you to create a new name for an existing data type. The data type may be one of the built-in types,

or a class, structure, union, or enumeration. The general form of
typedef is

typedef *type_specifier new_name*;

For example, to use the word **balance** in place of **float**, you would write

```
typedef float balance;
```

typeid

The **typeid** operator returns a reference to a **type_info** object that
describes the type of the object to which **typeid** is being applied.
typeid has this general form:

typeid(*object*)

typeid supports runtime type identification (RTTI) in C++.

NOTE: See **typeid** in Chapter 3.

typename

C++ supports the **typename** keyword. It may be used in place
of the keyword **class** in a **template** declaration or to signify an
undefined type.

union

A **union** is a special type of class that assigns two or more
variables to the same memory location. The form of its definition
and the way the . (dot) and –> (arrow) operators reference a
member are the same as for a class. By default, a **union**'s members
are public. The general form is

```
union class-name {
   // public members by default
private:
   // private members
} object-list;
```

The *class-name* is the type name for the union.

NOTE: In C, unions can contain only data members and the *private* specifier is not allowed.

For example, this creates a union between a **double** and a character string and creates one variable called **my_var**.

```
union my_union {
   char time[30];
   double offset;
} my_var;
```

The **union** is covered in more detail in Chapter 1.

unsigned

unsigned is a data type modifier that declares unsigned integers. Unsigned integers can hold only positive values.

using

See **namespace**.

virtual

The **virtual** function specifier creates a virtual function. A virtual function is a member of a base class that can be overridden by a derived class. If the function is not overridden by a derived class, the base class' definition is used.

A *pure virtual function* is a member function that has no definition. This means that a pure virtual function *must be* overridden in a derived class. A pure virtual function is prototyped like this:

> virtual *ret-type fname*(*param-list*) = 0;

Here, *ret-type* is the return type of the function, *fname* is the function's name, and *param-list* specifies any parameters. The important feature is the **= 0**. This tells the compiler that the virtual function has no definition relative to the base class.

Runtime polymorphism is attained when virtual functions are accessed through a base class pointer. When this is done, the type of object pointed to determines which version of the virtual function is called.

void

The **void** type specifier is primarily used to explicitly declare functions that return no value. It is also used to create **void** pointers (pointers to **void**), which are generic pointers that are capable of pointing to any type of object.

In C, **void** is also used to declare an empty parameter list in a function declaration.

➤ Programming Tip

A class that contains at least one pure virtual function is called *abstract*. Abstract classes cannot be used to instantiate objects. They also cannot be used as function parameter types or as return types. However, you can create a pointer to an abstract class.

A class that inherits an abstract class and does not override all of the pure virtual functions will, itself, be abstract. A derived class must override all pure virtual functions of all of its base classes before the derived class becomes concrete and objects of its class can be created.

volatile

The **volatile** modifier tells the compiler that a variable may have its contents altered in ways not explicitly defined by the program. For example, variables that are changed by hardware such as real-time clocks, interrupts, or other inputs should be declared as **volatile**.

wchar_t

5

wchar_t specifies a wide-character type. Wide characters are 16 bits long.

while

The while **loop** has the general form:

```
while(condition) {
    statement block
}
```

If a single statement is the object of the **while**, then the braces may be omitted.

The **while** tests the *condition* at the top of the loop. Therefore, if the *condition* is false to begin with, the loop will not execute even once. The *condition* may be any expression.

The following is an example of a **while** loop. It will read 100 characters and store them into a character array.

```
char s[256];

t = 0;
while(t<100) {
  s[t] = stream.get();
  t++;
}
```

Chapter 6
The Standard C I/O Functions

This chapter describes the standard C I/O functions. It includes the functions defined by C89 and those added by C99. The functions defined by C89 are also supported by C++, and there is no fundamental reason that you cannot use them in your C++ program when you deem it appropriate.

In C, the header associated with the I/O functions is **<stdio.h>**. In C++, this header is called **<cstdio>**. For ease of discussion, this chapter will use the C header name, but references to **<stdio.h>** also apply to **<cstdio>**.

The **<stdio.h>** header defines several macros and types required by the C file system. The most important type is **FILE**, which is used to declare a file pointer. Two other frequently used types are **size_t** and **fpos_t**. The **size_t** type, which is some form of unsigned integer, is the type of the result returned by **sizeof**. The **fpos_t** type defines an object that can uniquely specify each location within a file. The most commonly used macro defined by the header is **EOF**, which is the value that indicates end of file. Other data types and macros in **<stdio.h>** are described in conjunction with the functions to which they relate.

Many of the I/O functions set the built-in global integer variable **errno** when an error occurs. Your program can check this variable to obtain more information about the error. The values that **errno** may have are implementation dependent.

The C I/O system operates through *streams*. A stream is a logical device that is connected to an actual physical device, which is referred to as the *file* when a file is opened. In the C I/O system, all streams have the same capabilities, but files may have differing qualities. For example, a disk file allows random access, but a modem does not. Thus, the C I/O system provides a level of abstraction between the programmer and the physical device. The abstraction is the stream and the device is the file. In this way, a consistent logical interface can be maintained, even though the actual physical devices may differ.

A stream is connected to a file via a call to **fopen( )**. Streams are operated upon through the file pointer (which is a pointer of type **FILE ***). In a sense, the file pointer is the glue that holds the system together.

107

When a C program begins execution, three predefined streams are automatically opened. They are **stdin**, **stdout**, and **stderr**, referring to standard input, standard output, and standard error, respectively. By default, these are connected to the console, but they may be redirected to any other type of device.

C99 adds the **restrict** qualifier to certain parameters of several functions originally defined by C89. When this is the case, the function will be shown using its C89 prototype (which is also the prototype used by C++), but the **restrict**-qualified parameters will be pointed out in the function's description.

clearerr

```
#include <stdio.h>
void clearerr(FILE *stream);
```

The **clearerr( )** function resets (i.e., sets to zero) the error flag associated with the stream pointed to by *stream*. The end-of-file indicator is also reset.

The error flags for each stream are initially set to zero by a successful call to **fopen( )**. File errors can occur for a wide variety of reasons, many of which are system dependent. The exact nature of the error can be determined by calling **perror( )**, which displays a message describing the error. See **perror( )**.

Related functions are **feof( )**, **ferror( )**, and **perror( )**.

fclose

```
#include <stdio.h>
int fclose(FILE *stream);
```

The **fclose( )** function closes the file associated with *stream* and flushes its buffer. After a call to **fclose( )**, *stream* is no longer connected with the file, and any automatically allocated buffers are deallocated.

If **fclose( )** is successful, zero is returned; otherwise, **EOF** is returned. Trying to close a file that has already been closed is an error. Removing the storage media before closing a file will also generate an error, as will lack of sufficient free disk space.

Related functions are **fopen( )**, **freopen( )**, and **fflush( )**.

feof

```
#include <stdio.h>
int feof(FILE *stream);
```

The **feof( )** function determines if the end of the file associated with *stream* has been reached. A nonzero value is returned if the file position indicator is at end-of-file; zero is returned otherwise.

6

Once the end of the file has been reached, subsequent read operations will return **EOF** until either **rewind( )** is called or the file position indicator is moved using **fseek( )**.

The **feof( )** function is particularly useful when working with binary files because the end-of-file marker is also a valid binary integer. Explicit calls must be made to **feof( )** rather than simply testing the return value of **getc( )**, for example, to determine when the end of a binary file has been reached.

Related functions are **clearerr( )**, **ferror( )**, **perror( )**, **putc( )**, and **getc( )**.

ferror

```
#include <stdio.h>
int ferror(FILE *stream);
```

The **ferror( )** function checks for a file error on the given *stream*. A return value of zero indicates that no error has occurred, while a nonzero value means an error.

To determine the exact nature of the error, use the **perror( )** function.

Related functions are **clearerr( )**, **feof( )**, and **perror( )**.

fflush

```
#include <stdio.h>
int fflush(FILE *stream);
```

If *stream* is associated with a file opened for writing, a call to **fflush( )** causes the contents of the output buffer to be physically written to the file. The file remains open.

A return value of zero indicates success; **EOF** indicates that a write error has occurred.

All buffers are automatically flushed upon normal termination of the program or when they are full. Also, closing a file flushes its buffer.

Related functions are **fclose( )**, **fopen( )**, **fread( )**, **fwrite( )**, **getc( )**, and **putc( )**.

fgetc

```
#include <stdio.h>
int fgetc(FILE *stream);
```

The **fgetc( )** function returns the next character from the specified input stream and increments the file position indicator. The character is read as an **unsigned char** that is converted to an integer.

If the end of the file is reached, **fgetc( )** returns **EOF**. However, since **EOF** is a valid integer value, when working with binary files you must use **feof( )** to check for the end of the file. If **fgetc( )** encounters an error, **EOF** is also returned. If working with binary files, you must use **ferror( )** to check for file errors.

Related functions are **fputc( )**, **getc( )**, **putc( )**, and **fopen( )**.

fgetpos

```
#include <stdio.h>
int fgetpos(FILE *stream, fpos_t *position);
```

For the specified stream, the **fgetpos( )** function stores the current value of the file position indicator in the object pointed to by *position*. The object pointed to by *position* must be of type **fpos_t**. The value stored there is useful only in a subsequent call to **fsetpos( )**.

In C99, both *stream* and *position* are qualified by **restrict**.

If an error occurs, **fgetpos( )** returns nonzero; otherwise, it returns zero.

Related functions are **fsetpos( )**, **fseek( )**, and **ftell( )**.

6

fgets

```
#include <stdio.h>
char *fgets(char *str, int num, FILE *stream);
```

The **fgets( )** function reads up to *num–1* characters from *stream* and stores them in the character array pointed to by *str*. Characters are read until either a newline or an **EOF** is received or until the specified limit is reached. After the characters have been read, a null is stored in the array immediately after the last character read. A newline character will be retained and will be part of the array pointed to by *str*.

In C99, *str* and *stream* are qualified by **restrict**.

If successful, **fgets( )** returns *str*; a null pointer is returned upon failure. If a read error occurs, the contents of the array pointed to by *str* are indeterminate. Because a null pointer will be returned either when an error has occurred or when the end of the file is reached, you should use **feof( )** or **ferror( )** to determine what has actually happened.

Related functions are **fputs( )**, **fgetc( )**, **gets( )**, and **puts( )**.

fopen

```
#include <stdio.h>
FILE *fopen(const char *fname, const char *mode);
```

The **fopen( )** function opens a file whose name is pointed to by *fname* and returns the stream that is associated with it. The types of operations that will be allowed on the file are defined by the value of *mode*. The legal values for *mode* are shown in the following table. The filename must be a string of characters comprising a valid filename as defined by the operating system and may include a path specification if the environment supports it.

In C99, *fname* and *mode* are qualified by **restrict**.

Mode	Meaning
"r"	Open text file for reading
"w"	Create a text file for writing
"a"	Append to text file
"rb"	Open binary file for reading
"wb"	Create binary file for writing
"ab"	Append to a binary file
"r+"	Open text file for read/write
"w+"	Create text file for read/write
"a+"	Open text file for read/write
"rb+" or "r+b"	Open binary file for read/write
"wb+" or "w+b"	Create binary file for read/write
"ab+" or "a+b"	Open binary file for read/write

If **fopen( )** is successful in opening the specified file, a **FILE** pointer is returned. If the file cannot be opened, a null pointer is returned.

As the table shows, a file can be opened in either text or binary mode. In text mode, some character translations may occur. For example, newlines may be converted into carriage return/linefeed sequences. No such translations occur on binary files.

The correct method of opening a file is illustrated by this code fragment:

```
FILE *fp;

if ((fp = fopen("test", "w"))==NULL) {
  printf("Cannot open file.\n");
  exit(1);
}
```

This method detects any error in opening a file, such as a write-protected or a full disk, before attempting to write to it.

If you use **fopen( )** to open a file for output, any preexisting file by that name will be erased and a new file started. If no file by that name exists, one will be created. Opening a file for read operations requires that the file exists. If it does not exist, an error will be returned. If you want to add to the end of the file, you must use mode "a". If the file does not exist, it will be created.

6

➤ Programming Tip

Any file can be opened as either a text file or a binary file. It does not matter what the file actually contains. For example, a file that holds ASCII text can still be opened and operated upon as a binary file. As far as the standard C file system is concerned, the only difference between a text file and a binary file is that no character translations will take place when operating on a file opened in binary mode.

You might want to open a file that contains text as a binary file when you are performing various non-text-based manipulations on it. For example, file utilities that compare, compress, or sort will typically open the files for binary access. Also, file encryption programs will almost always need to operate in binary mode.

The key point is that the difference between a text file and a binary file is not what the file contains, but rather the mode in which you open it.

When accessing a file opened for read/write operations, you cannot follow an output operation with an input operation without first calling **fflush( )**, **fseek( )**, **fsetpos( )**, or **rewind( )**. Also, you cannot follow an input operation with an output operation without first calling one of the previously mentioned functions, except when the end of the file is reached during input. That is, output can directly follow input at the end of the file.

A minimum of **FOPEN_MAX** files can be open at any one time. **FOPEN_MAX** is defined in **<stdio.h>**.

Related functions are **fclose( )**, **fread( )**, **fwrite( )**, **putc( )**, and **getc( )**.

fprintf

```
#include <stdio.h>
int fprintf(FILE *stream, const char *format, ...);
```

The **fprintf( )** function outputs the values of the arguments that comprise the argument list as specified in the *format* string to the stream pointed to by *stream.* The return value is the number of characters actually printed. If an error occurs, a negative number is returned.

In C99, *stream* and *format* are qualified by **restrict**.

The operations of the format control string and commands are identical to those in **printf( )**; see **printf( )** for a complete description.

Related functions are **printf( )** and **fscanf( )**.

fputc

```
#include <stdio.h>
int fputc(int ch, FILE *stream);
```

The **fputc( )** function writes the character *ch* to the specified stream at the current file position and then advances the file position indicator. Even though *ch* is declared to be an **int** for historical reasons, it is converted by **fputc( )** into an **unsigned char**. Because a character argument is elevated to an integer at the time of the call, you will generally see character values used as arguments. If an integer were used, the high-order byte(s) would simply be discarded.

The value returned by **fputc( )** is the value of the character written. If an error occurs, **EOF** is returned. For files opened for binary operations, an **EOF** may be a valid character, and the function **ferror( )** will need to be used to determine whether an error has actually occurred.

Related functions are **fgetc( )**, **fopen( )**, **fprintf( )**, **fread( )**, and **fwrite( )**.

fputs

6

```
#include <stdio.h>
int fputs(const char *str, FILE *stream);
```

The **fputs( )** function writes the contents of the string pointed to by *str* to the specified stream. The null terminator is not written.

In C99, *str* and *stream* are qualified by **restrict**.

The **fputs( )** function returns nonnegative on success and **EOF** on failure.

If the stream is opened in text mode, certain character translations may take place. This means that there may not be a one-to-one mapping of the string onto the file. However, if the stream is opened in binary mode, no character translations will occur, and a one-to-one mapping between the string and the file will exist.

Related functions are **fgets( )**, **gets( )**, **puts( )**, **fprintf( )**, and **fscanf( )**.

fread

```
#include <stdio.h>
size_t fread(void *buf, size_t size, size_t count, FILE *stream);
```

The **fread( )** function reads *count* number of objects, each object being *size* bytes in length, from the stream pointed to by *stream* and stores them in the array pointed to by *buf*. The file position indicator is advanced by the number of characters read.

In C99, *buf* and *stream* are qualified by **restrict**.

The **fread( )** function returns the number of items actually read. If fewer items are read than are requested in the call, either an error has occurred or the end of the file has been reached. You must use **feof( )** or **ferror( )** to determine what has taken place.

If the stream is opened for text operations, certain character translations, such as carriage return/linefeed sequences being transformed into newlines, may occur.

Related functions are **fwrite( )**, **fopen( )**, **fscanf( )**, **fgetc( )**, and **getc( )**.

freopen

```
#include <stdio.h>
FILE *freopen(const char *fname, const char *mode, FILE *stream);
```

The **freopen( )** function associates an existing stream with a different file. The end-of-file and error flags are cleared in the process. The new file's name is pointed to by *fname*, the access mode is pointed to by *mode*, and the stream to be reassigned is pointed to by *stream*. The *mode* parameter uses the same format as **fopen( )**; a complete discussion is found in the **fopen( )** description.

In C99, *fname*, *mode*, and *stream* are qualified by **restrict**.

When called, **freopen( )** first tries to close a file that may currently be associated with *stream*. However, if the attempt to close the file fails, the **freopen( )** function still continues to open the other file.

The **freopen( )** function returns a pointer to *stream* on success and a null pointer otherwise.

The main use of **freopen( )** is to redirect the system-defined files **stdin**, **stdout**, and **stderr** to some other file.

Related functions are **fopen( )** and **fclose( )**.

fscanf

```
#include <stdio.h>
int fscanf(FILE *stream, const char *format, ...);
```

The **fscanf( )** function works exactly like the **scanf( )** function, except that it reads the information from the stream specified by *stream* instead of **stdin**. See **scanf( )**.

In C99, *stream* and *format* are qualified by **restrict**.

The **fscanf( )** function returns the number of arguments actually assigned values. This number does not include skipped fields. A return value of **EOF** means that a failure occurred before the first assignment was made.

Related functions are **scanf( )** and **fprintf( )**.

fseek

```
#include <stdio.h>
int fseek(FILE *stream, long int offset, int origin);
```

The **fseek( )** function sets the file position indicator associated with *stream* according to the values of *offset* and *origin*. Its purpose is to support random access I/O operations. The *offset* is the number of bytes from *origin* to seek to. The values for *origin* must be one of these macros (defined in **<stdio.h>**):

Name	Meaning
SEEK_SET	Seek from start of file
SEEK_CUR	Seek from current location
SEEK_END	Seek from end of file

A return value of zero means that **fseek( )** succeeded. A nonzero value indicates failure.

In general, **fseek( )** should be used only with binary files. If used on a text file, then *origin* must be **SEEK_SET** and *offset* must be a value obtained by calling **ftell( )** on the same file, or zero (to set the file position indicator to the start of the file).

The **fseek( )** function clears the end-of-file flag associated with the specified stream. Furthermore, it nullifies any prior **ungetc( )** on the same stream. See **ungetc( )**.

Related functions are **ftell( )**, **rewind( )**, **fopen( )**, **fgetpos( )**, and **fsetpos( )**.

fsetpos

```
#include <stdio.h>
int fsetpos(FILE *stream, const fpos_t *position);
```

The **fsetpos( )** function moves the file position indicator to the location specified by the object pointed to by *position*. This value must have been previously obtained through a call to **fgetpos( )**. After **fsetpos( )** is executed, the end-of-file indicator is reset. Also, any previous call to **ungetc( )** is nullified.

If **fsetpos( )** fails, it returns nonzero. If it is successful, it returns zero.

Related functions are **fgetpos( )**, **fseek( )**, and **ftell( )**.

ftell

```
#include <stdio.h>
long int ftell(FILE *stream);
```

The **ftell( )** function returns the current value of the file position indicator for the specified stream. In the case of binary streams, the value is the number of bytes the indicator is from the beginning of the file. For text streams, the return value may not be meaningful except as an argument to **fseek( )** because of possible character translations, such as carriage return/linefeeds being substituted for newlines, which affect the apparent size of the file.

The **ftell( )** function returns –1 when an error occurs.

Related functions are **fseek( )** and **fgetpos( )**.

fwrite

```
#include <stdio.h>
size_t fwrite(const void *buf, size_t size, size_t count,
              FILE *stream);
```

The **fwrite( )** function writes *count* number of objects, each object being *size* bytes in length, to the stream pointed to by *stream* from the character array pointed to by *buf*. The file position indicator is advanced by the number of characters written.

In C99, *buf* and *stream* are qualified by **restrict**.

The **fwrite( )** function returns the number of items actually written, which, if the function is successful, will equal the number requested. If fewer items are written than are requested, an error has occurred.

Related functions are **fread( )**, **fscanf( )**, **getc( )**, and **fgetc( )**.

getc

```
#include <stdio.h>
int getc(FILE *stream);
```

The **getc( )** function returns the next character from the specified input stream and increments the file position indicator. The character is read as an **unsigned char** that is converted to an integer.

If the end of the file is reached, **getc( )** returns **EOF**. However, since **EOF** is a valid integer value, when working with binary files you must use **feof( )** to check for the end-of-file condition. If **getc( )** encounters an error, **EOF** is also returned. If working with binary files, you must use **ferror( )** to check for file errors.

The functions **getc( )** and **fgetc( )** are identical except that in most implementations, **getc( )** is defined as a macro.

Related functions are **fputc( )**, **fgetc( )**, **putc( )**, and **fopen( )**.

getchar

```
#include <stdio.h>
int getchar(void);
```

The **getchar( )** function returns the next character from **stdin**. The character is read as an **unsigned char** that is converted to an integer.

If the end of the file is reached, **getchar( )** returns **EOF**. If **getchar( )** encounters an error, **EOF** is also returned.

The **getchar( )** function is often implemented as a macro.

Related functions are **fputc( )**, **fgetc( )**, **putc( )**, and **fopen( )**.

gets

```
#include <stdio.h>
char *gets(char *str);
```

The **gets( )** function reads characters from **stdin** and places them into the character array pointed to by *str*. Characters are read until a newline or an **EOF** is received. The newline character is not made part of the string; instead, it is translated into a null to terminate the string.

If successful, **gets( )** returns *str*; a null pointer is returned upon failure. If a read error occurs, the contents of the array pointed to by *str* are indeterminate. Because a null pointer will be returned either when an error has occurred or when the end of the file is reached, you should use **feof( )** or **ferror( )** to determine what has actually happened.

There is no way to limit the number of characters that **gets( )** will read, which means that the array pointed to by *str* could be overrun. Thus, this function is inherently dangerous. Its use should be limited to sample programs or utilities for your own use. It should not be used for production code.

Related functions are **fputs( )**, **fgetc( )**, **fgets( )**, and **puts( )**.

➤ Programming Tip

When using **gets( )**, it is possible to overrun the array that is being used to receive the characters entered by the user, because **gets( )** provides no bounds checking. One way around this problem is to use **fgets( )**, specifying **stdin** for the input stream. Since **fgets( )** requires you to specify a maximum length, it is possible to prevent an array overrun. The only trouble is that **fgets( )** does not remove the newline character that terminates input and **gets( )** does, so you will have to manually remove it, as shown in the following program:

```
#include <stdio.h>
#include <string.h>

int main(void)
{
  char str[10];
  int i;

  printf("Enter a string: ");
  fgets(str, 10, stdin);

  /* remove newline, if present */
  i = strlen(str)-1;
  if(str[i]=='\n') str[i] = '\0';

  printf("This is your string: %s", str);

  return 0;
}
```

Although using **fgets( )** requires a little more work, its advantage over **gets( )** is that you can prevent the input array from being overrun.

6

perror

```
#include <stdio.h>
void perror(const char *str);
```

The **perror( )** function maps the value of the global variable **errno** onto a string and writes that string to **stderr**. If the value of *str* is not null, that string is written first, followed by a colon, and then the implementation-defined error message.

printf

```
#include <stdio.h>
int printf(const char *format, ...);
```

The **printf( )** function writes to **stdout** the arguments that comprise the argument list as specified by the string pointed to by *format*.

In C99, *format* is qualified with **restrict**.

The string pointed to by *format* consists of two types of items. The first type is made up of characters that will be printed on the screen. The second type contains format specifiers that define the way the arguments are displayed. A format specifier begins with a percent sign and is followed by the format code. There must be exactly the same number of arguments as there are format specifiers, and the format specifiers and the arguments are matched in order. For example, the following **printf( )** call displays "Hi c 10 there!":

```
printf("Hi %c %d %s", 'c', 10, "there!");
```

If there are insufficient arguments to match the format specifiers, the output is undefined. If there are more arguments than format specifiers, the remaining arguments are discarded. The format specifiers are shown here.

Code	Format
%a	Hexadecimal output in the form 0x*h.hhhh*p+*d*. (C99 only)
%A	Hexadecimal output in the form 0X*h.hhhh*P+*d*. (C99 only)
%c	Character
%d	Signed decimal integers
%i	Signed decimal integers
%e	Scientific notation (lowercase e)
%E	Scientific notation (uppercase E)
%f	Decimal floating point
%F	Decimal floating point (C99 only; produces uppercase INF, INFINITY, or NAN when applied to infinity or a value that is not-a-number. The %f specifier produces lowercase equivalents.)
%g	Uses %e or %f, whichever is shorter
%G	Uses %E or %F, whichever is shorter
%o	Unsigned octal
%s	String of characters
%u	Unsigned decimal integers
%x	Unsigned hexadecimal (lowercase letters)
%X	Unsigned hexadecimal (uppercase letters)
%p	Displays a pointer
%n	The associated argument must be a pointer to an integer. This specifier causes the number of characters written (up to the point at which the %n is encountered) to be stored in that integer.
%%	Prints a % sign

The **printf( )** function returns the number of characters actually printed. A negative return value indicates that an error has taken place.

The format codes can accept modifiers that specify the field width, precision, and left-justification. An integer placed between the % sign and the format code acts as a *minimum field-width specifier*. This pads the output with spaces or 0's to ensure that it is at least a certain minimum length. If the string or number is greater than that minimum, it will be printed in full, even if it overruns the minimum. The default padding is done with spaces. If you want to pad with 0's, place a 0 before the field-width specifier. For example, **%05d** will pad a number of less than 5 digits with 0's so that its total length is 5.

The exact meaning of the *precision modifier* depends on the format code being modified. To add a precision modifier, place a decimal point followed by the precision after the field-width specifier. For **a**, **A**, **e**, **E**, **f**, and **F** formats, the precision modifier determines the number of decimal places printed. For example, **%10.4f** will display a number at least ten characters wide with four decimal places. When the precision modifier is applied to the **g** or **G** format code, it determines the maximum number of significant digits displayed. When applied to integers, the precision modifier specifies the minimum number of digits that will be displayed. Leading zeros are added, if necessary.

When the precision modifier is applied to strings, the number following the period specifies the maximum field length. For example, **%5.7s** will display a string that will be at least five characters long and will not exceed seven. If the string is longer than the maximum field width, the characters will be truncated off the end.

By default, all output is *right-justified*: if the field width is larger than the data printed, the data will be placed on the right edge of the field. You can force the information to be left-justified by putting a minus sign directly after the %. For example, **%-10.2f** will left-justify a floating-point number with two decimal places in a ten-character field.

There are two format modifiers that allow **printf( )** to display short and long integers. These modifiers can be applied to the **d**, **i**, **o**, **u**, **x**, and **X** type specifiers. The l modifier tells **printf( )** that a long data type follows. For example, **%ld** means that a **long int** is to be displayed. The **h** modifier tells **printf( )** to display a short integer. Therefore, **%hu** indicates that the data is of type **short unsigned int**.

If you are using a modern compiler that supports the wide-character features added in 1995, then you can use the l modifier with the **c** specifier to indicate a wide character. You can also use the l modifier with the **s** format command to indicate a wide-character string.

An **L** modifier can prefix the floating-point commands of **a**, **A**, **e**, **E**, **f**, **F**, **g**, and **G**, and indicates that a **long double** follows.

The **n** command causes the number of characters that have been written at the time the **n** is encountered to be placed in an integer variable whose pointer is specified in the argument list. For example, this code fragment displays the number 14 after the line "this is a test":

```
int i;

printf("This is a test%n", &i);
printf("%d", i);
```

You can apply the **l** modifier to the **n** specifier to indicate that the corresponding argument points to a long integer. You can specify the **h** modifier to indicate that the corresponding argument points to a short integer.

The **#** has a special meaning when used with some **printf( )** format codes. Preceding **a**, **A**, **g**, **G**, **f**, **e**, or **E** with a **#** ensures that the decimal point will be present, even if there are no decimal digits. If you precede the **x** or **X** format code with a **#**, the hexadecimal number will be printed with a **0x** prefix. If you precede the **o** format with a **#**, the octal value will be printed with a **0** prefix. The **#** cannot be applied to any other format specifiers.

The minimum field-width and precision specifiers may be provided by arguments to **printf( )** instead of by constants. To accomplish this, use an ***** as a placeholder. When the format string is scanned, **printf( )** will match each ***** to an argument in the order in which they occur.

Format Modifiers Added to printf( ) by C99

C99 adds several format modifiers to **printf( )**: **hh**, **ll**, **j**, **z**, and **t**. The **hh** modifier can be applied to **d**, **i**, **o**, **u**, **x**, **X**, or **n**. It specifies that the corresponding argument is a **signed** or **unsigned char** value, or in the case of **n**, a pointer to a **signed char** variable. The **ll** modifier also can be applied to **d**, **i**, **o**, **u**, **x**, **X**, or **n**. It specifies that the corresponding argument is a **signed** or **unsigned long long int** value, or in the case of **n**, a pointer to a **long long int**.

The **j** format modifier, which applies to **d**, **i**, **o**, **u**, **x**, **X**, or **n**, specifies that the matching argument is of type **intmax_t** or **uintmax_t**. These types are declared in **<stdint.h>** and specify greatest-width integers.

The **z** format modifier, which applies to **d**, **i**, **o**, **u**, **x**, **X**, or **n**, specifies that the matching argument is of type **size_t**. This type is declared in **<stddef.h>** and specifies the result of **sizeof**.

The **t** format modifier, which applies to **d**, **i**, **o**, **u**, **x**, **X**, or **n**, specifies that the matching argument is of type **ptrdiff_t**. This type is declared in **<stddef.h>** and specifies the difference between two pointers.

C99 also allows the l to be applied to the floating-point specifiers **a**, **A**, **e**, **E**, **f**, **F**, **g**, and **G**, but it has no effect.

Related functions are **scanf( )** and **fprintf( )**.

putc

```
#include <stdio.h>
int putc(int ch, FILE *stream);
```

The **putc( )** function writes the character contained in the least significant byte of *ch* to the output stream pointed to by *stream*. Because character arguments are elevated to integer at the time of the call, you can use character values as arguments to **putc( )**. **putc( )** is often implemented as a macro.

The **putc( )** function returns the character written if successful, or **EOF** if an error occurs. If the output stream has been opened in binary mode, **EOF** is a valid value for *ch*. This means that you may need to use **ferror( )** to determine whether an error has occurred.

Related functions are **fgetc( )**, **fputc( )**, **getchar( )**, and **putchar( )**.

putchar

```
#include <stdio.h>
int putchar(int ch);
```

The **putchar( )** function writes the character contained in the least significant byte of *ch* to **stdout**. It is functionally equivalent to **putc(ch, stdout)**. Because character arguments are elevated to integer at the time of the call, you can use character values as arguments to **putchar( )**.

The **putchar( )** function returns the character written if successful, or **EOF** if an error occurs.

A related function is **putc( )**.

puts

```
#include <stdio.h>
int puts(const char *str);
```

The **puts( )** function writes the string pointed to by *str* to the standard output device. The null terminator is translated to a newline.

The **puts( )** function returns a nonnegative value if successful and an **EOF** upon failure.

Related functions are **putc( )**, **gets( )**, and **printf( )**.

6

remove

```
#include <stdio.h>
int remove(const char *fname);
```

The **remove( )** function erases the file specified by *fname*. It returns zero if the file was successfully deleted and nonzero if an error occurred.

A related function is **rename( )**.

rename

```
#include <stdio.h>
int rename(const char *oldfname, const char *newfname);
```

The **rename( )** function changes the name of the file specified by *oldfname* to *newfname*. The *newfname* must not match any existing directory entry.

The **rename( )** function returns zero if successful and nonzero if an error has occurred.

A related function is **remove( )**.

rewind

```
#include <stdio.h>
void rewind(FILE *stream);
```

The **rewind( )** function moves the file position indicator to the start of the specified stream. It also clears the end-of-file and error flags associated with *stream*.

A related function is **fseek( )**.

scanf

```
#include <stdio.h>
int scanf(const char *format, ...);
```

The **scanf( )** function is a general-purpose input routine that reads the stream **stdin** and stores the information in the variables pointed to in its argument list. It can read all the built-in data types and automatically converts them into the proper internal format.

In C99, *format* is qualified with **restrict**.

The control string pointed to by *format* consists of three classifications of characters:

    Format specifiers
    Whitespace characters
    Nonwhitespace characters

The input format specifiers begin with a % sign and tell **scanf( )** what type of data is to be read next. The format specifiers are listed in the following table. For example, **%s** reads a string while **%d** reads an integer. The format string is read left to right and the format specifiers are matched, in order, with the arguments that comprise the argument list.

Code	Meaning
%a	Read a floating-point value (C99 only)
%A	Same as %a (C99 only)
%c	Read a single character
%d	Read a decimal integer
%i	Read an integer in either decimal, octal, or hexadecimal format
%e	Read a floating-point number
%E	Same as %e
%f	Read a floating-point number
%F	Same as %f (C99 only)
%g	Read a floating-point number
%G	Same as %g
%o	Read an octal number
%s	Read a string
%x	Read a hexadecimal number
%X	Same as %x
%p	Read a pointer
%n	Receive an integer value equal to the number of characters read so far
%u	Read an unsigned decimal integer
%[ ]	Scan for a set of characters
%%	Read a percent sign

To read a long integer, put an l (*ell*) in front of the format specifier. To read a short integer, put an **h** in front of the format specifier. These modifiers can be used with the **d**, **i**, **o**, **u**, and **x** format codes.

By default, the **a**, **f**, **e**, and **g** tell **scanf( )** to assign data to a **float**. If you put an l (*ell*) in front of one of these specifiers, **scanf( )** assigns the data to a **double**. Using an **L** tells **scanf( )** that the variable receiving the data is a **long double**.

If you are using a modern compiler that supports the wide-character features added in 1995, then you can use the l modifier with the **c** format code to indicate a pointer to a wide character of type **whcar_t**. You can also use the l modifier with the **s** format

code to indicate a pointer to a wide-character string. The l may
also be used to modify a scanset to indicate wide characters.

A whitespace character in the format string causes **scanf( )** to
skip over zero or more whitespace characters in the input stream.
A whitespace character is either a space, a tab character, or a
newline. In essence, one whitespace character in the control string
will cause **scanf( )** to read, but not store, any number (including
zero) of whitespace characters up to the first nonwhitespace
character.

A nonwhitespace character in the format string causes **scanf( )** to
read and discard a matching character. For example, **%d,%d** causes
scanf( ) to first read an integer, then read and discard a comma,
and finally read another integer. If the specified character is not
found, **scanf( )** will terminate.

All the variables used to receive values through **scanf( )** must be
passed by their addresses. This means that all arguments must be
pointers to the variables.

In the input stream, items must be separated by spaces, tabs, or
newlines. Punctuation such as commas, semicolons, and the like
do not count as separators. This means that

```
scanf("%d%d", &r, &c);
```

will accept an input of **10 20** but fail with **10,20**.

An * placed after the % and before the format code will read data
of the specified type but suppress its assignment. Thus, the
following command:

```
scanf("%d%*c%d", &x, &y);
```

given the input **10/20**, will put the value 10 into **x**, discard the
divide sign, and give **y** the value 20.

The format commands can specify a maximum field-length
modifier. This is an integer number placed between the % and the
format code that limits the number of characters read for any field.
For example, if you wish to read no more than 20 characters into
address, then you would write the following:

```
scanf("%20s", address);
```

If the input stream were greater than 20 characters, a subsequent
call to input would begin where this call left off. Input for a field

may terminate before the maximum field length is reached if a whitespace is encountered. In this case, **scanf( )** moves on to the next field.

Although spaces, tabs, and newlines are used as field separators, when reading a single character, these are read like any other character. For example, given an input stream of **x y**,

```
scanf("%c%c%c", &a, &b, &c);
```

will return with the character *x* in **a**, a space in **b**, and the character *y* in **c**.

Remember that any non-format specifiers in the control string—including spaces, tabs, and newlines—will be used to match and discard characters from the input stream. Any character that matches is discarded. For example, given the input stream **10t20**,

```
scanf("%dt%d", &x, &y);
```

will store 10 in **x** and 20 in **y**. The **t** is discarded because of the **t** in the control string.

Another feature of **scanf( )** is called a *scanset*. A scanset defines a set of characters that will be read by **scanf( )** and assigned to the corresponding character array. A scanset is defined by putting the characters you want to scan for inside square brackets. The beginning square bracket must be prefixed by a percent sign. For example, this scanset tells **scanf( )** to read only the characters A, B, and C:

```
%[ABC]
```

When a scanset is used, **scanf( )** continues to read characters and put them into the corresponding character array until a character that is not in the scanset is encountered. The corresponding variable must be a pointer to a character array. Upon return from **scanf( )**, the array will contain a null-terminated string comprised of the characters read.

You can specify an inverted set if the first character in the set is a ^. When the ^ is present, it instructs **scanf( )** to accept any character that *is not* defined by the scanset.

For many implementations, you can specify a range using a hyphen. For example, this tells **scanf( )** to accept the characters A through Z:

```
%[A-Z]
```

One important point to remember is that the scanset is case sensitive. Therefore, if you want to scan for both uppercase and lowercase letters, they must be specified individually.

The **scanf( )** function returns a number equal to the number of fields that were successfully assigned values. This number will not include fields that were read but not assigned because the * modifier was used to suppress the assignment. **EOF** is returned if an error occurs before the first field is assigned.

Format Modifiers Added to scanf( ) by C99

C99 adds several format modifiers to **scanf( )**: **hh, ll, j, z,** and **t.** The **hh** modifier can be applied to **d, i, o, u, x,** or **n.** It specifies that the corresponding argument is a pointer to a **signed** or **unsigned char** value. The **ll** modifier also can be applied to **d, i, o, u, x,** or **n.** It specifies that the corresponding argument is a pointer to a **signed** or **unsigned long long int** value.

The **j** format modifier, which applies to **d, i, o, u, x,** or **n,** specifies that the matching argument is a pointer to an object of type **intmax_t** or **uintmax_t.** These types are declared in **<stdint.h>** and specify greatest-width integers.

The **z** format modifier, which applies to **d, i, o, u, x,** or **n,** specifies that the matching argument is a pointer to an object of type **size_t.** This type is declared in **<stddef.h>** and specifies the result of **sizeof.**

The **t** format modifier, which applies to **d, i, o, u, x,** or **n,** specifies that the matching argument is a pointer to an object of type **ptrdiff_t.** This type is declared in **<stddef.h>** and specifies the difference between two pointers.

Related functions are **printf( )** and **fscanf( ).**

setbuf

```
#include <stdio.h>
void setbuf(FILE *stream, char *buf);
```

The **setbuf( )** function specifies the buffer that *stream* will use or, if called with *buf* set to null, turns off buffering. If a programmer-defined buffer is to be specified, it must be **BUFSIZ** characters long. **BUFSIZ** is defined in **<stdio.h>**.

In C99, *stream* and *buf* are qualified by **restrict**.

Related functions are **fopen( )**, **fclose( )**, and **setvbuf( )**.

setvbuf

```
#include <stdio.h>
int setvbuf(FILE *stream, char *buf, int mode, size_t size);
```

The **setvbuf( )** function allows the programmer to specify a buffer, its size, and its mode for the specified stream. The character array pointed to by *buf* is used as the buffer for I/O operations on *stream*. The size of the buffer is set by *size* and *mode* determines how buffering will be handled. If *buf* is null, **setvbuf( )** will allocate its own buffer.

In C99, *stream* and *buf* are qualified by **restrict**.

The legal values of *mode* are **_IOFBF**, **_IONBF**, and **_IOLBF**. These are defined in **<stdio.h>**. When *mode* is set to **_IOFBF**, full buffering will take place. If *mode* is **_IOLBF**, the stream will be line buffered. For output streams, this means that the buffer will be flushed each time a newline character is written. The buffer is also flushed when full. For input streams, input is buffered until a newline is read. If mode is **_IONBF**, no buffering takes place.

The **setvbuf( )** function returns zero on success and nonzero on failure.

A related function is **setbuf( )**.

snprintf

```
#include <stdio.h>
int snprintf(char * restrict buf, size_t num,
             const char * restrict format, ...)
```

The **snprintf( )** function was added by C99.

The **snprintf( )** function is identical to **sprintf( )** except that a maximum of *num*–1 characters will be stored into the array pointed to by *buf*. On completion, this array is null-terminated. Thus, **snprintf( )** allows you to prevent *buf* from being overrun.

Related functions are **printf( )**, **sprintf( )**, and **fsprintf( )**.

sprintf

```
#include <stdio.h>
int sprintf(char *buf, const char *format, ...);
```

The **sprintf( )** function is identical to **printf( )** except that the output is put into the array pointed to by *buf* instead of being written to the **stdout**. The array pointed to by *buf* is null-terminated. See **printf( )**.

In C99, *buf* and *format* are qualified by **restrict**.

The return value is equal to the number of characters actually placed into the array.

It is important to understand that **sprintf( )** provides no bounds checking on the array pointed to by *buf*. This means that the array will be overrun if the output generated by **sprintf( )** is greater than the array can hold. See **snprintf( )** for an alternative.

Related functions are **printf( )** and **fsprintf( )**.

sscanf

```
#include <stdio.h>
int sscanf(const char *buf, const char *format, ...);
```

The **sscanf( )** function is identical to **scanf( )** except that data is read from the array pointed to by *buf* rather than **stdin**. See **scanf( )**.

In C99, *buf* and *format* are qualified by **restrict**.

The return value is equal to the number of variables that were actually assigned values. This number does not include fields that were skipped through the use of the * format command modifier.

A value of zero means that no fields were assigned, and **EOF** indicates that an error occurred prior to the first assignment.

Related functions are **scanf( )** and **fscanf( )**.

tmpfile

```
#include <stdio.h>
FILE *tmpfile(void);
```

The **tmpfile( )** function opens a temporary binary file for read/write operations and returns a pointer to the stream. The function automatically uses a unique filename to avoid conflicts with existing files.

The **tmpfile( )** function returns a null pointer on failure; otherwise, it returns a pointer to the stream.

The temporary file created by **tmpfile( )** is automatically removed when the file is closed or when the program terminates.

You can open **TMP_MAX** temporary files (up to the limit set by **FOPEN_MAX**).

A related function is **tmpnam( )**.

tmpnam

```
#include <stdio.h>
char *tmpnam(char *name);
```

The **tmpnam( )** function generates a unique filename and stores it in the array pointed to by *name*. This array must be at least **L_tmpnam** characters long. (**L_tmpnam** is defined in **<stdio.h>**.) The main purpose of **tmpnam( )** is to generate a temporary filename that is different from any other file in the current disk directory.

The function can be called up to **TMP_MAX** times. **TMP_MAX** is defined in **<stdio.h>**, and it will be at least 25. Each time **tmpnam( )** is called, it will generate a new temporary filename.

A pointer to *name* is returned on success; otherwise, a null pointer is returned. If *name* is null, then the temporary filename is held in a static array owned by **tmpnam( )** and a pointer to this array is returned. This array will be overwritten by a subsequent call.

A related function is **tmpfile( )**.

ungetc

```
#include <stdio.h>
int ungetc(int ch, FILE *stream);
```

The **ungetc( )** function returns the character specified by the low-order byte of *ch* to the input stream *stream*. This character will then be obtained by the next read operation on *stream*. A call to **fflush( )**, **fseek( )**, or **rewind( )** undoes an **ungetc( )** operation and discards the character.

A one-character pushback is guaranteed; however, some implementations will accept more.

You may not unget an **EOF**.

A call to **ungetc( )** clears the end-of-file flag associated with the specified stream. The value of the file position indicator for a text stream is undefined until all pushed-back characters are read, in which case it will be the same as it was prior to the first **ungetc( )** call. For binary streams, each **ungetc( )** call decrements the file position indicator.

The return value is equal to *ch* on success and **EOF** on failure.

A related function is **getc( )**.

vprintf, vfprintf, vsprintf, and vsnprintf

```
#include <stdarg.h>
#include <stdio.h>
int vprintf(char *format, va_list arg_ptr);
int vfprintf(FILE *stream, const char *format,
```

```
                   va_list arg_ptr);
int vsprintf(char *buf, const char *format,
                   va_list arg_ptr);
int vsnprintf(char * restrict buf, size_t num,
                   const char * restrict format,  va_list arg_ptr);
```

The functions **vprintf( )**, **vfprintf( )**, **vsprintf( )**, and **vsnprint( )**
are functionally equivalent to **printf( )**, **fprintf( )**, **sprintf( )**, and
snprintf( ), respectively, except that the argument list has been
replaced by a pointer to a list of arguments. This pointer must
be of type **va_list**, which is defined in the header **<stdarg.h>**.

In C99, *buf* and *format* are qualified by **restrict**. The **vsnprintf( )**
function was added by C99.

Related functions are **vscanf( )**, **vfscanf( )**, **vsscanf( )**, **va_arg( )**,
va_start( ), and **va_end( )**.

vscanf, vfscanf, and vsscanf

```
#include <stdarg.h>
#include <stdio.h>
int vscanf(char * restrict format, va_list arg_ptr);
int vfscanf(FILE * restrict stream, const char * restrict format,
            va_list arg_ptr);
int vsscanf(char * restrict buf, const char * restrict format,
            va_list arg_ptr);
```

These functions were added by C99.

The functions **vscanf( )**, **vfscanf( )**, and **vsscanf( )** are functionally
equivalent to **scanf( )**, **fscanf( )**, and **sscanf( )**, respectively, except
that the argument list has been replaced by a pointer to a list of
arguments. This pointer must be of type **va_list**, which is defined
in the header **<stdarg.h>**.

Related functions are **vprintf( )**, **vfprintf( )**, **vsprintf( )**, **va_arg( )**,
va_start( ), and **va_end( )**.

Chapter 7
The String and Character Functions

The C/C++ function library has a rich and varied set of string-
and character-handling functions. The string functions operate
on null-terminated arrays of characters. In C, the string functions
require the header **<string.h>** and the character functions use
<ctype.h>. In C++, the string and character function headers are
<cstring> and **<cctype>**, respectively. For ease of discussion, this
chapter will use the C header names.

Because C/C++ has no bounds checking on array operations, it
is the programmer's responsibility to prevent an array overflow
when working with strings. Neglecting this may cause your
program to crash.

In C/C++, a *printable character* is one that can be displayed on a
terminal. In ASCII environments, these are the characters between
a space (0x20) and tilde (0xFE). *Control characters* have values
between zero and 0x1F, and DEL (0x7F) in ASCII environments.

For historical reasons, the arguments to the character functions
are integers, but only the low-order byte is used; the character
functions automatically convert their arguments to **unsigned char**.
Of course, you are free to call these functions with character
arguments because characters are automatically elevated to
integers at the time of the call.

The header **<string.h>** defines the **size_t** type, which is the result
of the **sizeof** operator and is some form of unsigned integer.

C99 adds the **restrict** qualifier to certain parameters of several
functions originally defined by C89. When this is the case, the
function will be shown using its C89 prototype, which is also the
prototype used by C++; but the **restrict**-qualified parameters will
be pointed out in the function's description.

isalnum

```
#include <ctype.h>
int isalnum(int ch);
```

The **isalnum( )** function returns nonzero if its argument is either a letter of the alphabet or a digit. If the character is not alphanumeric, zero is returned.

Related functions are **isalpha( )**, **iscntrl( )**, **isdigit( )**, **isgraph( )**, **isprint( )**, **ispunct( )**, and **isspace( )**.

isalpha

```
#include <ctype.h>
int isalpha(int ch);
```

The **isalpha( )** function returns nonzero if *ch* is a letter of the alphabet; otherwise, zero is returned. What constitutes a letter of the alphabet may vary from language to language. For English, these are the uppercase and lowercase letters A through Z.

Related functions are **isalnum( )**, **iscntrl( )**, **isdigit( )**, **isgraph( )**, **isprint( )**, **ispunct( )**, and **isspace( )**.

isblank

```
#include <ctype.h>
int isblank(int ch);
```

The **isblank( )** function was added by C99.

The **isblank( )** function returns nonzero if *ch* is a character for which **isspace( )** returns true *and* is used to separate words. Thus, for English, the blank characters are space and horizontal tab.

Related functions are **isalnum( )**, **isalpha( )**, **iscntrl( )**, **isdigit( )**, **isgraph( )**, **ispunct( )**, and **isspace( )**.

iscntrl

```
#include <ctype.h>
int iscntrl(int ch);
```

The **iscntrl( )** function returns nonzero if *ch* is a control character, which in ASCII environments is a value between zero and 0x1F, or equal to 0x7F (DEL). Otherwise, zero is returned.

Related functions are **isalnum( )**, **isalpha( )**, **isdigit( )**, **isgraph( )**, **isprint( )**, **ispunct( )**, and **isspace( )**.

isdigit

```
#include <ctype.h>
int isdigit(int ch);
```

The **isdigit( )** function returns nonzero if *ch* is a digit—that is, 0 through 9. Otherwise, zero is returned.

Related functions are **isalnum( )**, **isalpha( )**, **iscntrl( )**, **isgraph( )**, **isprint( )**, **ispunct( )**, and **isspace( )**.

isgraph

```
#include <ctype.h>
int isgraph(int ch);
```

The **isgraph( )** function returns nonzero if *ch* is any printable character other than a space; otherwise, zero is returned. For ASCII environments, printable characters are in the range 0x21 through 0x7E.

Related functions are **isalnum( )**, **isalpha( )**, **iscntrl( )**, **isdigit( )**, **isprint( )**, **ispunct( )**, and **isspace( )**.

islower

```
#include <ctype.h>
int islower(int ch);
```

The **islower( )** function returns nonzero if *ch* is a lowercase letter; otherwise, zero is returned.

A related function is **isupper( )**.

isprint

```
#include <ctype.h>
int isprint(int ch);
```

The **isprint( )** function returns nonzero if *ch* is a printable character, including a space; otherwise, zero is returned. In ASCII environments, printable characters are in the range 0x20 through 0x7E.

Related functions are **isalnum( )**, **isalpha( )**, **iscntrl( )**, **isdigit( )**, **isgraph( )**, **ispunct( )**, and **isspace( )**.

ispunct

```
#include <ctype.h>
int ispunct(int ch);
```

The **ispunct( )** function returns nonzero if *ch* is a punctuation character; otherwise, zero is returned. The term "punctuation," as defined by this function, includes all printing characters that are neither alphanumeric nor a space.

Related functions are **isalnum( )**, **isalpha( )**, **iscntrl( )**, **isdigit( )**, **isgraph( )**, **ispunct( )**, and **isspace( )**.

isspace

```
#include <ctype.h>
int isspace(int ch);
```

The **isspace( )** function returns nonzero if *ch* is a whitespace character, including space, horizontal tab, vertical tab, formfeed, carriage return, or newline characters; otherwise, zero is returned.

Related functions are **isalnum( )**, **isalpha( )**, **isblank( )**, **iscntrl( )**, **isdigit( )**, **isgraph( )**, and **ispunct( )**.

isupper

7

```
#include <ctype.h>
int isupper(int ch);
```

The **isupper( )** function returns nonzero if *ch* is an uppercase letter; otherwise, zero is returned.

A related function is **islower( )**.

isxdigit

```
#include <ctype.h>
int isxdigit(int ch);
```

The **isxdigit( )** function returns nonzero if *ch* is a hexadecimal digit; otherwise, zero is returned. A hexadecimal digit will be in one of these ranges: A–F, a–f, or 0–9.

Related functions are **isalnum( )**, **isalpha( )**, **iscntrl( )**, **isdigit( )**, **isgraph( )**, **ispunct( )**, and **isspace( )**.

memchr

```
#include <string.h>
void *memchr(const void *buffer, int ch, size_t count);
```

The **memchr( )** function searches the array pointed to by *buffer* for the first occurrence of *ch* in the first *count* characters.

The **memchr( )** function returns a pointer to the first occurrence of *ch* in *buffer*, or it returns a null pointer if *ch* is not found.

Related functions are **memcpy( )** and **isspace( )**.

memcmp

```
#include <string.h>
int memcmp(const void *buf1, const void *buf2,  size_t count);
```

The **memcmp( )** function compares the first *count* characters of the arrays pointed to by *buf1* and *buf2*.

The **memcmp( )** function returns an integer that is interpreted, as indicated here:

Value	Meaning
Less than zero	*buf1* is less than *buf2*
Zero	*buf1* is equal to *buf2*
Greater than zero	*buf1* is greater than *buf2*

Related functions are **memchr( )**, **memcpy( )**, and **strcmp( )**.

memcpy

```
#include <string.h>
void *memcpy(void *to, const void *from, size_t count);
```

The **memcpy( )** function copies *count* characters from the array pointed to by *from* into the array pointed to by *to*. If the arrays overlap, the behavior of **memcopy( )** is undefined.

In C99, *to* and *from* are qualified by **restrict**.

The **memcpy( )** function returns a pointer to *to*.

A related function is **memmove( )**.

memmove

```
#include <string.h>
void *memmove(void *to, const void *from, size_t count);
```

The **memmove( )** function copies *count* characters from the array pointed to by *from* into the array pointed to by *to*. If the arrays overlap, the copy will take place correctly, placing the correct contents into *to* but leaving *from* modified.

The **memmove( )** function returns a pointer to *to*.

A related function is **memcpy( )**.

memset

```
#include <string.h>
void *memset(void *buf, int ch, size_t count);
```

The **memset( )** function copies the low-order byte of *ch* into the first *count* characters of the array pointed to by *buf*. It returns *buf*.

The most common use of **memset( )** is to initialize a region of memory to some known value.

Related functions are **memcmp( )**, **memcpy( )**, and **memmove( )**.

strcat

```
#include <string.h>
char *strcat(char *str1, const char *str2);
```

The **strcat( )** function concatenates a copy of *str2* to *str1* and terminates *str1* with a null. The null terminator originally ending *str1* is overwritten by the first character of *str2*. The string *str2* is untouched by the operation. If the arrays overlap, the behavior of **strcat( )** is undefined.

In C99, *str1* and *str2* are qualified by **restrict**.

The **strcat( )** function returns *str1*.

Remember, no bounds checking takes place, so it is the programmer's responsibility to ensure that *str1* is large enough to hold both its original contents and also those of *str2*.

Related functions are **strchr( )**, **strcmp( )**, and **strcpy( )**.

strchr

```
#include <string.h>
char *strchr(const char *str, int ch);
```

The **strchr( )** function returns a pointer to the first occurrence of the low-order byte of *ch* in the string pointed to by *str*. If no match is found, a null pointer is returned.

Related functions are **strpbrk( )**, **strspn( )**, **strstr( )**, and **strtok( )**.

strcmp

```
#include <string.h>
int strcmp(const char *str1, const char *str2);
```

The **strcmp( )** function lexicographically compares two strings and returns an integer based on the outcome, as shown here:

Value	Meaning
Less than zero	*str1* is less than *str2*
Zero	*str1* is equal to *str2*
Greater than zero	*str1* is greater than *str2*

Related functions are **strchr( )**, **strcpy( )**, and **strncmp( )**.

strcoll

```
#include <string.h>
int strcoll(const char *str1, const char *str2);
```

The **strcoll( )** function compares the string pointed to by *str1* with the one pointed to by *str2*. The comparison is performed in accordance with the locale specified using the **setlocale( )** function. See **setlocale( )**.

The **strcoll( )** function returns an integer that is interpreted as indicated here:

Value	Meaning
Less than zero	*str1* is less than *str2*
Zero	*str1* is equal to *str2*
Greater than zero	*str1* is greater than *str2*

Related functions are **memcmp( )** and **strcmp( )**.

strcpy

```
#include <string.h>
char *strcpy(char *str1, const char *str2);
```

The **strcpy( )** function copies the contents of *str2* into *str1*. *str2* must be a pointer to a null-terminated string. The **strcpy( )** function returns a pointer to *str1*.

In C99, *str1* and *str2* are qualified by **restrict**.

If *str1* and *str2* overlap, the behavior of **strcpy( )** is undefined.

Related functions are **memcpy( )**, **strchr( )**, **strcmp( )**, and **strncmp( )**.

strcspn

```
#include <string.h>
size_t strcspn(const char *str1, const char *str2);
```

The **strcspn( )** function returns the length of the initial substring of the string pointed to by *str1* that is made up of only those characters not contained in the string pointed to by *str2*. Stated differently, **strcspn( )** returns the index of the first character in the string pointed to by *str1* that matches any of the characters in the string pointed to by *str2*.

Related functions are **strrchr( )**, **strpbrk( )**, **strstr( )**, and **strtok( )**.

strerror

```
#include <string.h>
char *strerror(int errnum);
```

The **strerror( )** function returns a pointer to an implementation-defined string associated with the value of *errnum*. Under no circumstances should you modify the string.

strlen

```
#include <string.h>
size_t strlen(const char *str);
```

The **strlen( )** function returns the length of the null-terminated string pointed to by *str*. The null terminator is not counted.

Related functions are **memcpy( )**, **strchr( )**, **strcmp( )**, and **strncmp( )**.

strncat

```
#include <string.h>
char *strncat(char *str1, const char *str2, size_t count);
```

The **strncat( )** function concatenates not more than *count* characters of the string pointed to by *str2* to the string pointed to by *str1* and terminates *str1* with a null. The null terminator originally ending *str1* is overwritten by the first character of *str2*. The string *str2* is untouched by the operation. If the strings overlap, the behavior is undefined.

In C99, *str1* and *str2* are qualified by **restrict**.

The **strncat( )** function returns *str1*.

Remember that no bounds checking takes place, so it is the programmer's responsibility to ensure that *str1* is large enough to hold both its original contents and also those of *str2*.

Related functions are **strcat( )**, **strnchr( )**, **strncmp( )**, and **strncpy( )**.

strncmp

```
#include <string.h>
int strncmp(const char *str1, const char *str2, size_t count);
```

The **strncmp( )** function lexicographically compares not more than *count* characters from the two null-terminated strings and returns an integer based on the outcome, as shown here:

Value	Meaning
Less than zero	*str1* is less than *str2*
Zero	*str1* is equal to *str2*
Greater than zero	*str1* is greater than *str2*

7

If there are less than *count* characters in either string, the comparison ends when the first null is encountered.

Related functions are **strcmp( )**, **strnchr( )**, and **strncpy( )**.

strncpy

```
#include <string.h>
char *strncpy(char *str1, const char *str2, size_t count);
```

The **strncpy( )** function copies up to *count* characters from the string pointed to by *str2* into the array pointed to by *str1*. *str2* must be a pointer to a null-terminated string.

In C99, *str1* and *str2* are qualified by **restrict**.

If *str1* and *str2* overlap, the behavior of **strncpy( )** is undefined.

If the string pointed to by *str2* has less than *count* characters, nulls will be appended to the end of *str1* until *count* characters have been copied.

Alternatively, if the string pointed to by *str2* is longer than *count* characters, the resultant array pointed to by *str1* will not be null terminated.

The **strncpy( )** function returns a pointer to *str1*.

Related functions are **memcpy( )**, **strchr( )**, **strncat( )**, and **strncmp( )**.

strpbrk

```
#include <string.h>
char *strpbrk(const char *str1, const char *str2);
```

The **strpbrk( )** function returns a pointer to the first character in the string pointed to by *str1* that matches any character in the string pointed to by *str2*. The null terminators are not included. If there are no matches, a null pointer is returned.

Related functions are **strspn( )**, **strrchr( )**, **strstr( )**, and **strtok( )**.

strrchr

```
#include <string.h>
char *strrchr(const char *str, int ch);
```

The **strrchr( )** function returns a pointer to the last occurrence of the low-order byte of *ch* in the string pointed to by *str*. If no match is found, a null pointer is returned.

Related functions are **strpbrk( )**, **strspn( )**, **strstr( )**, and **strtok( )**.

strspn

```
#include <string.h>
size_t strspn(const char *str1, const char *str2);
```

The **strspn( )** function returns the length of the initial substring of the string pointed to by *str1* that is made up of only those characters contained in the string pointed to by *str2*. Stated differently, **strspn( )** returns the index of the first character in the string pointed to by *str1* that does not match any of the characters in the string pointed to by *str2*.

Related functions are **strpbrk( )**, **strrchr( )**, **strstr( )**, and **strtok( )**.

strstr

```
#include <string.h>
char *strstr(const char *str1, const char *str2);
```

The **strstr( )** function returns a pointer to the first occurrence in the string pointed to by *str1* of the string pointed to by *str2*. It returns a null pointer if no match is found.

Related functions are **strchr( )**, **strcspn( )**, **strpbrk( )**, **strspn( )**, **strtok( )**, and **strrchr( )**.

strtok

```
#include <string.h>
char *strtok(char *str1, const char *str2);
```

The **strtok( )** function returns a pointer to the next token in the string pointed to by *str1*. The characters making up the string pointed to by *str2* are the delimiters that determine the token. A null pointer is returned when there is no token to return.

In C99, *str1* and *str2* are qualified by **restrict**.

To tokenize a string, the first call to **strtok( )** must have *str1* point to the string being tokenized. Subsequent calls must use a null pointer for *str1*. In this way, the entire string can be reduced to its tokens.

It is possible to use a different set of delimiters for each call to **strtok( )**.

Related functions are **strchr( )**, **strcspn( )**, **strpbrk( )**, **strrchr( )**, and **strspn( )**.

strxfrm

```
#include <string.h>
size_t strxfrm(char *str1, const char *str2, size_t count);
```

The **strxfrm( )** function transforms the string pointed to by *str2* so that it can be used by the **strcmp( )** function and puts the result into the string pointed to by *str1*. After the transformation, the outcome of a **strcmp( )** using *str1* and a **strcoll( )** using the original string pointed to by *str2* will be the same. Not more than *count* characters are written to the array pointed to by *str1*.

In C99, *str1* and *str2* are qualified by **restrict**.

The **strxfrm( )** function returns the length of the transformed string.

A related function is **strcoll( )**.

➤ Programming Tip

The **strtok( )** function provides a means by which you can reduce a string to its constituent parts. For example, the following program tokenizes the string "One, two, and three."

```c
#include <stdio.h>
#include <string.h>

int main(void)
{
  char *p;
  char str[] = "One, two, and three.";

  p = strtok(str, ",");
  printf(p);
  do {
    p = strtok(NULL, ",. ");
    if(p) printf("|%s", p);
  } while(p);

  return 0;
}
```

The output produced by this program is

```
One|two|and|three
```

Notice how **strtok( )** is first called with a pointer to the string to be tokenized, but subsequent calls use **NULL** for the first argument. The **strtok( )** function maintains an internal pointer into the string being tokenized. When **strtok( )**'s first argument points to a string, this internal pointer is reset to point to that string. When the first argument is **NULL**, **strtok( )** continues tokenizing the previous string from the point at which it left off, advancing the internal pointer as each token is obtained. This way, **strtok( )** can tokenize an entire string. Also notice how the string that defines the delimiters was changed between the first call and the subsequent calls. Each call can define the delimiters differently.

7

tolower

```
#include <ctype.h>
int tolower(int ch);
```

The **tolower( )** function returns the lowercase equivalent of *ch* if *ch* is a letter; otherwise, *ch* is returned unchanged.

A related function is **toupper( )**.

toupper

```
#include <ctype.h>
int toupper(int ch);
```

The **toupper( )** function returns the uppercase equivalent of *ch* if *ch* is a letter; otherwise, *ch* is returned unchanged.

A related function is **tolower( )**.

Chapter 8
The C Mathematical Functions

C and C++ define a rich and varied set of mathematical functions. Originally, both C and C++ supported the same set of 22 math functions. However, as C++ matured, it added to these original functions. Then, C99 greatly increased the size of the C math library. The net result of these changes is that today, the C and C++ math libraries have diverged. For this reason, the C math functions (including those added by C99) are described here. Chapter 9 describes the C++ math functions. Keep in mind that the original, core set of C math functions is still fully supported by all versions of C and C++.

All the math functions require the header **<math.h>**. In addition to declaring the math functions, this header defines one or more macros. For C89, the only macro defined by **<math.h>** is **HUGE_VAL**, which is a **double** value that indicates that an overflow has occurred. C99 defines several more, including the following:

HUGE_VALF	A **float** version of **HUGE_VAL**
HUGE_VALL	A **long double** version of **HUGE_VAL**
INFINITY	A value representing infinity
math_errhandling	Contains either **MATH_ERRNO** and/or **MATH_ERREXCEPT**
MATH_ERRNO	**errno** used to report errors
MATH_ERREXCEPT	Floating-point exception raised to report errors
NAN	Not a Number

C99 defines several function-like macros that classify a value. They are shown here:

int fpclassify(*fpval*)	Returns **FP_INFINITE**, **FP_NAN**, **FP_NORMAL**, **FP_SUBNORMAL**, or **FP_ZERO**, depending upon the value in *fpval*. These macros are defined by **<math.h>**.
int isfinite(*fpval*)	Returns nonzero if *fpval* is finite.

int isinf(*fpval*)	Returns nonzero if *fpval* is infinite.
int isnan(*fpval*)	Returns nonzero if *fpval* is not a number.
int isnormal(*fpval*)	Returns nonzero if *fpval* is a normal value.
int signbit(*fpval*)	Returns nonzero if *fpval* is negative (i.e., its sign bit is set).

C99 defines the following comparison macros. For each, *a* and *b* must be floating-point types.

int isgreater(*a*, *b*)	Returns nonzero if *a* is greater than *b*.
int isgreaterequal(*a*, *b*)	Returns nonzero if *a* is greater than or equal to *b*.
int isless(*a*, *b*)	Returns nonzero if *a* is less than *b*.
int islessequal(*a*, *b*)	Returns nonzero if *a* is less than or equal to *b*.
int islessgreater(*a*, *b*)	Returns nonzero if *a* is greater than or less than *b*.
int isunordered(*a*, *b*)	Returns 1 if *a* and *b* are unordered relative to each other; zero is returned if *a* and *b* are ordered.

The reason for these macros is that they gracefully handle values that are not numbers, without causing a floating-point exception.

The macros **EDOM** and **ERANGE** are also used by the math functions. These macros are defined in the header **<errno.h>**.

Errors are handled somewhat differently between C89 and C99. For C89, if an argument to a math function is not in the domain for which it is defined, an implementation-defined value is returned, and the built-in global integer variable **errno** is set equal to **EDOM**. For C99, a domain error also causes an implementation-defined value to be returned. However, the value of **math_errhandling** determines what other actions take place. If **math_errhandling** contains **MATH_ERRNO**, then the built-in global integer variable **errno** is set equal to **EDOM**. If **math_errhandling** contains **MATH_ERREXCEPT**, a floating-point exception is raised.

For C89, if a function produces a result that is too large to be represented, an overflow occurs. This causes the function to return **HUGE_VAL**, and **errno** is set to **ERANGE**, indicating a range error. If an underflow happens, the function returns zero and sets **errno** to **ERANGE**. For C99, an overflow error also causes the function to return **HUGE_VAL** and an underflow also causes the function to return zero. Then, if **math_errhandling** contains **MATH_ERRNO**, **errno** is set to **ERANGE**, indicating a range error. If **math_errhandling** contains **MATH_ERREXCEPT**, a floating-point exception is raised.

In C89, the mathematical functions were specified as operating on values of type **double**, and returning **double** values. C99 added **float** and **long double** versions of these functions, which use the **f** and **l** suffixes, respectively. For example, C89 defined **sin( )** as shown here:

double sin(double *arg*);

C99 keeps **sin( )** and adds **sinf( )** and **sinl( )**, shown next:

float sinf(float *arg*);
long double sinl(long double *arg*);

The operations of all three functions are the same, except for the data upon which they operate. The addition of the **f** and **l** math functions allows you to use the version that precisely fits the data upon which you are operating.

Since C99 has added so many new functions, it is helpful to list those functions that are supported by C89. They are shown here. These are also the math functions that C has in common with C++.

acos	asin	atan	atan2	ceil
cos	cosh	exp	fabs	floor
fmod	frexp	ldexp	log	log10
modf	pow	sin	sinh	sqrt
tan	tanh			

One last point: Throughout, all angles are in radians.

acos

```
#include <math.h>
float acosf(float arg);
double acos(double arg);
long double acosl(long double arg);
```

acosf( ) and **acosl( )** were added by C99.

The **acos( )** family of functions returns the arc cosine of *arg*. The argument must be in the range −1 to 1; otherwise, a domain error will occur.

Related functions are **asin( )**, **atan( )**, **atan2( )**, **sin( )**, **cos( )**, **tan( )**, **sinh( )**, **cosh( )**, and **tanh( )**.

acosh

```
#include <math.h>
float acoshf(float arg);
double acosh(double arg);
long double acoshl(long double arg);
```

acosh( ), **acoshf( )**, and **acoshl( )** were added by C99.

The **acosh( )** family of functions returns the arc hyperbolic cosine of *arg*. The argument must be zero or greater; otherwise, a domain error will occur.

Related functions are **asinh( )**, **atanh( )**, **sinh( )**, **cosh( )**, and **tanh( )**.

asin

```
#include <math.h>
float asinf(float arg);
double asin(double arg);
long double asinl(long double arg);
```

asinf( ) and **asinl( )** were added by C99.

The **asin( )** family of functions returns the arc sine of *arg*. The argument must be in the range −1 to 1; otherwise, a domain error will occur.

Related functions are **acos( )**, **atan( )**, **atan2( )**, **sin( )**, **cos( )**, **tan( )**, **sinh( )**, **cosh( )**, and **tanh( )**.

asinh

```
#include <math.h>
float asinhf(float arg);
double asinh(double arg);
long double asinhl(long double arg);
```

asinh( ), **asinhf( )**, and **asinl( )** were added by C99.

The **asinh( )** family of functions returns the arc hyperbolic sine of *arg*.

Related functions are **acosh( )**, **atanh( )**, **sinh( )**, **cosh( )**, and **tanh( )**.

atan

```
#include <math.h>
float atanf(float arg);
double atan(double arg);
long double atanl(long double arg);
```

atanf( ) and **atanl( )** were added by C99.

The **atan( )** family of functions returns the arc tangent of *arg*.

Related functions are **asin( )**, **acos( )**, **atan2( )**, **tan( )**, **cos( )**, **sin( )**, **sinh( )**, **cosh( )**, and **tanh( )**.

8

atanh

```
#include <math.h>
float atanhf(float arg);
double atanh(double arg);
long double atanhl(long double arg);
```

atanh( ), **atanhf( )**, and **atanl( )** were added by C99.

The **atanh( )** family of functions returns the arc hyperbolic tangent of *arg*. This argument must be in the range –1 to 1; otherwise a domain error will occur. If *arg* equals 1 or –1 a range error is possible.

Related functions are **acosh( )**, **asinh( )**, **sinh( )**, **cosh( )**, and **tanh( )**.

atan2

```
#include <math.h>
float atan2f(float a, float b);
double atan2(double a, double b);
long double atan2l(long double a, long double b);
```

atan2f( ) and **atan2l( )** were added by C99.

The **atan2( )** family of functions returns the arc tangent of *a/b*. It uses the signs of its arguments to compute the quadrant of the return value.

Related functions are **asin( )**, **acos( )**, **atan( )**, **tan( )**, **cos( )**, **sin( )**, **sinh( )**, **cosh( )**, and **tanh( )**.

cbrt

```
#include <math.h>
float cbrtf(float num);
double cbrt(double num);
long double cbrtl(long double num);
```

cbrt( ), **cbrtf( )**, and **cbrtl( )** were added by C99.

The **cbrt( )** family of functions returns cube root of *num*.

A related function is **sqrt( )**.

ceil

```
#include <math.h>
float ceilf(float num);
```

```
double ceil(double num);
long double ceill(long double num);
```

ceilf( ) and **ceill( )** were added by C99.

The **ceil( )** family of functions returns the smallest integer (represented as a floating-point value) not less than *num*. For example, given 1.02, **ceil( )** would return 2.0. Given −1.02, **ceil( )** would return −1.

Related functions are **floor( )** and **fmod( )**.

copysign

```
#include <math.h>
float copysignf(float val, float signval);
double copysign(double val, double signval);
long double copysignl(long double val, long double
                      signval);
```

copysign( ), **copysignf( )**, and **copysignl( )** were added by C99.

The **copysign( )** family of functions gives *val* the same sign as the value passed in *signval* and returns the result. Thus, the value returned has a magnitude equal to *val*, but with the same sign as that of *signval*.

A related function is **fabs( )**.

cos

```
#include <math.h>
float cosf(float arg);
double cos(double arg);
long double cosl(long double arg);
```

cosf( ) and **cosl( )** were added by C99.

The **cos( )** family of functions returns the cosine of *arg*. The value of *arg* must be in radians.

Related functions are **asin( )**, **acos( )**, **atan2( )**, **atan( )**, **tan( )**, **sin( )**, **sinh( )**, **cos( )**, and **tanh( )**.

cosh

```
#include <math.h>
float coshf(float arg);
double cosh(double arg);
long double coshl(long double arg);
```

coshf( ) and **coshl( )** were added by C99.

The **cosh( )** family of functions returns the hyperbolic cosine of *arg*.

Related functions are **asin( )**, **acos( )**, **atan2( )**, **atan( )**, **tan( )**, **sin( )**, **cosh( )**, and **tanh( )**.

erf

```
#include <math.h>
float erff(float arg);
double erf(double arg);
long double erfl(long double arg);
```

erf( ), **erff( )**, and **erfl( )** were added by C99.

The **erf( )** family of functions returns the error function of *arg*.

A related function is **erfc( )**.

erfc

```
#include <math.h>
float erfcf(float arg);
double erfc(double arg);
long double erfcl(long double arg);
```

erfc( ), **erfcf( )**, and **erfcl( )** were added by C99.

The **erfc( )** family of functions returns the complementary error function of *arg*.

A related function is **erf( )**.

exp

```
#include <math.h>
float expf(float arg);
double exp(double arg);
long double expl(long double arg);
```

expf( ) and **expl( )** were added by C99.

The **exp( )** family of functions returns the natural logarithm *e* raised to the *arg* power.

Related functions are **exp2( )** and **log( )**.

exp2

```
#include <math.h>
float exp2f(float arg);
double exp2(double arg);
long double exp2l(long double arg);
```

exp2( ), **exp2f( )**, and **exp2l( )** were added by C99.

The **exp2** family of functions returns 2 raised to the *arg* power.

Related functions are **exp( )** and **log( )**.

expm1

```
#include <math.h>
float expm1f(float arg);
double expm1(double arg);
long double expm1l(long double arg);
```

expm1( ), **expm1f( )**, and **expm1l( )** were added by C99.

The **expm1** family of functions returns the natural logarithm *e* raised to the *arg* power, minus 1. That is, it returns $e^{arg} - 1$.

Related functions are **exp( )** and **log( )**.

fabs

```
#include <math.h>
float fabsf(float num);
double fabs(double num);
long double fabsl(long double num);
```

fabsf( ) and **fabsl( )** were added by C99.

The **fabs( )** family of functions returns the absolute value of *num*.

A related function is **abs( )**.

fdim

```
#include <math.h>
float fdimf(float a, float b);
double fdim(double a, double b);
long double fdiml(long double a, long double b);
```

fdim( ), **fdimf( )**, and **fdiml( )** were defined by C99.

The **fdim( )** family of functions returns zero if *a* is less than or equal to *b*. Otherwise, the result of *a* − *b* is returned.

Related functions are **remainder( )** and **remquo( )**.

floor

```
#include <math.h>
float floorf(float num);
```

```
double floor(double num);
long double floorl(long double num);
```

floorf( ) and **floorl( )** were added by C99.

The **floor( )** family of functions returns the largest integer (represented as a floating-point value) not greater than num. For example, given 1.02, **floor( )** would return 1.0. Given –1.02, **floor( )** would return –2.0.

Related functions are **fceil( )** and **fmod( )**.

fma

```
#include <math.h>
float fmaf(float a, float b, float c);
double fma(double a, double b, double c);
long double fmal(long double a, long double b, long
                double c);
```

fma( ), **fmaf( )**, and **fmal( )** were defined by C99.

The **fma( )** family of functions returns the value of $a * b + c$. Rounding takes place only once, after the entire operation has been completed.

Related functions are **round( )**, **lround( )**, and **llround( )**.

8

fmax

```
#include <math.h>
float fmaxf(float a, float b);
double fmax(double a, double b);
long double fmaxl(long double a, long double b);
```

fmax( ), **fmaxf( )**, and **fmaxl( )** were defined by C99.

The **fmax( )** family of functions returns the greater of a and b.

A related function is **fmin( )**.

fmin

```
#include <math.h>
float fminf(float a, float b);
double fmin(double a, double b);
long double fminl(long double a, long double b);
```

fmin( ), **fminf( )**, and **fminl( )** were defined by C99.

The **fmin( )** family of functions returns the lesser of *a* and *b*.

A related function is **fmax( )**.

fmod

```
#include <math.h>
float fmodf(float a, float b);
double fmod(double a, double b);
long double fmodl(long double a, long double b);
```

fmodf( ) and **fmodl( )** were added by C99.

The **fmod( )** family of functions returns the remainder of *a/b*.

Related functions are **ceil( )**, **floor( )**, and **fabs( )**.

frexp

```
#include <math.h>
float frexpf(float num, int *exp);
double frexp(double num, int *exp);
long double frexpl(long double num, int *exp);
```

frexpf( ) and **frexpl( )** were added by C99.

The **frexp( )** family of functions decompose the number *num* into a mantissa in the range 0.5 to less than 1, and an integer exponent such that $num = mantissa * 2^{exp}$. The mantissa is returned by the function, and the exponent is stored at the variable pointed to by *exp*.

A related function is **ldexp( )**.

hypot

```
#include <math.h>
float hypotf(float side1, float side2);
double hypot(double side1, double side2);
long double hypotl(long double side1, long double
                   side2);
```

hypot( ), **hypotf( )**, and **hypotl( )** functions were added by C99.

The **hypot( )** family of functions returns the length of the hypotenuse given the lengths of the two opposing sides. That is, it returns the square root of the sum of the squares of *side1* and *side2*.

A related function is **sqrt( )**.

ilogb

```
#include <math.h>
int ilogbf(float num);
int ilogb(double num);
int ilogbl(long double num);
```

ilogb( ), **ilogbf( )**, and **ilogbl( )** were added by C99.

The **ilogb( )** family of functions returns the exponent of *num*. This value is returned as an **int** value.

A related function is **logb( )**.

ldexp

```
#include <math.h>
float ldexpf(float num, int exp);
double ldexp(double num, int exp);
long double ldexpl(long double num, int exp);
```

8

ldexpf( ) and **ldexpl( )** were added by C99.

The **ldexp( )** family of functions returns the value of *num* $* 2^{exp}$.

Related functions are **frexp( )** and **modf( )**.

lgamma

```
#include <math.h>
float lgammaf(float arg);
double lgamma(double arg);
long double lgammal(long double arg);
```

lgamma( ), **lgammaf( )**, and **lgammal( )** were added by C99.

The **lgamma( )** family of functions computes the absolute value of the gamma of *arg* and returns its natural logarithm.

A related function is **tgamma( )**.

llrint

```
#include <math.h>
long long int llrintf(float arg);
long long int llrint(double arg);
long long int llrintl(long double arg);
```

llrint( ), **llrintf( )**, and **llrintl( )** were added by C99.

The **llrint( )** family of functions returns the value of *arg* rounded to the nearest **long long** integer.

Related functions are **lrint( )** and **rint( )**.

llround

```
#include <math.h>
long long int llroundf(float arg);
```

```
long long int llround(double arg);
long long int llroundl(long double arg);
```

llround( ), **llroundf( )**, and **llroundl( )** were added by C99.

The **llround( )** family of functions returns the value of *arg* rounded to the nearest **long long** integer. Values precisely between two values, such as 3.5, are rounded up.

Related functions are **lround( )** and **round( )**.

log

```
#include <math.h>
float logf(float num);
double log(double num);
long double logl(long double num);
```

logf( ) and **logl( )** were added by C99.

The **log( )** family of functions returns the natural logarithm for *num*. A domain error occurs if *num* is negative. If *num* is zero, a range error is possible.

Related functions are **log10( )** and **log2( )**.

log1p

```
#include <math.h>
float log1pf(float num);
double log1p(double num);
long double log1pl(long double num);
```

log1p( ), **log1pf( )**, and **log1pl( )** were added by C99.

The **log1p( )** family of functions returns the natural logarithm for *num* + 1. A domain error occurs if *num* is negative. If *num* is −1, a range error is possible.

A related function is **log( )**.

log10

```
#include <math.h>
float log10f(float num);
double log10(double num);
long double log10l(long double num);
```

log10f( ) and **log10l( )** were added by C99.

The **log10( )** family of functions returns the base 10 logarithm for *num*. A domain error occurs if *num* is negative. If *num* is zero, a range error is possible.

Related functions are **log( )** and **log2( )**.

log2

```
#include <math.h>
float log2f(float num);
double log2(double num);
long double log2l(long double num);
```

log2( ), **log2f( )**, and **log2l( )** were added by C99.

The **log2( )** family of functions returns the base 2 logarithm for *num*. A domain error occurs if *num* is negative. If *num* is zero, a range error is possible.

Related functions are **log( )** and **log10( )**.

logb

```
#include <math.h>
float logbf(float num);
```

```
double logb(double num);
long double logbl(long double num);
```

logb( ), **logbf( )**, and **logbl( )** functions were added by C99.

The **logb( )** family of functions returns the exponent of *num*. This value is returned as a floating-point integer value. A domain error is possible when *num* is zero.

A related function is **ilogb( )**.

lrint

```
#include <math.h>
long int lrintf(float arg);
long int lrint(double arg);
long int lrintl(long double arg);
```

lrint( ), **lrintf( )**, and **lrintl( )** were added by C99.

The **lrint( )** family of functions returns the value of *arg* rounded to the nearest **long** integer.

Related functions are **llrint( )** and **rint( )**.

lround

```
#include <math.h>
long int lroundf(float arg);
long int lround(double arg);
long int lroundl(long double arg);
```

lround( ), **lroundf( )**, and **lroundl( )** were added by C99.

The **lround( )** family of functions returns the value of *arg* rounded to the nearest **long** integer. Values precisely between two values, such as 3.5, are rounded up.

Related functions are **llround( )** and **round( )**.

modf

```
#include <math.h>
float modff(float num, float *i);
double modf(double num, double *i);
long double modfl(long double num, long double *i);
```

modff( ) and **modfl( )** were added by C99.

The **modf( )** family of functions decomposes *num* into its integer and fractional parts. The functions return the fractional portion and place the integer part in the variable pointed to by *i*.

Related functions are **frexp( )** and **ldexp( )**.

nan

```
float nanf(const char *content);
double nan(const char *content);
long double nanl(const char *content);
```

nan( ), **nanf( )**, and **nanl( )** were defined by C99.

The **nan( )** family of functions returns a value that is not a number and that contains the string pointed to by *content*.

A related function is **isnan( )**.

nearbyint

```
#include <math.h>
float nearbyintf(float arg);
```

```
double nearbyint(double arg);
long double nearbyintl(long double arg);
```

nearbyint( ), **nearbyintf( )**, and **nearbyintl( )** were added by C99.

The **nearbyint( )** family of functions returns the value of *arg* rounded to the nearest integer. However, the number is returned as a floating-point value.

Related functions are **rint( )** and **round( )**.

nextafter

```
#include <math.h>
float nextafterf(float from, float towards);
double nextafter(double from, double towards);
long double nextafterl(long double from, long double towards);
```

nextafter( ), **nextafterf( )**, and **nextafterl( )** were defined by C99.

The **nextafter( )** family of functions returns the next value after *from* that is closer to *towards*.

A related function is **nexttoward( )**.

nexttoward

```
#include <math.h>
float nexttowardf(float from, long double towards);
double nexttoward(double from, long double towards);
long double nexttowardl(long double from, long double towards);
```

nexttoward( ), **nexttowardf( )**, and **nexttowardl( )** were defined by C99.

The **nexttoward( )** family of functions returns the next value after *from* that is closer to *towards*. They are the same as the **nextafter( )** family, except that *towards* is a **long double** for all three functions.

A related function is **nextafter( )**.

pow

```
#include <math.h>
float powf(float base, float exp);
double pow(double base, double exp);
long double powl(long double base, long double exp);
```

powf( ) and **powl( )** were added by C99.

The **pow( )** family of functions returns *base* raised to the *exp* power *(base^{exp})*. A domain error may occur if *base* is zero and *exp* is less than or equal to zero. It will also happen if *base* is negative and *exp* is not an integer. A range error is possible.

Related functions are **exp( )**, **log( )**, and **sqrt( )**.

remainder

```
#include <math.h>
float remainderf(float a, float b);
double remainder(double a, double b);
long double remainderl(long double a, long double b);
```

remainder( ), **remainderf( )**, and **remainderl( )** were added by C99.

The **remainder( )** family of functions returns the remainder of *a/b*.

A related function is **remquo( )**.

remquo

```
#include <math.h>
float remquof(float a, float b, int *quo);
double remquo(double a, double b, int *quo);
long double remquol(long double a, long double b, int *quo);
```

remquo( ), **remquof( )**, and **remquol( )** were added by C99.

The **remquo( )** family of functions returns the remainder of *a/b*. On return, the integer pointed to by *quo* will contain the quotient.

A related function is **remainder( )**.

rint

```
#include <math.h>
float rintf(float arg);
double rint(double arg);
long double rintl(long double arg);
```

rint( ), **rintf( )**, and **rintl( )** were added by C99.

The **rint( )** family of functions returns the value of *arg* rounded to the nearest integer. However, the number is returned as a floating-point value. It is possible that a floating-point exception will be raised.

Related functions are **nearbyint( )**, **round( )**, and **rint( )**.

round

8

```
#include <math.h>
float roundf(float arg);
double round(double arg);
long double roundl(long double arg);
```

round( ), **roundf( )**, and **roundl( )** were added by C99.

The **round( )** family of functions returns the value of *arg* rounded to the nearest integer. However, the number is returned as a floating-point value. Values precisely between two values, such as 3.5, are rounded up.

Related functions are **lround( )** and **llround( )**.

scalbn

```
#include <math.h>
float scalbnf(float val, int exp);
```

```
double scalbn(double val, int exp);
long double scalbnl(long double val, int exp);
```

scalbn( ), **scalbnf( )**, and **scalbnl( )** were added by C99.

The **scalbn( )** family of functions returns the product of *val* and **FLT_RADIX** raised to the *exp* power. That is,

$$val * FLT\_RADIX^{exp}$$

The macro **FLT_RADIX** is defined in **<float.h>** and its value is the radix of exponent representation.

A related function is **scalbln( )**.

scalbln

```
#include <math.h>
float scalblnf(float val, long int exp);
double scalbln(double val, long int exp);
long double scalblnl(long double val, long int exp);
```

scalbln( ), **scalblnf( )**, and **scalblnl( )** were added by C99.

The **scalbln( )** family of functions returns the product of *val* and **FLT_RADIX** raised to the *exp* power. That is,

$$val * FLT\_RADIX^{exp}$$

The macro **FLT_RADIX** is defined in **<float.h>** and its value is the radix of exponent representation.

A related function is **scalbn( )**.

sin

```
#include <math.h>
float sinf(float arg);
```

```
double sin(double arg);
long double sinl(long double arg);
```

sinf( ) and **sinl( )** were added by C99.

The **sin( )** family of functions returns the sine of *arg*. The value of *arg* must be in radians.

Related functions are **asin( )**, **acos( )**, **atan2( )**, **atan( )**, **tan( )**, **cos( )**, **sinh( )**, **cosh( )**, and **tanh( )**.

sinh

```
#include <math.h>
float sinhf(float arg);
double sinh(double arg);
long double sinhl(long double arg);
```

sinhf( ) and **sinhl( )** were added by C99.

The **sinh( )** family of functions returns the hyperbolic sine of *arg*.

Related functions are **asin( )**, **acos( )**, **atan2( )**, **atan( )**, **tan( )**, **cos( )**, **tanh( )**, **cosh( )**, and **sin( )**.

sqrt

```
#include <math.h>
float sqrtf(float num);
double sqrt(double num);
long double sqrtl(long double num);
```

sqrtf( ) and **sqrtl( )** were added by C99.

The **sqrt( )** family of functions returns the square root of *num*. If they are called with a negative argument, a domain error will occur.

Related functions are **exp( )**, **log( )**, and **pow( )**.

tan

```
#include <math.h>
float tanf(float arg);
double tan(double arg);
long double tanl(long double arg);
```

tanf( ) and **tanl( )** were added by C99.

The **tan( )** family of functions returns the tangent of *arg*. The value of *arg* must be in radians.

Related functions are **acos( )**, **asin( )**, **atan( )**, **atan2( )**, **cos( )**, **sin( )**, **sinh( )**, **cosh( )**, and **tanh( )**.

tanh

```
#include <math.h>
float tanhf(float arg);
double tanh(double arg);
long double tanhl(long double arg);
```

tanhf( ) and **tanhl( )** were added by C99.

The **tanh( )** family of functions returns the hyperbolic tangent of *arg*.

Related functions are **acos( )**, **asin( )**, **atan( )**, **atan2( )**, **cos( )**, **sin( )**, **cosh( )**, **sinh( )**, and **tan( )**.

tgamma

```
#include <math.h>
float tgammaf(float arg);
double tgamma(double arg);
long double tgammal(long double arg);
```

tgamma( ), **tgammaf( )**, and **tgammal( )** were added by C99.

The **tgamma( )** family of functions returns the gamma function of *arg*.

A related function is **lgamma( )**.

trunc

```
#include <math.h>
float truncf(float arg);
double trunc(double arg);
long double truncl(long double arg);
```

trunc( ), **truncf( )**, and **truncl( )** were added by C99.

The **trunc( )** family of functions returns the truncated value of *arg*.

A related function is **nearbyint( )**.

8

Chapter 9
The C++ Mathematical Functions

As explained in Chapter 8, both C and C++ originally supported the same set of 22 math functions. However, as C++ matured, it added overloaded versions of these original functions. Then, C99 greatly increased the size of the C math library in ways that C++ does not support. The net result of these changes is that today, the C and C++ math libraries have diverged, although both still support the original core set of math functions. Because of the differences between C and C++ in this area, the C math functions (including those added by C99) are described in Chapter 8. This chapter describes the math functions defined by C++.

In C++, the math functions require the header **<cmath>**. In addition to declaring the math functions, this header defines the macro called **HUGE_VAL**. The macros **EDOM** and **ERANGE** are also used by the math functions. These macros are defined in the header **<cerrno>**. If an argument to a math function is not in the domain for which it is defined, an implementation-defined value is returned, and the built-in global integer variable **errno** is set equal to **EDOM**. If a routine produces a result that is too large to be represented, an overflow occurs. This causes the routine to return **HUGE_VAL**, and **errno** is set to **ERANGE**, indicating a range error. If an underflow happens, the function returns zero and sets **errno** to **ERANGE**.

C++ supports the original math functions defined by C89. However, in C89, these functions operate only on floating-point values of type **double**. To these functions, C++ adds overloaded versions that explicitly accommodate values of type **float** and **long double**. The operation of the functions is otherwise unchanged.

All angles are in radians.

acos

```
#include <cmath>
float acos(float arg);
```

181

```
double acos(double arg);
long double acos(long double arg);
```

The **acos( )** function returns the arc cosine of *arg*. The argument to **acos( )** must be in the range –1 to 1; otherwise, a domain error will occur.

Related functions are **asin( )**, **atan( )**, **atan2( )**, **sin( )**, **cos( )**, **tan( )**, **sinh( )**, **cosh( )**, and **tanh( )**.

asin

```
#include <cmath>
float asin(float arg);
double asin(double arg);
long double asin(long double arg);
```

The **asin( )** function returns the arc sine of *arg*. The argument to **asin( )** must be in the range –1 to 1; otherwise, a domain error will occur.

Related functions are **acos( )**, **atan( )**, **atan2( )**, **sin( )**, **cos( )**, **tan( )**, **sinh( )**, **cosh( )**, and **tanh( )**.

atan

```
#include <cmath>
float atan(float arg);
double atan(double arg);
long double atan(long double arg);
```

The **atan( )** function returns the arc tangent of *arg*.

Related functions are **asin( )**, **acos( )**, **atan2( )**, **tan( )**, **cos( )**, **sin( )**, **sinh( )**, **cosh( )**, and **tanh( )**.

atan2

```
#include <cmath>
float atan2(float y, float x);
double atan2(double y, double x);
long double atan2(long double y, long double x);
```

The **atan2( )** function returns the arc tangent of y/x. It uses the signs of its arguments to compute the quadrant of the return value.

Related functions are **asin( )**, **acos( )**, **atan( )**, **tan( )**, **cos( )**, **sin( )**, **sinh( )**, **cosh( )**, and **tanh( )**.

ceil

```
#include <cmath>
float ceil(float num);
double ceil(double num);
long double ceil(long double num);
```

The **ceil( )** function returns the smallest integer (represented as a floating-point value) not less than *num*. For example, given 1.02, **ceil( )** would return 2.0. Given −1.02, **ceil( )** would return −1.

Related functions are **floor( )** and **fmod( )**.

9

cos

```
#include <cmath>
float cos(float arg);
double cos(double arg);
long double cos(long double arg);
```

The **cos( )** function returns the cosine of *arg*. The value of *arg* must be in radians.

Related functions are **asin( )**, **acos( )**, **atan2( )**, **atan( )**, **tan( )**, **sin( )**, **sinh( )**, **cos( )**, and **tanh( )**.

cosh

```
#include <cmath>
float cosh(float arg);
double cosh(double arg);
long double cosh(long double arg);
```

The **cosh( )** function returns the hyperbolic cosine of *arg*.

Related functions are **asin( )**, **acos( )**, **atan2( )**, **atan( )**, **tan( )**, **sin( )**, **cosh( )**, and **tanh( )**.

exp

```
#include <cmath>
float exp(float arg);
double exp(double arg);
long double exp(long double arg);
```

The **exp( )** function returns the natural logarithm *e* raised to the *arg* power.

A related function is **log( )**.

fabs

```
#include <cmath>
float fabs(float num);
double fabs(double num);
long double fabs(long double num);
```

The **fabs( )** function returns the absolute value of *num*.

A related function is **abs( )**.

floor

```
#include <cmath>
float floor(float num);
double floor(double num);
long double floor(long double num);
```

The **floor( )** function returns the largest integer (represented as a floating-point value) not greater than *num*. For example, given 1.02, **floor( )** would return 1.0. Given –1.02, **floor( )** would return –2.0.

Related functions are **fceil( )** and **fmod( )**.

fmod

```
#include <cmath>
float fmod(float x, float y);
double fmod(double x, double y);
long double fmod(long double x, long double y);
```

The **fmod( )** function returns the remainder of *x/y*.

Related functions are **ceil( )**, **floor( )**, and **fabs( )**.

frexp

```
#include <cmath>
float frexp(float num, int *exp);
double frexp(double num, int *exp);
long double frexp(long double num, int *exp);
```

The **frexp( )** function decomposes the number *num* into a mantissa in the range 0.5 to less than 1, and an integer exponent such that

$num = mantissa * 2^{exp}$. The mantissa is returned by the function, and the exponent is stored at the variable pointed to by *exp*.

A related function is **ldexp( )**.

ldexp

```
#include <cmath>
float ldexp(float num, int exp);
double ldexp(double num, int exp);
long double ldexp(long double num, int exp);
```

The **ldexp( )** returns the value of $num * 2^{exp}$. If overflow occurs, **HUGE_VAL** is returned.

Related functions are **frexp( )** and **modf( )**.

log

```
#include <cmath>
float log(float num);
double log(double num);
long double log(long double num);
```

The **log( )** function returns the natural logarithm for *num*. A domain error occurs if *num* is negative, and a range error occurs if the argument is zero.

A related function is **log10( )**.

log10

```
#include <cmath>
float log10(float num);
```

```
double log10(double num);
long double log10(long double num);
```

The **log10( )** function returns the base 10 logarithm for *num*. A domain error occurs if *num* is negative, and a range error occurs if the argument is zero.

A related function is **log( )**.

modf

```
#include <cmath>
float modf(float num, float *i);
double modf(double num, double *i);
long double modf(long double num, long double *i);
```

The **modf( )** function decomposes *num* into its integer and fractional parts. It returns the fractional portion and places the integer part in the variable pointed to by *i*.

Related functions are **frexp( )** and **ldexp( )**.

pow

9

```
#include <cmath>
float pow(float base, float exp);
float pow(float base, int exp);
double pow(double base, double exp);
double pow(double base, int exp);
long double pow(long double base, long double exp);
long double pow(long double base, int exp);
```

The **pow( )** function returns *base* raised to the *exp* power *(base^{exp})*. A domain error may occur if *base* is zero and *exp* is less than or equal to zero. It will also happen if *base* is negative and *exp* is not an integer. An overflow produces a range error.

Related functions are **exp( )**, **log( )**, and **sqrt( )**.

sin

```
#include <cmath>
float sin(float arg);
double sin(double arg);
long double sin(long double arg);
```

The **sin( )** function returns the sine of *arg*. The value of *arg* must be in radians.

Related functions are **asin( )**, **acos( )**, **atan2( )**, **atan( )**, **tan( )**, **cos( )**, **sinh( )**, **cosh( )**, and **tanh( )**.

sinh

```
#include <cmath>
float sinh(float arg);
double sinh(double arg);
long double sinh(long double arg);
```

The **sinh( )** function returns the hyperbolic sine of *arg*.

Related functions are **asin( )**, **acos( )**, **atan2( )**, **atan( )**, **tan( )**, **cos( )**, **tanh( )**, **cosh( )**, and **sin( )**.

sqrt

```
#include <cmath>
float sqrt(float num);
double sqrt(double num);
long double sqrt(long double num);
```

The **sqrt( )** function returns the square root of *num*. If it is called with a negative argument, a domain error will occur.

Related functions are **exp( )**, **log( )**, and **pow( )**.

tan

```
#include <cmath>
float tan(float arg);
double tan(double arg);
long double tan(long double arg);
```

The **tan( )** function returns the tangent of *arg*. The value of *arg* must be in radians.

Related functions are **acos( )**, **asin( )**, **atan( )**, **atan2( )**, **cos( )**, **sin( )**, **sinh( )**, **cosh( )**, and **tanh( )**.

tanh

```
#include <cmath>
float tanh(float arg);
double tanh(double arg);
long double tanh(long double arg);
```

The **tanh( )** function returns the hyperbolic tangent of *arg*.

Related functions are **acos( )**, **asin( )**, **atan( )**, **atan2( )**, **cos( )**, **sin( )**, **cosh( )**, **sinh( )**, and **tan( )**.

9

Chapter 10
Time, Date, and Localization Functions

The C/C++ standard library defines several functions that deal with the date and time. It also defines functions that handle the geopolitical information associated with a program. These functions are described here.

In C, the time and date functions require the header **<time.h>**. For C++, the header is **<ctime>**. For ease of discussion, this chapter will use the C header name, but references to **<time.h>** also apply to **<ctime>**.

In **<time.h>** are defined three time-related types: **clock_t**, **time_t**, and **tm**. The types **clock_t** and **time_t** are capable of representing the system time and date as some sort of integer. This is called the *calendar time*. The structure type **tm** holds the date and time broken down into its elements. The **tm** structure contains the following members:

```
int tm_sec;   /* seconds, 0-60 */
int tm_min;   /* minutes, 0-59 */
int tm_hour;  /* hours, 0-23 */
int tm_mday;  /* day of the month, 1-31 */
int tm_mon;   /* months since Jan, 0-11 */
int tm_year;  /* years from 1900 */
int tm_wday;  /* days since Sunday, 0-6 */
int tm_yday;  /* days since Jan 1, 0-365 */
int tm_isdst  /* Daylight Saving Time indicator */
```

The value of **tm_isdst** will be positive if Daylight Saving Time is in effect, zero if it is not in effect, and negative if there is no information available. This form of the time and date is called the *broken-down time*.

In addition, **<time.h>** defines the macro **CLOCKS_PER_SEC**, which is the number of system clock ticks per second.

The geopolitical environmental functions require the C header **<locale.h>** or the C++ header **<clocale>**. It defines the structure **lconv**, which is described under the function **localeconv( )**.

10

asctime

```
#include <time.h>
char *asctime(const struct tm *ptr);
```

The **asctime( )** function returns a pointer to a string that contains
the information stored in the structure pointed to by *ptr* converted
into the following form:

  day month date hours:minutes:seconds year\n\0

For example:

  Fri Apr 15 12:05:34 2005

The structure pointed to by *ptr* is usually obtained from either
localtime( ) or **gmtime( )**.

The buffer used by **asctime( )** to hold the formatted output string is
a statically allocated character array and is overwritten each time
the function is called. If you want to save the contents of the string,
you must copy it elsewhere.

Related functions are **localtime( )**, **gmtime( )**, **time( )**, and **ctime( )**.

clock

```
#include <time.h>
clock_t clock(void);
```

The **clock( )** function returns a value that approximates the amount
of time the calling program has been running. To transform this
value into seconds, divide it by **CLOCKS_PER_SEC**. A value of –1
is returned if the time is not available.

Related functions are **time( )**, **asctime( )**, and **ctime( )**.

ctime

```
#include <time.h>
char *ctime(const time_t *time);
```

The **ctime( )** function returns a pointer to a string of the form

day month year hours:minutes:seconds year\n\0

given a pointer to the calendar time. The calendar time is often obtained through a call to **time( )**.

The buffer used by **ctime( )** to hold the formatted output string is a statically allocated character array and is overwritten each time the function is called. If you want to save the contents of the string, it is necessary to copy it elsewhere.

Related functions are **localtime( )**, **gmtime( )**, **time( )**, and **asctime( )**.

difftime

```
#include <time.h>
double difftime(time_t time2, time_t time1);
```

The **difftime( )** function returns the difference, in seconds, between *time1* and *time2.* That is, *time2 – time1.*

Related functions are **localtime( )**, **gmtime( )**, **time( )**, and **asctime( )**.

10

gmtime

```
#include <time.h>
struct tm *gmtime(const time_t *time);
```

The **gmtime( )** function returns a pointer to the broken-down form of *time* in the form of a **tm** structure. The time is represented in

Coordinated Universal Time (UTC), which is essentially Greenwich mean time. The *time* pointer is usually obtained through a call to **time( )**. If the system does not support Coordinated Universal Time, **NULL** is returned.

The structure used by **gmtime( )** to hold the broken-down time is statically allocated and is overwritten each time the function is called. If you want to save the contents of the structure, you must copy it elsewhere.

Related functions are **localtime( )**, **time( )**, and **asctime( )**.

localeconv

```
#include <locale.h>
struct lconv *localeconv(void);
```

The **localeconv( )** function returns a pointer to a structure of type **lconv**, which contains various geopolitical environmental information relating to the way numbers are formatted. The **lconv** structure contains the following members:

```
char *decimal_point;      /* Decimal point character
                             for nonmonetary values. */
char *thousands_sep;      /* Thousands separator
                             for nonmonetary values. */
char *grouping;           /* Specifies grouping for
                             nonmonetary values. */
char *int_curr_symbol;    /* International currency symbol. */
char *currency_symbol;    /* Local currency symbol. */
char *mon_decimal_point;  /* Decimal point character for
                             monetary values. */
char *mon_thousands_sep;  /* Thousands separator for
                             monetary values. */
char *mon_grouping;       /* Specifies grouping for
                             monetary values. */
char *positive_sign;      /* Positive value indicator for
                             monetary values. */
char *negative_sign;      /* Negative value indicator for
                             monetary values. */
char int_frac_digits;     /* Number of digits displayed to the
                             right of the decimal point for
                             monetary values displayed using
                             international format. */
```

```
char frac_digits;        /* Number of digits displayed to the
                            right of the decimal point for
                            monetary values displayed using
                            local format. */
char p_cs_precedes;      /* 1 if currency symbol precedes
                            positive value, 0 if currency
                            symbol follows value. */
char p_sep_by_space;     /* 1 if currency symbol is
                            separated from value by a space,
                            0 otherwise. In C99, contains a
                            value that indicates separation. */
char n_cs_precedes;      /* 1 if currency symbol precedes
                            a negative value, 0 if currency
                            symbol follows value. */
char n_sep_by_space;     /* 1 if currency symbol is
                            separated from a negative
                            value by a space, 0 if
                            currency symbol follows value.
                            In C99, contains a value that
                            indicates separation. */
char p_sign_posn;        /* Indicates position of
                            positive value symbol. */
char n_sign_posn;        /* Indicates position of
                            negative value symbol. */

/* The following members were added by C99. */
char _p_cs_precedes;     /* 1 if currency symbol precedes
                            positive value, 0 if currency
                            symbol follows value. Applies to
                            internationally formatted values. */
char _p_sep_by_space;    /* Indicates the separation between the
                            currency symbol, sign, and a positive value.
                            Applies to internationally formatted values.
*/
char _n_cs_precedes;     /* 1 if currency symbol precedes
                            a negative value, 0 if currency
                            symbol follows value. Applies to
                            internationally formatted values. */
char _n_sep_by_space;    /* Indicates the separation between the
                            currency symbol, sign, and a negative value.
                            Applies to internationally formatted values.
*/
char _p_sign_posn;       /* Indicates position of
                            positive value symbol. Applies to
                            internationally formatted values.  */
char _n_sign_posn;       /* Indicates position of
                            negative value symbol. Applies to
                            internationally formatted values.  */
```

10

The **localeconv( )** function returns a pointer to the **lconv** structure.
You must not alter the contents of this structure. Refer to your
compiler's documentation for implementation-specific information
relating to the **lconv** structure.

A related function is **setlocale( )**.

localtime

```
#include <time.h>
struct tm *localtime(const time_t *time);
```

The **localtime( )** function returns a pointer to the broken-down form of *time* in the form of a **tm** structure. The time is represented in local time. The *time* pointer is usually obtained through a call to **time( )**.

The structure used by **localtime( )** to hold the broken-down time is statically allocated and is overwritten each time the function is called. If you want to save the contents of the structure, you must copy it elsewhere.

Related functions are **gmtime( )**, **time( )**, and **asctime( )**.

mktime

```
#include <time.h>
time_t mktime(struct tm *time);
```

The **mktime( )** function returns the calendar-time equivalent of the broken-down time found in the structure pointed to by *time.* The elements **tm_wday** and **tm_yday** are set by the function, so they need not be defined at the time of the call.

If **mktime( )** cannot represent the information as a valid calendar time, −1 is returned.

Related functions are **time( )**, **gmtime( )**, **asctime( )**, and **ctime( )**.

➤ Programming Tip

The **mktime( )** function is especially useful when you want to know the day of the week a given date falls on. For example, what day of the week is Jan 12, 2012? To find out, call the **mktime( )** function with that date and then examine the **tm_wday** member of the **tm** structure after the function returns. It will contain the day of the week. The following program demonstrates this method:

```c
/* Find day of week for January 12, 2012. */
#include <stdio.h>
#include <time.h>

char day[][20] = {
  "Sunday",
  "Monday",
  "Tuesday",
  "Wednesday",
  "Thursday",
  "Friday",
  "Saturday"
};

int main(void)
{
  struct tm t;

  t.tm_mday = 12;
  t.tm_mon = 0;
  t.tm_year = 112;
  t.tm_hour = 0;
  t.tm_min = 0;
  t.tm_sec = 0;
  t.tm_isdst = 0;

  mktime(&t); /* fill in day of week */

  printf("Day of week is %s.\n", day[t.tm_wday]);

  return 0;
}
```

When this program is run, **mktime( )** automatically computes the day of the week, which is Thursday in this case. Since the return value of **mktime( )** is not needed, it is simply ignored.

10

setlocale

```
#include <locale.h>
char *setlocale(int type, const char *locale);
```

The **setlocale( )** function allows certain parameters that are sensitive to the geopolitical environment of a program's execution to be queried or set. If *locale* is null, **setlocale( )** returns a pointer to the current localization string. Otherwise, **setlocale( )** attempts to use the string specified by *locale* to set the locale parameters as specified by *type*. To specify the standard C locale, use the string "C". To specify the native environment, use the null-string "". Refer to your compiler's documentation for the localization strings that it supports.

At the time of the call, *type* must be one of the following macros (defined in **<locale.h>**):

LC_ALL
LC_COLLATE
LC_CTYPE
LC_MONETARY
LC_NUMERIC
LC_TIME

LC_ALL refers to all localization categories. **LC_COLLATE** affects the operation of the **strcoll( )** function. **LC_CTYPE** alters the way the character functions work. **LC_MONETARY** determines the monetary format. **LC_NUMERIC** changes the decimal-point character for formatted input/output functions. Finally, **LC_TIME** determines the behavior of the **strftime( )** function.

The **setlocale( )** function returns a pointer to a string associated with the *type* parameter.

Related functions are **localeconv( )**, **time( )**, **strcoll( )**, and **strftime( )**.

strftime

```
#include <time.h>
size_t strftime(char *str, size_t maxsize,   const char *fmt,
                const struct tm *time);
```

The **strftime( )** function stores time and date information, along with other information, into the string pointed to by *str* according to the format commands found in the string pointed to by *fmt* and using the broken-down time pointed to by *time*. A maximum of *maxsize* characters will be placed into *str*.

In C99, *str*, *fmt*, and *time* are qualified by **restrict**.

The **strftime( )** function works a little like **sprintf( )** in that it recognizes a set of format commands that begin with the percent sign (%) and it stores its formatted output into a string. The format commands are used to specify the exact way various time and date information is represented in *str*. Any other characters found in the format string are placed into *str* unchanged. The time and date displayed are in local time. The format commands are shown in the table below. Notice that many of the commands are case sensitive.

The **strftime( )** function returns the number of characters stored in the string pointed to by *str* or zero if an error occurs.

Command	Replaced By
%a	Abbreviated weekday name
%A	Full weekday name
%b	Abbreviated month name
%B	Full month name
%c	Standard date and time string
%C	Last two digits of year
%d	Day of month as a decimal (1–31)
%D	month/day/year (added by C99)
%e	Day of month as a decimal (1–31) in a 2-character field (added by C99)
%F	Year-month-day (added by C99)
%g	Last two digits of year using a week-based year (added by C99)
%G	The year using a week-based year (added by C99)
%h	Abbreviated month name (added by C99)
%H	Hour (0–23)
%I	Hour (1–12)
%j	Day of year as a decimal (1–366)
%m	Month as decimal (1–12)
%M	Minute as decimal (0–59)
%n	A newline (added by C99)
%p	Locale's equivalent of A.M. or P.M.

10

Command	Replaced By
%r	12-hour time (added by C99)
%R	hh:mm (added by C99)
%S	Second as decimal (0–60)
%t	Horizontal tab (added by C99)
%T	hh:mm:ss (added by C99)
%u	Day of week; Monday is first day of week (1–7) (added by C99)
%U	Week of year, Sunday being first day (0–53)
%V	Week of year using a week-based year (added by C99)
%w	Weekday as a decimal (0–6, Sunday being 0)
%W	Week of year, Monday being first day (0–53)
%x	Standard date string
%X	Standard time string
%y	Year in decimal without century (0–99)
%Y	Year including century as decimal
%z	Offset from UTC (added by C99)
%Z	Time zone name
%%	The percent sign

C99 allows certain of the **strftime( )** format commands to be modified by **E** or **O**. The **E** can modify **c**, **C**, **x**, **X**, **y**, **Y**, **d**, **e**, and **H**. The **O** can modify **I**, **m**, **M**, **S**, **u**, **U**, **V**, **w**, **W**, and **y**. These modifiers cause an alternative representation of the time and/or date to be displayed. Consult your compiler's documentation for details.

A week-based year is used by the **%g**, **%G**, and **%V** format commands. With this representation, Monday is the first day of the week and the first week of a year must include January 4th.

Related functions are **time( )**, **localtime( )**, and **gmtime( )**.

time

```
#include <time.h>
time_t time(time_t *time);
```

The **time( )** function returns the current calendar time of the system. If the system has no time, −1 is returned.

The **time( )** function can be called either with a null pointer or with a pointer to a variable of type **time_t**. If the latter is used, the variable will also be assigned the calendar time.

Related functions are **localtime( )**, **gmtime( )**, **strftime( )**, and **ctime( )**.

10

Chapter 11
The Dynamic
Allocation Functions

This chapter describes the C/C++ dynamic allocation functions.
At their core are **malloc( )** and **free( )**. Each time **malloc( )** is called,
a portion of the remaining free memory is allocated. Each time
free( ) is called, memory is returned to the system. The region of
free memory from which memory is allocated is called the *heap*.
For a C program, the prototypes for the dynamic allocation
functions are in **<stdlib.h>**. For C++, the header is **<cstdlib>**.
For ease of discussion, this chapter will use the C header name,
but references to **<stdlib.h>** also apply to **<cstdlib>**.

All C/C++ compilers will include at least these four dynamic
allocation functions: **calloc( )**, **malloc( )**, **free( )**, **realloc( )**.
However, your compiler will almost certainly contain several
variants on these functions to accommodate various options
and environmental differences. You will want to refer to your
compiler's documentation.

While C++ supports the dynamic allocation functions described
here, you will typically not use them in a C++ program. The reason
for this is that C++ provides dynamic allocation operators called
new and **delete**. There are several advantages to using C++'s
dynamic allocation operators. First, **new** automatically allocates
the correct amount of memory for the type of data being allocated.
Second, it returns the correct type of pointer to that memory. Third,
both **new** and **delete** can be overloaded. Since **new** and **delete**
have advantages over the dynamic allocation functions, their use
is recommended for C++ programs. (For a discussion of **new** and
delete, see Chapter 5.)

11

calloc

```
#include <stdlib.>
void *calloc(size_t num, size_t size);
```

203

The **calloc( )** function allocates memory the size of which is equal to *num* * *size*. That is, **calloc( )** allocates sufficient memory for an array of *num* objects of size *size*. All bits in the allocated memory are initially set to zero.

The **calloc( )** function returns a pointer to the first byte of the allocated region. If there is not enough memory to satisfy the request, a null pointer is returned. It is always important to verify that the return value is not null before attempting to use it.

Related functions are **free( )**, **malloc( )**, and **realloc( )**.

free

```
#include <stdlib.h>
void free(void *ptr);
```

The **free( )** function returns the memory pointed to by *ptr* to the heap. This makes the memory available for future allocation.

It is imperative that **free( )** only be called with a pointer that was previously allocated using one of the dynamic allocation system's functions. Attempting to free an invalid pointer will most likely destroy the memory management mechanism and possibly cause a system crash. If you pass a null pointer, **free( )** performs no operation.

Related functions are **calloc( )**, **malloc( )**, and **realloc( )**.

malloc

```
#include <stdlib.h>
void *malloc(size_t size);
```

The **malloc( )** function returns a pointer to the first byte of a region of memory of size *size* that has been allocated from the heap. If there is insufficient memory in the heap to satisfy the request, **malloc( )** returns a null pointer. It is always important to verify that the return value is not null before attempting to use it. Attempting to use a null pointer will usually result in a system crash.

Related functions are **free( )**, **realloc( )**, and **calloc( )**.

➤ Programming Tip

If you are writing 16-bit programs for the 8086 family of
processors (such as the Pentium), then your compiler will
provide additional allocation functions that accommodate
the segmented memory model used by these processors
when operating in 16-bit mode. For example, there will be
functions that allocate memory from the FAR heap (the heap
that is outside the default data segment), that can allocate
pointers to memory that are larger than one segment, and
that free such memory.

---

realloc

```
#include <stdlib.h>
void *realloc(void *ptr, size_t size);
```

The precise operation of **realloc( )** is slightly different in C99 than it
is in C++ and C89, although the net effect is the same. For C++ and
C89, **realloc( )** changes the size of the previously allocated memory
pointed to by *ptr* to that specified by *size*. The value of *size* can be
greater or less than the original. A pointer to the memory block is
returned because it may be necessary for **realloc( )** to move the
block in order to change its size. If this occurs, the contents of the
old block (up to *size* bytes) are copied into the new block.

For C99, the block of memory pointed to by *ptr* is freed and a new
block is allocated. The new block contains the same contents as the
original block (up to the length passed in *size*). A pointer to the
new block is returned. It is permissible, however, for the new block
and the old block to begin at the same address. That is, the pointer
returned by **realloc( )** might be the same as the one passed in *ptr*.

If *ptr* is null, **realloc( )** simply allocates *size* bytes of memory and returns
a pointer to it. If *size* is zero, the memory pointed to by *ptr* is freed.

If there is not enough free memory in the heap to allocate *size* bytes,
a null pointer is returned and the original block is left unchanged.

Related functions are **free( )**, **malloc( )**, and **calloc( )**.

11

Chapter 12
Miscellaneous Functions

The standard function library defines several utility functions. They include various conversions, variable-length argument processing, sorting and searching, and random number generation. Many of the functions covered here require the use of the C header **<stdlib.h>** or its C++ equivalent **<cstdlib>**. This chapter will use the C header name, but references to **<stdlib.h>** also apply to **<cstdlib>**.

In **<stdlib.h>** are declared the types **div_t** and **ldiv_t**, which are the types of the values returned by **div( )** and **ldiv( )**, respectively. C99 adds the **lldiv_t** type and the **lldiv( )** function. Also declared are the types **size_t** and **wchar_t**. The following macros are also defined:

Macro	Meaning
MB_CUR_MAX	Maximum length (in bytes) of a multibyte character
NULL	A null pointer
RAND_MAX	The maximum value that can be returned by the **rand( )** function
EXIT_FAILURE	The value returned to the calling process if program termination is unsuccessful
EXIT_SUCCESS	The value returned to the calling process if program termination is successful

If a function requires a header other than **<stdlib.h>**, that function description will discuss it.

abort

12

```
#include <stdlib.h>
void abort(void);
```

The **abort( )** function causes immediate abnormal termination of a program. Generally, no files are flushed. In environments that support it, **abort( )** will return an implementation-defined value to the calling process (usually the operating system) indicating failure.

Related functions are **exit( )** and **atexit( )**.

abs

```
#include <stdlib.h>
int abs(int num);
```

The **abs( )** function returns the absolute value of *num*.

A related function is **fabs( )**.

assert

```
#include <assert.h>
void assert(int exp);
```

The **assert( )** macro, defined in the headers **<assert.h>** and **<cassert>**, writes error information to **stderr** and then aborts program execution if the expression *exp* evaluates to zero. Otherwise, **assert( )** does nothing. Although the exact output is implementation defined, many compilers use a message similar to this:

    Assertion failed: *<expression>*, file *<file>*, line *<linenum>*

For C99, the message will also include the name of the function that contained **assert( )**.

The **assert( )** macro is generally used to help verify that a program is operating correctly, with the expression being devised in such a way that it evaluates to true only when no errors have taken place.

It is not necessary to remove the **assert( )** statements from the source code once a program is debugged because if the macro **NDEBUG** is defined (as anything), the **assert( )** macros will be ignored.

A related function is **abort( )**.

atexit

```
#include <stdlib.h>
int atexit(void (*func)(void));
```

The **atexit( )** function causes the function pointed to by *func* to be called upon normal program termination. The **atexit( )** function returns zero if the function is successfully registered as a termination function and nonzero otherwise.

At least 32 termination functions can be registered, and they will be called in the reverse order of their registration.

Related functions are **exit( )** and **abort( )**.

atof

```
#include <stdlib.h>
double atof(const char *str);
```

The **atof( )** function converts the string pointed to by *str* into a **double** value. The string must contain a valid floating-point number. If this is not the case, the returned value is undefined.

The number can be terminated by any character that cannot be part of a valid floating-point number. This includes whitespace, punctuation (other than periods), and characters other than E or e. This means that if **atof( )** is called with "100.00HELLO", the value 100.00 will be returned.

Related functions are **atoi( )** and **atol( )**.

12

atoi

```
#include <stdlib.h>
int atoi(const char *str);
```

The **atoi( )** function converts the string pointed to by *str* into an **int** value. The string must contain a valid integer number. If this is not the case, the returned value is undefined.

The number can be terminated by any character that cannot be part of an integer number. This includes whitespace, punctuation, and characters. This means that if **atoi( )** is called with "123.23", the integer value 123 will be returned, and the ".23" is ignored.

Related functions are **atof( )** and **atol( )**.

atol

```
#include <stdlib.h>
long int atol(const char *str);
```

The **atol( )** function converts the string pointed to by *str* into a **long int** value. The string must contain a valid integer number. If this is not the case, the returned value is undefined.

The number can be terminated by any character that cannot be part of an integer number. This includes whitespace, punctuation, and characters. This means that if **atol( )** is called with "123.23", the long integer value 123L will be returned, and the ".23" is ignored.

Related functions are **atof( )**, **atoi( )**, and **atoll( )**.

atoll

```
#include <stdlib.h>
long long int atoll(const char *str);
```

atoll( ) was added by C99.

The **atoll( )** function converts the string pointed to by *str* into a **long long int** value. It is otherwise similar to **atol( )**.

Related functions are **atof( )**, **atoi( )**, and **atol( )**.

bsearch

```
#include <stdlib.h>
void *bsearch(const void *key, const void *buf,
              size_t num, size_t size,
              int (*compare)(const void *, const void *));
```

The **bsearch( )** function performs a binary search on the sorted array pointed to by *buf* and returns a pointer to the first member that matches the key pointed to by *key*. The number of elements in the array is specified by *num*, and the size (in bytes) of each element is described by *size*.

The function pointed to by *compare* is used to compare an element of the array with the key. The form of the *compare* function must be as follows:

int *func_name*(const void **arg1*, const void **arg2*);

It must return values as described in the following table:

Comparison	Value Returned
arg1 is less than *arg2*	Less than zero
arg1 is equal to *arg2*	Zero
arg1 is greater than *arg2*	Greater than zero

12

The array must be sorted in ascending order with the lowest address containing the lowest element.

If the array does not contain the key, a null pointer is returned.

A related function is **qsort( )**.

div

```
#include <stdlib.h>
div_t div(int numerator, int denominator);
```

The **div( )** function returns the quotient and the remainder of the operation *numerator / denominator* in a structure of type **div_t**.

The structure type **div_t** has these two fields:

```
int quot; /* quotient */
int rem;  /* remainder */
```

Related functions are **ldiv( )** and **lldiv( )**.

exit

```
#include <stdlib.h>
void exit(int exit_code);
```

The **exit( )** function causes immediate, normal termination of a program. This means that termination functions registered by **atexit( )** are called and any open files are flushed and closed.

The value of *exit_code* is passed to the calling process, usually the operating system, if the environment supports it. By convention, if the value of *exit_code* is zero, or **EXIT_SUCCESS**, normal program termination is assumed. A nonzero value, or **EXIT_FAILURE**, is used to indicate an implementation-defined error.

Related functions are **atexit( )**, **abort( )**, and **_Exit( )**.

_Exit

```
#include <stdlib.h>
void _Exit(int exit_code);
```

_Exit( ) was added by C99.

The **_Exit( )** function is similar to **exit( )** except for the following:

- No calls to termination functions registered by **atexit( )** are made.
- No calls to signal handlers registered by **signal( )** are made.
- Open files are not necessarily flushed or closed.

Related functions are **atexit( )**, **abort( )**, and **exit( )**.

getenv

```
#include <stdlib.h>
char *getenv(const char *name);
```

The **getenv( )** function returns a pointer to environmental information associated with the string pointed to by *name* in the implementation-defined environmental information table. The information must not be changed by your code.

The environment of a program may include such things as path names and devices online. The exact nature of this data is implementation defined. You will need to refer to your compiler's documentation for details.

If a call is made to **getenv( )** with an argument that does not match any of the environment data, a null pointer is returned.

A related function is **system( )**.

labs

12

```
#include <stdlib.h>
long int labs(long int num);
```

The **labs( )** function returns the absolute value of *num*.

Related functions are **abs( )** and **llabs( )**.

ldiv

```
#include <stdlib.h>
ldiv_t ldiv(long int numerator, long int denominator);
```

The **ldiv( )** function returns the quotient and remainder of the operation *numerator* / *denominator* in an **ldiv_t** structure.

The structure type **ldiv_t** has these two fields:

```
long int quot; /* quotient */
long int rem;  /* remainder */
```

Related functions are **div( )** and **lldiv( )**.

llabs

```
#include <stdlib.h>
long long int llabs(long long int num);
```

llabs( ) was added by C99.

The **llabs( )** function returns the absolute value of *num*. It is similar to **labs( )** except that it operates on values of type **long long int**.

Related functions are **abs( )** and **labs( )**.

lldiv

```
#include <stdlib.h>
lldiv_t lldiv(long long int numerator, long long int denominator);
```

lldiv( ) was added by C99.

The **lldiv( )** function returns the quotient and remainder of the operation *numerator* / *denominator* in an **lldiv_t** structure. It is similar to **ldiv( )** except that it operates on **long long** integers.

The structure type **lldiv_t** has these two fields:

```
long long int quot; /* quotient */
long long int rem;  /* remainder */
```

Related functions are **div( )** and **ldiv( )**.

longjmp

```
#include <setjmp.h>
void longjmp(jmp_buf envbuf, int status);
```

The **longjmp( )** function causes program execution to resume at the point of the last call to **setjmp( )**. Thus, **longjmp( )** and **setjmp( )** provide a means of jumping between functions. Notice that the header **<setjmp.h>** is required. For C++, use the header **<csetjmp>**.

The **longjmp( )** function operates by resetting the stack to the state as described in *envbuf,* which must have been set by a prior call to **setjmp( )**. This causes program execution to resume at the statement following the **setjmp( )** invocation. That is, the computer is "tricked" into thinking that it never left the function that called **setjmp( )**. (As a somewhat graphic explanation, the **longjmp( )** function "warps" across time and (memory) space to a previous point in your program without having to perform the normal function return process.)

The buffer *evnbuf* is of type **jmp_buf**, which is defined in the header **<setjmp.h>**. Again, the buffer must have been set through a call to **setjmp( )** prior to calling **longjmp( )**.

The value of *status* becomes the return value of **setjmp( )** and is used to determine where the long jump came from. The only value that is not allowed is zero. Zero is returned by **setjmp( )** when it is actually called directly by your program, not indirectly through the execution of **longjmp( )**.

By far the most common use of **longjmp( )** is to return from a deeply nested set of routines when an error occurs.

A related function is **setjmp( )**.

12

mblen

```
#include <stdlib.h>
int mblen(const char *str, size_t size);
```

The **mblen( )** function returns the length (in bytes) of a multibyte character pointed to by *str*. Only the first *size* number of characters are examined. It returns –1 on error.

If *str* is null, then **mblen( )** returns nonzero if multibyte characters have state-dependent encodings. If they do not, zero is returned.

Related functions are **mbtowc( )** and **wctomb( )**.

mbstowcs

```
#include <stdlib.h>
size_t mbstowcs(wchar_t *out, const char *in, size_t size);
```

The **mbstowcs( )** function converts the multibyte string pointed to by *in* into a wide-character string and puts that result in the array pointed to by *out*. Only *size* number of bytes will be stored in *out*.

In C99, *out* and *in* are qualified by **restrict**.

The **mbstowcs( )** function returns the number of multibyte characters that are converted. If an error occurs, the function returns –1.

Related functions are **wcstombs( )** and **mbtowc( )**.

mbtowc

```
#include <stdlib.h>
int mbtowc(wchar_t *out, const char *in, size_t size);
```

The **mbtowc( )** function converts the multibyte character in the array pointed to by *in* into its wide-character equivalent and puts that result in the object pointed to by *out*. Only *size* number of characters will be examined.

In C99, *out* and *in* are qualified by **restrict**.

This function returns the number of bytes that are put into *out*. –1 is returned if an error occurs. If *in* is null, then **mbtowc( )** returns nonzero if multibyte characters have state-dependent encodings. If they do not, zero is returned.

Related functions are **mblen( )** and **wctomb( )**.

qsort

```
#include <stdlib.h>
void qsort(void *buf, size_t num, size_t size,
           int (*compare) (const void *, const void *));
```

The **qsort( )** function sorts the array pointed to by *buf* using a Quicksort (developed by C.A.R. Hoare). The Quicksort is generally considered the best general-purpose sorting algorithm. The number of elements in the array is specified by *num*, and the size (in bytes) of each element is described by *size*.

The function pointed to by *compare* is used to compare two elements of the array. The form of the *compare* function must be as follows:

int *func_name*(const void *arg1*, const void *arg2*);

It must return values as described here:

Comparison	Value Returned
arg1 is less than *arg2*	Less than zero
arg1 is equal to *arg2*	Zero
arg1 is greater than *arg2*	Greater than zero

The array is sorted into ascending order with the lowest address containing the lowest element.

A related function is **bsearch( )**.

12

> ## ➤ Programming Tip

When using **qsort( )**, if you want to sort an array in descending order (that is, high to low), simply reverse the conditions used by the comparison function. That is, have the comparison function return the following values:

Comparison	Value Returned
arg1 is less than *arg2*	Greater than zero
arg1 is equal to *arg2*	Zero
arg1 is greater than *arg2*	Less than zero

Also, if you want to use the **bsearch( )** function on an array that is sorted in descending order, you will need to use a reversed comparison function.

raise

```
#include <signal.h>
int raise(int signal);
```

The **raise( )** function sends the signal specified by *signal* to the executing program. It returns zero if successful and nonzero otherwise. Its uses the header **<signal.h>**, or **<csignal>** in a C++ program.

The following signals are defined by Standard C. Of course, your compiler is free to provide additional signals:

Macro	Meaning
SIGABRT	Termination error
SIGFPE	Floating-point error
SIGILL	Bad instruction
SIGINT	User pressed CTRL-C
SIGSEGV	Illegal memory access
SIGTERM	Terminate program

A related function is **signal( )**.

rand

```
#include <stdlib.h>
int rand(void);
```

The **rand( )** function generates a sequence of pseudorandom numbers. Each time it is called, an integer between zero and **RAND_MAX** is returned. **RAND_MAX** will be at least 32,767.

A related function is **srand( )**.

setjmp

```
#include <setjmp.h>
int setjmp(jmp_buf envbuf);
```

The **setjmp( )** macro saves the contents of the system stack in the buffer *envbuf* for later use by **longjmp( )**. It uses the header **<setjmp.h>**, or **<csetjmp>** in a C++ program.

The **setjmp( )** macro returns zero upon invocation. However, **longjmp( )** passes an argument to **setjmp( )**, and it is this value (always nonzero) that will appear to be the value of **setjmp( )** after a call to **longjmp( )** has occurred. See **longjmp( )**.

A related function is **longjmp( )**.

signal

12

```
#include <signal.h>
void (*signal(int signal, void (*func)(int))) (int);
```

The **signal( )** function registers the function pointed to by *func* as a handler for the signal specified by *signal*. That is, the function pointed to by *func* will be called when *signal* is received by your program. It uses the header **<signal.h>**, or **<csignal>** in a C++ program.

The value of *func* can be the address of a signal handler function or one of the following macros, defined in **<signal.h>**:

Macro	Meaning
SIG_DFL	Use default signal handling
SIG_IGN	Ignore the signal

If a function address is used, the specified handler will be executed when its signal is received. Check your compiler's documentation for additional details.

On success, **signal( )** returns the address of the previously defined function for the specified signal. On error, **SIG_ERR** (defined in **<signal.h>**) is returned.

A related function is **raise( )**.

srand

```
#include <stdlib.h>
void srand(unsigned int seed);
```

The **srand( )** function sets a starting point for the sequence generated by **rand( )**. (The **rand( )** function returns pseudorandom numbers.)

srand( ) is often used to allow multiple program runs to use different sequences of pseudorandom numbers by specifying different starting points. Conversely, you can also use **srand( )** to generate the same pseudorandom sequence over and over again by calling it with the same seed before starting the sequence.

A related function is **rand( )**.

strtod

```
#include <stdlib.h>
double strtod(const char *start, char **end);
```

The **strtod( )** function converts the string representation of a number stored in the string pointed to by *start* into a **double** and returns the result.

In C99, *start* and *end* are qualified by **restrict**.

The **strtod( )** function works as follows. First, any whitespace in the string pointed to by *start* is stripped. Next, each character that comprises the number is read. Any character that cannot be part of a floating-point number will cause this process to stop. This includes whitespace, punctuation (other than periods), and characters other than E or e. Finally, *end* is set to point to the remainder, if any, of the original string. This means that if **strtod( )** is called with "100.00 Pliers", the value 100.00 will be returned and *end* will point to the space that precedes "Pliers".

If overflow occurs, either **HUGE_VAL** or **–HUGE_VAL** (indicating positive or negative overflow) is returned, and the global variable **errno** is set to **ERANGE**, indicating a range error. If underflow occurs, the function returns zero and the global variable **errno** is set to **ERANGE**. If *start* does not point to a number, no conversion takes place and zero is returned.

Related functions are **atof( )**, **strtold( )**, and **strtof( )**.

strtof

12

```
#include <stdlib.h>
long double strtof(const char * restrict start,
                   char restrict ** restrict end);
```

strtof( ) was added by C99.

The **strtof( )** function is similar to **strtod( )** except that it returns a **float** value. If overflow occurs, then either **HUGE_VALF** or –**HUGE_VALF** is returned, and the global variable **errno** is set to **ERANGE**, indicating a range error. If *start* does not point to a number, no conversion takes place and zero is returned.

Related functions are **atof( )**, **strtod( )**, and **strtold( )**.

strtol

```
#include <stdlib.h>
long int strtol(const char *start, char **end, int radix);
```

The **strtol( )** function converts the string representation of a number stored in the string pointed to by *start* into a **long int** and returns the result. The base of the number is determined by *radix*. If *radix* is zero, the base is determined by the rules that govern constant specification. If *radix* is other than zero, it must be in the range 2 through 36.

In C99, *start* and *end* are qualified by **restrict**.

The **strtol( )** function works as follows. First, any whitespace in the string pointed to by *start* is stripped. Next, each character that comprises the number is read. Any character that cannot be part of a long integer number will cause this process to stop. This includes whitespace, punctuation, and characters. Finally, *end* is set to point to the remainder, if any, of the original string. This means that if **strtol( )** is called with " 100 Pliers", the value 100L will be returned, and *end* will point to the space that precedes "Pliers".

If the result cannot be represented by a **long int**, **LONG_MAX** or **LONG_MIN** is returned, and the global **errno** is set to **ERANGE**, indicating a range error. If *start* does not point to a number, no conversion takes place and zero is returned.

Related functions are **atol( )** and **strtoll( )**.

strtold

```
#include <stdlib.h>
long double strtold(const char * restrict start,
                char restrict ** restrict end);
```

strtold( ) was added by C99.

The **strtold( )** is similar to **strtod( )** except that it returns a **long double** value. If overflow occurs, then either **HUGE_VALL** or –**HUGE_VALL** is returned, and the global variable **errno** is set to **ERANGE**, indicating a range error. If *start* does not point to a number, no conversion takes place and zero is returned.

Related functions are **atof( )**, **strtod( )**, and **strtof( )**.

strtoll

```
#include <stdlib.h>
long long int strtoll(const char * restrict start,
                char ** restrict end, int radix);
```

strtoll( ) was added by C99.

The **strtoll( )** function is similar to **strtol( )** except that it returns a **long long int**. If the result cannot be represented by a long integer, **LLONG_MAX** or **LLONG_MIN** is returned, and the global **errno** is set to **ERANGE**, indicating a range error. If *start* does not point to a number, no conversion takes place and zero is returned.

Related functions are **atol( )** and **strtol( )**.

12

strtoul

```
#include <stdlib.h>
unsigned long int strtoul(const char *start, char **end,
                int radix);
```

The **strtoul( )** function converts the string representation of a number stored in the string pointed to by *start* into an **unsigned long int** and returns the result. The base of the number is determined by *radix*. If *radix* is zero, the base is determined by the rules that govern constant specification. If the radix is specified, it must be in the range 2 through 36.

In C99, *start* and *end* are qualified by **restrict**.

The **strtoul( )** function works as follows. First, any whitespace in the string pointed to by *start* is stripped. Next, each character that comprises the number is read. Any character that cannot be part of an unsigned integer number will cause this process to stop. This includes whitespace, punctuation, and characters. Finally, *end* is set to point to the remainder, if any, of the original string. This means that if **strtoul( )** is called with " 100 Pliers", the value 100L will be returned, and *end* will point to the space that precedes "Pliers".

If the result cannot be represented as an unsigned long integer, **ULONG_MAX** is returned and the global variable **errno** is set to **ERANGE**, indicating a range error. If *start* does not point to a number, no conversion takes place and zero is returned.

Related functions are **strtol( )** and **strtoull( )**.

strtoull

```
#include <stdlib.h>
unsigned long long int strtoull(const char *start, char **end,
                                int radix);
```

strtoull( ) was added by C99.

The **strtoull( )** function is similar to **strtoul( )** except that it returns an **unsigned long long int**. If the result cannot be represented as an unsigned long integer **ULLONG_MAX** is returned and the global variable **errno** is set to **ERANGE**. If *start* does not point to a number, no conversion takes place and zero is returned.

Related functions are **strtol( )** and **strtoul( )**.

system

```
#include <stdlib.h>
int system(const char *str);
```

The **system( )** function passes the string pointed to by *str* as a command to the command processor of the operating system.

If **system( )** is called with a null pointer, it will return nonzero if a command processor is present, and zero otherwise. (Programs executed in unhosted environments will not have access to a command processor.) For all other cases, the return value of **system( )** is implementation defined, but typically, zero is returned if the command was successfully executed and a nonzero return value indicates an error.

A related function is **exit( )**.

va_arg, va_start, va_end, and va_copy

```
#include <stdarg.h>
type va_arg(va_list argptr, type);
void va_copy(va_list target, va_list source);
void va_end(va_list argptr);
void va_start(va_list argptr, last_parm);
```

va_copy( ) was added by C99.

The **va_arg( )**, **va_start( )**, and **va_end( )** macros work together to allow a variable number of arguments to be passed to a function. The most common example of a function that takes a variable number of arguments is **printf( )**. The type **va_list** is defined by **<stdarg.h>**, or **<cstdarg>** for C++.

The general procedure for creating a function that can take a variable number of arguments is as follows. The function must

12

have at least one known parameter, but may have more, prior to the variable parameter list. The rightmost known parameter is called the *last_parm*. The name of *last_parm* is used as the second parameter in a call to **va_start( )**. Before any of the variable-length parameters can be accessed, the argument pointer *argptr* must be initialized through a call to **va_start( )**. After that, parameters are returned via calls to **va_arg( )**, with *type* being the type of the next parameter. Finally, once all the parameters have been read and prior to returning from the function, a call to **va_end( )** must be made to ensure that the stack is properly restored. If **va_end( )** is not called, a program crash is very likely.

The **va_copy( )** macro copies the argument list in *source* to *target*.

A related function is **vprintf( )**.

➤ Programming Tip

The proper use of **va_start( )**, **va_end( )**, and **va_arg( )** is best illustrated with an example. This program uses **sum_series( )** to return the sum of a series of numbers. The first argument contains a count of the number of arguments to follow. In this example, the first five elements of the following series are summed:

$$\frac{1}{2} + \frac{1}{4} + \frac{1}{8} + \frac{1}{16} \ldots + \frac{1}{2^n}$$

The output displayed is "0.968750".

```
/* Variable length argument example - sum a series.*/

#include <stdio.h>
#include <stdarg.h>

double sum_series(int, ...);

int main(void)
{
```

```
    double d;

    d = sum_series(5, 0.5, 0.25, 0.125, 0.0625, 0.03125);
    printf("Sum of series is %f\n",d);

    return 0;
}

double sum_series(int num, ...)
{
    double sum = 0.0, t;
    va_list argptr;

    /* initialize argptr */
    va_start(argptr, num);

    /* sum the series */
    for(; num; num--) {
     t = va_arg(argptr, double);
     sum += t;
    }

    /* do orderly shutdown */
    va_end(argptr);
    return sum;
}
```

wcstombs

```
#include <stdlib.h>
size_t wcstombs(char *out, const wchar_t *in, size_t size);
```

The **wcstombs( )** function converts the wide-character array
pointed to by *in* into its multibyte equivalent and puts the result
in the array pointed to by *out*. Only the first *size* bytes of *in* are
converted. Conversion stops before that if the null terminator is
encountered.

In C99, *out* and *in* are qualified by **restrict**.

If successful, **wcstombs( )** returns the number of bytes written. On failure, −1 is returned.

Related functions are **wctomb( )** and **mbstowcs( )**.

wctomb

```
#include <stdlib.h>
int wctomb(char *out,  wchar_t in);
```

The **wctomb( )** function converts the wide character in *in* into its multibyte equivalent and puts the result in the object pointed to by *out*. The array pointed to by *out* must be at least **MB_CUR_MAX** characters long.

If successful, **wctomb( )** returns the number of bytes contained in the multibyte character. On failure, −1 is returned.

If *out* is null, then **wctomb( )** returns nonzero if the multibyte character has state-dependent encodings, and zero if it does not.

Related functions are **wcstombs( )** and **mbtowc( )**.

Chapter 13
The Wide-Character Functions

In 1995, a number of wide-character functions were added to the C89 standard, and were later incorporated into C99 and C++. The wide-character functions operate on characters of type **wchar_t**, which are 16 bits. For the most part, these functions parallel their **char** equivalents. For example, the function **iswspace( )** is the wide-character version of **isspace( )**. In general, the wide-character functions use the same names as their **char** equivalents, except that a "w" is added.

For C, the wide-character functions use the headers **<wchar.h>** and **<wctype.h>**. For C++, the headers are **<cwchar>** and **<cwctype>**. This chapter will use the C header names, but references to **<wchar.h>** and **<wctype.h>** also apply to **<cwchar>** and **<cwctype>**, respectively.

The header **<wctype.h>** defines the types **wint_t**, **wctrans_t**, and **wctype_t**. Many of the wide-character functions receive a wide character as a parameter. The type of this parameter is **wint_t**. It is capable of holding a wide character. The use of the **wint_t** type in the wide-character functions parallels the use of **int** in the **char**-based functions. The types **wctrans_t** and **wctype_t** are the types of objects used to represent a character mapping (i.e., character translation) and the classification of a character, respectively. Also defined is the wide-character EOF mark, which is defined as **WEOF**.

In addition to defining **win_t**, the header **<wchar.h>** defines the types **wchar_t**, **size_t**, and **mbstate_t**. The **wchar_t** type creates a wide-character object, and **size_t** is the type of value returned by **sizeof**. The **mbstate_t** type describes an object that holds the state of a multibyte to wide-character conversion. The **<wchar.h>** header also defines the macros **NULL**, **WEOF**, **WCHAR_MAX**, and **WCHAR_MIN**. The last two define the maximum and minimum value that can be held in an object of type **wchar_t**.

13

Since most of the wide-character functions simply parallel their **char** equivalents, only a brief description of these functions is provided.

The Wide-Character Classification Functions

The header **<wctype.h>** provides the prototypes for the wide-character functions that support character classification. These functions categorize wide characters as to their type or convert the case of a character. The following table lists these functions along with their **char** equivalents, which are described in Chapter 7.

Function	char Equivalent
int iswalnum(wint_t *ch*)	isalnum( )
int iswalpha(wint_t *ch*)	isalpha( )
int iswblank(wint_t *ch*)	isblank( ) (Added by C99)
int iswcntrl(wint_t *ch*)	iscntrl( )
int iswdigit(wint_t *ch*)	isdigit( )
int iswgraph(wint_t *ch*)	isgraph( )
int iswlower(wint_t *ch*)	islower( )
int iswprint(wint_t *ch*)	isprint( )
int iswpunct(wint_t *c*)	ispunct( )
int iswspace(wint_t *ch*)	isspace( )
int iswupper(wint_t *ch*)	isupper( )
int iswxdigit(wint_t *ch*)	isxdigit( )
wint_t towlower(wint_t *ch*)	tolower( )
wint_t towupper(wint_t *ch*)	toupper( )

In addition to the functions shown above, **<wctype.h>** defines the following, which provide an open-ended means of classifying characters:

wctype_t wctype(const char *attr*);

int iswctype(wint_t *ch*, wctype_t *attr_ob*);

The function **wctype( )** returns a value that can be passed as the *attr_ob* parameter to **iswctype( )**. The string pointed to by *attr* specifies a property that a character must have. This value can then be used to determine if *ch* is a character that has that property. If it has, **iswctype( )** returns nonzero. Otherwise, it returns zero. The following property strings are defined for all execution environments:

alnum	alpha	cntrl	digit
graph	lower	print	punct
space	upper	xdigit	

For C99, the string "blank" is also defined.

The functions **wctrans( )** and **towctrans( )** are also defined in **<wctype.h>**. They are shown here:

wctrans_t wctrans(const char *mapping);

wint_t towctrans(wint_t ch, wctrans_t mapping_ob);

The function **wctrans( )** returns a value that can be passed as the mapping_ob parameter to **towctrans( )**. The string pointed to by mapping specifies a mapping of one character to another. This value can then be used by **towctrans( )** to map ch. The mapped value is returned. The following mapping strings are supported in all execution environments:

tolower   toupper

The Wide-Character I/O Functions

Several of the I/O functions described in Chapter 6 have wide-character implementations. These functions are shown in the following table. The wide-character I/O functions use the header **<wchar.h>**. Notice that **swprintf( )** and **vswprintf( )** require an additional parameter not needed by their **char** equivalents.

Function	char Equivalent
win_t fgetwc(FILE *stream)	fgetc( )
wchar_t *fgetws(wchar_t *str, int num, FILE *stream)	fgets( ) In C99, str and stream are qualified by **restrict**.
wint_t fputwc(wchar_t ch, FILE *stream)	fputc( )
int fputws(const wchar_t *str, FILE *stream)	fputs( ) In C99, str and stream are qualified by **restrict**.

13

Function	char Equivalent
int fwprintf(FILE *stream, const wchar_t *fmt, ...)	fprintf( ) In C99, str and fmt are qualified by **restrict**.
int fwscanf(FILE *stream, const wchar_t *fmt, ...)	fscanf( ) In C99, str and fmt are qualified by **restrict**.
wint_t getwc(FILE *stream)	getc( )
wint_t getwchar(void)	getchar( )
wint_t putwc(wchar_t ch, FILE *stream)	putc( )
wint_t putwchar(wchar_t ch)	putchar( )
int swprintf(wchar_t *str, size_t num, const wchar_t *fmt, ...)	sprintf( ) Note the addition of the parameter num, which limits the number of characters written to str. In C99, str and fmt are qualified by **restrict**.
int swscanf(const wchar_t *str, const wchar_t *fmt, ...)	sscanf( ) In C99, str and fmt are qualified by **restrict**.
wint_t ungetwc(wint_t ch, FILE *stream)	ungetc( )
int vfwprintf(FILE *stream, const wchar_t *fmt, va_list arg)	vfprintf( ) In C99, str and fmt are qualified by **restrict**.
int vfwscanf(FILE * restrict stream, const wchar_t * restrict fmt, va_list arg);	vfscanf( ) (Added by C99.)
int vswprintf(wchar_t *str, size_t num, const wchar_t *fmt, va_list arg)	vsprintf( ) Note the addition of the parameter num, which limits the number of characters written to str. In C99, str and fmt are qualified by **restrict**.
int vswscanf(const wchar_t * restrict str, const wchar_t * restrict fmt, va_list arg);	vsscanf( ) (Added by C99.)
int vwprintf(const wchar_t *fmt, va_list arg)	vprintf( ) In C99, str and fmt are qualified by **restrict**.

Function	char Equivalent
int vwscanf(const wchar_t * restrict *fmt*, va_list *arg*);	vscanf( ) (Added by C99.)
int wprintf(const wchar_t *fmt*, ...)	printf( ) In C99, *fmt* is qualified by **restrict**.
int wscanf(const wchar_t *fmt*, ...)	scanf( ) In C99, *fmt* is qualified by **restrict**.

In addition to those shown in the table, the following wide-character I/O function has been added:

    int fwide(FILE *stream*, int *how*);

If *how* is positive, **fwide( )** makes *stream* a wide-character stream. If *how* is negative, **fwide( )** makes *stream* into a **char** stream. If *how* is zero, *stream* is unaffected. If the stream has already been oriented to either wide or normal characters, it will not be changed. The function returns positive if the stream uses wide characters, negative if the stream uses **chars**, and zero if the stream has not yet been oriented. A stream's orientation is also determined by its first use.

The Wide-Character String Functions

There are wide-character versions of the string manipulation functions described in Chapter 7. These are shown in the following table. They use the header **<wchar.h>**. Note that **wcstok( )** requires an additional parameter not used by its **char** equivalent.

Function	char Equivalent
wchar_t *wcscat(wchar_t *str1*, const wchar_t *str2*)	strcat( ) In C99, *str1* and *str2* are qualified by **restrict**.
wchar_t *wcschr(const wchar_t *str*, wchar_t *ch*)	strchr( )

13

Function	char Equivalent
int wcscmp(const wchar_t *str1, const wchar_t *str2)	strcmp( )
int wcscoll(const wchar_t *str1, const wchar_t *str2)	strcoll( )
size_t wcscspn(const wchar_t *str1, const wchar_t *str2)	strcspn( )
wchar_t *wcscpy(wchar_t *str1, const wchar_t *str2)	strcpy( ) In C99, str1 and str2 are qualified by **restrict**.
size_t wcslen(const wchar_t *str)	strlen( )
wchar_t *wcsncpy(wchar_t *str1, const wchar_t str2, size_t num)	strncpy( ) In C99, str1 and str2 are qualified by **restrict**.
wchar_t *wcsncat(wchar_t *str1, const wchar_t str2, size_t num)	strncat( ) In C99, str1 and str2 are qualified by **restrict**.
int wcsncmp(const wchar_t *str1, const wchar_t *str2, size_t num)	strncmp( )
wchar_t *wcspbrk(const wchar_t *str1, const wchar_t *str2)	strpbrk( )
wchar_t *wcsrchr(const wchar_t *str, wchar_t ch)	strrchr( )
size_t wcsspn(const wchar_t *str1, const wchar_t *str2)	strspn( )
wchar_t *wcstok(wchar_t *str1, const wchar_t *str2, wchar_t **endptr)	strtok( ) Here, endptr is a pointer that holds information necessary to continue the tokenizing process. In C99, str1, str2, and endptr are qualified by **restrict**.
wchar_t *wcsstr(const wchar_t *str1, const wchar_t *str2)	strstr( )
size_t wcsxfrm(wchar_t *str1, const wchar_t *str2, size_t num)	strxfrm( ) In C99, str1 and str2 are qualified by **restrict**.

Wide-Character String Conversion Functions

The functions shown in the following table provide wide-character versions of the standard numeric and time conversion functions. These functions use the header **<wchar.h>**.

Function	char Equivalent

size_t wcsftime(wchar_t *str, size_t max,
                const wchar_t *fmt,
                const struct tm *ptr)
	strftime( )
	In C99, str, fmt, and ptr
	are qualified by **restrict**.

double wcstod(const wchar_t *start, wchar_t **end);	strtod( ) In C99, start and end are qualified by **restrict**.
float wcstof(const wchar_t * restrict start, wchar_t ** restrict end);	strtof( ) (Added by C99)

long double wcstold(const wchar_t *
                    restrict start,
                    wchar_t ** restrict end);
	strtold( ) (Added by C99)

long int wcstol(const wchar_t *start,
                wchar_t **end,
                int radix)
	strtol( )
	In C99, start and end are
	qualified by **restrict**.

long long int wcstoll(const wchar_t *
                      restrict start,
                      wchar_t ** restrict end,
                      int radix)
	strtoll( ) (Added by C99)

unsigned long int wcstoul(
                    const wchar_t * restrict
                    start,
                    wchar_t ** restrict end,
                    int radix)
	strtoul( )
	In C99, start and end are
	qualified by **restrict**.

unsigned long long int wcstoull(
                    const wchar_t *start,
                    wchar_t **end,
                    int radix)
	strtoull( ) (Added
	by C99)

13

Wide-Character Array Functions

The standard character array-manipulation functions, such as **memcpy( )**, also have wide-character equivalents. They are shown in the following table. These functions use the header **<wchar.h>**.

Function	char Equivalent
wchar_t *wmemchr(const wchar_t *str, wchar_t ch, size_t num)	memchr( )
int wmemcmp(const wchar_t *str1, const wchar_t *str2, size_t num)	memcmp( )
wchar_t *wmemcpy(wchar_t *str1, const wchar_t *str2, size_t num)	memcpy( ) In C99, str1 and str2 are qualified by **restrict**.
wchar_t *wmemmove(wchar_t *str1, const wchar_t *str2, size_t num)	memmove( )
wchar_t *wmemset(wchar_t *str, wchar_t ch, size_t num)	memset( )

Multibyte/Wide-Character Conversion Functions

The standard library supplies various functions that support conversions between multibyte and wide characters. These functions, shown in the following table, use the header **<wchar.h>**. Many of these functions are *restartable* versions of the normal multibyte functions. The restartable version utilizes the state information passed to it in a parameter of type **mbstate_t**. If this parameter is null, the function will provide its own **mbstate_t** object.

Function	Description
win_t btowc(int *ch*)	Converts *ch* into its wide-character equivalent and returns the result. Returns **WEOF** on error or if *ch* is not a one-byte, multibyte character.
size_t mbrlen(const char **str*, size_t *num*, mbstate_t **state*)	Restartable version of **mblen( )** as described by *state*. Returns a positive value that indicates the length of the next multibyte character. Zero is returned if the next character is null. A negative value is returned if an error occurs. In C99, *str* and *state* are qualified by **restrict**.
size_t mbrtowc(wchar_t **out*, const char **in*, size_t *num*, mbstate_t **state*)	Restartable version of **mbtowc( )** as described by *state*. Returns a positive value that indicates the length of the next multibyte character. Zero is returned if the next character is null. A value of −1 is returned if an error occurs and the macro **EILSEQ** is assigned to **errno**. If the conversion is incomplete, −2 is returned. In C99, *out*, *in*, and *state* are qualified by **restrict**.
int mbsinit(const mbstate_t **state*)	Returns true if *state* represents an initial conversion state.

13

Function	Description
size_t mbsrtowcs(wchar_t *out, const char **in, size_t num, mbstate_t state)	Restartable version of **mbstowcs( )** as described by *state*. Also, **mbsrtowcs( )** differs from **mbstowcs( )** in that *in* is an indirect pointer to the source array. If an error occurs, the macro **EILSEQ** is assigned to **errno**. In C99, *out*, *in*, and *state* are qualified by **restrict**.
size_t wcrtomb(char *out, wchar_t ch, mbstate_t *state)	Restartable version of **wctomb( )** as described by *state*. If an error occurs, the macro **EILSEQ** is assigned to **errno**. In C99, *out* and *state* are qualified by **restrict**.
size_t wcsrtombs(char *out, const wchar_t **in, size_t num, mbstate_t *state)	Restartable version of **wcstombs( )** as described by *state*. Also, **wcsrtombs( )** differs from **wcstombs( )** in that *in* is an indirect pointer to the source array. If an error occurs, the macro **EILSEQ** is assigned to **errno**. In C99, *out*, *in*, and *state* are qualified by **restrict**.
int wctob(wint_t ch)	Converts *ch* into its one-byte multibyte equivalent. It returns **EOF** on failure.

Chapter 14
The Old-Style C++ I/O System

Because C++ includes the entire C library, it supports the use of C's I/O system. However, C++ also defines its own class-based, object-oriented I/O system, which is referred to as the *iostream library*. When writing C++ programs, you will usually want to use the iostream library rather than C-based I/O.

At the time of this writing there are two versions of the iostream library in widespread use: the older one that is based upon the original specifications for C++ and the modern one defined by the ANSI/ISO Standard for C++. Today, most C++ compilers support both the old-style and modern iostream libraries. However, the old-style iostream library is obsolete and should not be used for new code. New code should use the modern approach as defined by the ANSI/ISO C++ Standard. The old-style iostream library is described in this chapter for the benefit of those programmers maintaining old code, or porting old code to the modern standard. The modern approach is described in Chapter 15.

For the most part, both the old-style and modern I/O systems work the same way. If you know how to use one, you can easily use the other. However, there are several important differences between the two.

First, the old-style iostream classes were defined in the global name space. The modern iostream library is contained in the **std** namespace.

Second, the modern iostream library is defined using a complex, interrelated set of template classes and functions. The old-style library uses a less complicated, nontemplatized class hierarchy. Fortunately, the names of the classes that you will use in your programs remain the same.

Third, the modern iostream library defines many new data types.

Fourth, to use the old library, you need to include **.h** header files, such as **iostream.h**. These header files define the old-style iostream classes and put them into the global name space. By contrast, to use the modern iostream library, include the new style header **<iostream>** in your program.

14

239

One final point: Since the old-style iostream library is nonstandard, its precise implementation will differ between compilers, and may differ slightly from that described here.

The Basic Stream Classes

The old-style iostream library uses the header file **iostream.h**. This file defines the foundational class hierarchy that supports I/O operations. If you will be performing file I/O, then you will need to also include **fstream.h**. To use array-based I/O, you will need to include **strstrea.h**.

The lowest-level class is called **streambuf**. This class provides the basic input and output operations. It is used primarily as a base class for other classes. Unless you are deriving your own I/O classes, you will not use **streambuf** directly.

The class **ios** is the base of the class hierarchy that you will typically use when using the C++ I/O system. It provides formatting, error checking, and status information. From **ios** are derived several classes—sometimes through intermediary classes. The classes derived either directly or indirectly from **ios** that you will typically use are listed here:

Class	Purpose
istream	General input
ostream	General output
iostream	General input/output
ifstream	File input
ofstream	File output
fstream	File input/output
istrstream	Array-based input
ostrstream	Array-based output
strstream	Array-based input/output

C++'s Predefined Streams

When a C++ program begins execution, four built-in streams are automatically opened. They are listed here:

Stream	Meaning	Default Device
cin	Standard input	Keyboard
cout	Standard output	Screen
cerr	Standard error output	Screen
clog	Buffered version of cerr	Screen

By default, the standard streams are used to communicate with the console. However, in environments that support I/O redirection (such as DOS, UNIX, and Windows), the standard streams can be redirected to other devices or files.

The Format Flags

In the C++ I/O system, each stream has associated with it a set of format flags that control the way information is formatted by a stream. In **ios** are defined the following enumerated values. These values are used to set or clear the format flags.

adjustfield	basefield	dec	fixed
floatfield	hex	internal	left
oct	right	scientific	showbase
showpoint	showpos	skipws	stdio
unitbuf	uppercase		

Since these flags are defined within the **ios** class, you will need to explicitly specify this when using them in a program. For example, to refer to **left** you will write **ios::left**.

When the **skipws** flag is set, leading whitespace characters (spaces, tabs, and newlines) are discarded when performing input on a stream. When **skipws** is cleared, whitespace characters are not discarded.

When the **left** flag is set, output is left-justified. When **right** is set, output is right-justified. When the **internal** flag is set, a numeric value is padded to fill a field by inserting spaces between any sign or base character. If none of these flags is set, output is right-justified by default.

By default, numeric values are output in decimal. However, it is possible to change the number base. Setting the **oct** flag causes output to be displayed in octal. Setting the **hex** flag causes output

14

to be displayed in hexadecimal. To return output to decimal, set the **dec** flag.

Setting **showbase** causes the base of numeric values to be shown. For example, if the conversion base is hexadecimal, the value 1F will be displayed as 0x1F.

By default, when scientific notation is displayed, the **e** is in lowercase. Also, when a hexadecimal value is displayed, the **x** is in lowercase. When **uppercase** is set, these characters are displayed in uppercase.

Setting **showpos** causes a leading plus sign to be displayed before positive values.

Setting **showpoint** causes a decimal point and trailing zeros to be displayed for all floating-point output—whether needed or not.

By setting the **scientific** flag, floating-point numeric values are displayed using scientific notation. When **fixed** is set, floating-point values are displayed using normal notation. When neither flag is set, the compiler chooses an appropriate method.

When **unitbuf** is set, the buffer is flushed after each insertion operation.

When **stdio** is set, **stdout** and **stderr** are flushed after each output.

Since it is common to refer to the **oct, dec,** and **hex** fields, they can be collectively referred to as **ios::basefield.** Similarly, the **left, right,** and **internal** fields can be referred to as **ios::adjustfield.** Finally, the **scientific** and **fixed** fields can be referenced as **ios::floatfield.**

The format flags are typically stored in a **long** integer and may be set by various member functions of the **ios** class.

The I/O Manipulators

In addition to setting or clearing the format flags directly, there is another way in which you may alter the format parameters of a stream. This second way is through the use of special functions called *manipulators*, which can be included in an I/O expression. The manipulators defined by the old-style iostream library are shown in the following table:

Manipulator	Purpose	Input/Output
dec	Use decimal integers	Input/output
endl	Output a newline character and flush the stream	Output
ends	Output a null	Output
flush	Flush a stream	Output
hex	Use hexadecimal integers	Input/output
oct	Use octal integers	Input/output
resetiosflags (long f)	Turn off the flags specified in f	Input/output
setbase(int base)	Set the number base to base	Output
setfill(int ch)	Set the fill character to ch	Output
setiosflags (long f)	Turn on the flags specified in f	Input/output
setprecision (int p)	Set the number of digits of precision	Output
setw(int w)	Set the field width to w	Output
ws	Skip leading whitespace	Input

To access manipulators that take parameters, such as **setw( )**, you must include **iomanip.h** in your program.

The Old-Style Iostream Functions

The most commonly used of the old-style iostream functions are described next.

bad

```
#include <iostream.h>
int bad() const;
```

The **bad( )** function is a member of **ios**.

The **bad( )** function returns nonzero if a fatal I/O error has occurred in the associated stream; otherwise, zero is returned.

A related function is **good( )**.

14

clear

```
#include <iostream.h>
void clear(int flags = 0);
```

The **clear( )** function is a member of **ios**.

The **clear( )** function clears the status flags associated with a stream. If *flags* is zero (as it is by default), then all error flags are cleared (reset to zero). Otherwise, the status flags will be set to whatever value is specified in *flags*.

A related function is **rdstate( )**.

eatwhite

```
#include <iostream.h>
void eatwhite();
```

The **eatwhite( )** function is a member of **istream**.

The **eatwhite( )** function reads and discards all leading whitespace from the associated input stream and advances the get pointer to the first nonwhitespace character.

A related function is **ignore( )**.

eof

```
#include <iostream.h>
int eof() const;
```

The **eof( )** function is a member of **ios**.

The **eof( )** function returns nonzero when the end of the associated input file has been encountered; otherwise, it returns zero.

Related functions are **bad( )**, **fail( )**, **good( )**, **rdstate( )**, and **clear( )**.

fail

```
#include <iostream.h>
int fail() const;
```

The **fail( )** function is a member of **ios**.

The **fail( )** function returns nonzero if an I/O error has occurred in the associated stream. Otherwise, it returns zero.

Related functions are **good( )**, **eof( )**, **bad( )**, **clear( )**, and **rdstate( )**.

fill

```
#include <iostream.h>
char fill() const;
char fill(char ch);
```

The **fill( )** function is a member of **ios**.

By default, when a field needs to be filled, it is filled with spaces. However, you can specify the fill character using the **fill( )** function and specifying the new fill character in *ch*. The old fill character is returned.

To obtain the current fill character, use the first form of **fill( )**, which returns the current fill character.

Related functions are **precision( )** and **width( )**.

flags

```
#include <iostream.h>
long flags() const;
long flags(long f);
```

The **flags( )** function is a member of **ios**.

14

The first form of **flags( )** simply returns the current format flags settings for the associated stream.

The second form of **flags( )** sets all format flags associated with a stream as specified by *f*. When you use this version, the bit pattern found in *f* is copied into the format flags associated with the stream. This version also returns the previous settings.

Related functions are **unsetf( )** and **setf( )**.

flush

```
#include <iostream.h>
ostream &flush();
```

The **flush( )** function is a member of **ostream**.

The **flush( )** function causes the buffer connected to the associated output stream to be physically written to the device. The function returns a reference to its associated stream.

Related functions are **put( )** and **write( )**.

fstream, ifstream, and ofstream

```
#include <fstream.h>
fstream();
fstream(const char *filename, int mode,
        int access=filebuf::openprot);
fstream(int fd);
fstream(int fd, char *buf, int size);

ifstream();
ifstream(const char *filename,
        int mode=ios::in,
        int access=filebuf::openprot);
ifstream(int fd);
ifstream(int fd, char *buf, int size);

ofstream();
ofstream(const char *filename,
        int mode=ios::out,
```

```
                int access=filebuf::openprot);
ofstream(int fd);
ofstream(int fd, char *buf, int size);
```

The **fstream( )**, **ifstream( )**, and **ofstream( )** are the constructors of the **fstream**, **ifstream**, and **ofstream** classes, respectively.

The versions of **fstream( )**, **ifstream( )**, and **ofstream( )** that take no parameters create a stream that is not associated with any file. This stream can then be linked to a file using **open( )**.

The versions of **fstream( )**, **ifstream( )**, and **ofstream( )** that take a filename for their first parameters are the most commonly used in application programs. Although it is entirely proper to open a file using the **open( )** function, most of the time you will not do so because these **ifstream**, **ofstream**, and **fstream** constructor functions automatically open the file when the stream is created. The constructor functions have the same parameters and defaults as the **open( )** function. (See **open** for details.) Therefore, the most common way you will see a file opened is shown in this example:

```
ifstream mystream("myfile");
```

If for some reason the file cannot be opened, the value of the associated stream variable will be zero. Therefore, whether you use a constructor function to open the file or an explicit call to **open( )**, you will want to confirm that the file has actually been opened by testing the value of the stream.

The versions of **fstream( )**, **ifstream( )**, and **ofstream( )** that take only one parameter, an already valid file descriptor, create a stream and then associate that stream with the file descriptor specified in *fd*.

The versions of **fstream( )**, **ifstream( )**, and **ofstream( )** that take a file descriptor, a pointer to a buffer, and a size create a stream and associate it with the file descriptor specified in *fd*. *buf* must be a pointer to memory that will serve as a buffer, and *size* specifies the length of the buffer, in bytes. (If *buf* is null and/or if *size* is 0, no buffering takes place.)

Related functions are **close( )** and **open( )**.

gcount

14

```
#include <iostream.h>
int gcount() const;
```

The **gcount( )** function is a member of **istream**.

The **gcount( )** function returns the number of characters read by the last input operation.

Related functions are **get( )**, **getline( )**, and **read( )**.

get

```
#include <iostream.h>
int get();
istream &get(char &ch):
istream &get(char *buf, int num, char delim = '\n');
istream &get(streambuf &buf, char delim = '\n');
```

The **get( )** function is a member of **istream**.

In general, **get( )** reads characters from an input stream. The parameterless form of **get( )** reads a single character from the associated stream and returns that value.

The form of **get( )** that takes a single character reference reads a character from the associated stream and puts that value in *ch*. It returns a reference to the stream. (Note that *ch* may also be of type **unsigned char *** or **signed char ***.)

The form of **get( )** that takes three parameters reads characters into the array pointed to by *buf* until either *num* characters have been read or the character specified by *delim* has been encountered. The array pointed to by *buf* will be null terminated by **get( )**. If no *delim* parameter is specified, by default a newline character acts as a delimiter. If the delimiter character is encountered in the input stream, it is *not* extracted. Instead, it remains in the stream until the next input operation. This function returns a reference to the stream. (Note that *buf* may also be of type **unsigned char *** or **signed char ***.)

The form of **get( )** that takes two parameters reads characters from the input stream into the **streambuf** (or derived) object. Characters are read until the specified delimiter is encountered. It returns a reference to the stream.

Related functions are **put( )**, **read( )**, and **getline( )**.

getline

```
#include <iostream.h>
istream &getline(char *buf, int num, char delim = '\n');
```

The **getline( )** function is a member of **istream**.

The **getline( )** function reads characters into the array pointed to by *buf* until either *num* characters have been read or the character specified by *delim* has been encountered. The array pointed to by *buf* will be null terminated by **getline( )**. If no *delim* parameter is specified, by default a newline character acts as a delimiter. If the delimiter character is encountered in the input stream, it is extracted but is not put into *buf*. This function returns a reference to the stream. (Note that *buf* may also be of type **unsigned char *** or **signed char ***.)

Related functions are **get( )** and **read( )**.

good

```
#include <iostream.h>
int good() const;
```

The **good( )** function is a member of **ios**.

The **good( )** function returns nonzero if no I/O errors have occurred in the associated stream; otherwise, it returns zero.

Related functions are **bad( )**, **fail( )**, **eof( )**, **clear( )**, and **rdstate( )**.

ignore

14

```
#include <iostream.h>
istream &ignore(int num = 1, int delim = EOF);
```

The **ignore( )** function is a member of **istream**.

You can use the **ignore( )** member function to read and discard characters from the input stream. It reads and discards characters until either *num* characters have been ignored (1 by default) or until the character specified by *delim* is encountered (**EOF** by default). If the delimiting character is encountered, it is removed from the input stream. The function returns a reference to the stream.

Related functions are **get( )** and **getline( )**.

open

```
#include <fstream.h>
  void open(const char *filename, int mode,
            int access=filebuf::openprot);
```

The **open( )** function is a member of **fstream**, **ifstream**, and **ofstream**.

A file is associated with a stream by using the **open( )** function. Here, *filename* is the name of the file, which may include a path specifier. The value of *mode* determines how the file is opened. It must be one (or more) of these values:

ios::app
ios::ate
ios::binary
ios::in
ios::nocreate
ios::noreplace
ios::out
ios::trunc

You can combine two or more of these values by ORing them together.

Including **ios::app** causes all output to that file to be appended to the end. This value can only be used with files capable of output. Including **ios::ate** causes a seek to the end of the file to occur when the file is opened. Although **ios::ate** causes a seek to the end of file, I/O operations can still occur anywhere within the file.

The **ios::binary** value causes the file to be opened for binary I/O operations. By default, files are opened in text mode.

The **ios::in** value specifies that the file is capable of input. The **ios::out** value specifies that the file is capable of output. However, creating a stream using **ifstream** implies input, and creating a stream using **ofstream** implies output, so in these cases it is unnecessary to supply these values.

The **ios::trunc** value causes the contents of a preexisting file by the same name to be destroyed and the file is truncated to zero length.

Including **ios::nocreate** causes the **open( )** function to fail if the file does not already exist. The **ios::noreplace** value causes the **open( )** function to fail if the file already exists and **ios::ate** or **ios::app** is not also specified.

The value of *access* determines how the file can be accessed. Its default value is **filebuf::openprot** (**filebuf** is a base class of the file classes), which means a normal file. Check your compiler's documentation for other legal values of *access*.

When opening a file, both *mode* and *access* will default. When opening an input file, *mode* will default to **ios::in**. When opening an output file, *mode* will default to **ios::out**. In either case, the default for *access* is a normal file. For example, this opens a file called "test" for output:

```
out.open("test"); // defaults to output and normal file
```

To open a stream for input and output, you must usually specify both the **ios::in** and the **ios::out** *mode* values, as shown here:

```
mystream.open("test", ios::in | ios::out);
```

For many compilers, no default value for *mode* is supplied when opening read/write files.

In all cases, if **open( )** fails, the stream will be zero. Therefore, before using a file, you should test to make sure that the open operation succeeded.

Related functions are **close( )**, **fstream( )**, **ifstream( )**, and **ofstream( )**.

14

➤ Programming Tip

To read from or write to a text file, you simply use the <<
and >> operators with the stream you opened. For example,
the following old-style program writes an integer, a floating-
point value, and a string to a file called "test" and then reads
them back:

```
// This is an old-style program.
#include <iostream.h>
#include <fstream.h>

int main()
{
  ofstream out("test");
  if(!out) {
    cout << "Cannot open file.\n";
    return 1;
  }

  // output data
  out << 10 << " " << 123.23 << "\n";
  out << "This is a short text file.\n";
  out.close();

  // now, read it back
  char ch;
  int i;
  float f;
  char str[80];

  ifstream in("test");
  if(!in) {
    cout << "Cannot open file.\n";
    return 1;
  }

  in >> i;
  in >> f;
  in >> ch;
  in >> str;
```

```
    cout << "Here is the data: ";
    cout << i << " " << f << " " << ch << "\n";
    cout << str;

    in.close();

    return 0;
}
```

When reading text files using the >> operator, keep in mind that certain character translations occur. For example, whitespace characters are omitted. If you want to prevent any character translations, you must open the file for binary I/O and use the binary I/O functions.

peek

```
#include <iostream.h>
int peek();
```

The **peek( )** function is a member of **istream**.

The **peek( )** function returns the next character in the stream or **EOF** if the end of the file is encountered. It does not, under any circumstances, remove the character from the stream.

A related function is **get( )**.

precision

```
#include <iostream.h>
int precision() const;
int precision(int p);
```

The **precision( )** function is a member of **ios**.

By default, six digits of precision are displayed after the decimal point when floating-point values are output. However, using the

14

second form of **precision( )**, you can set this number to the value specified in *p*. The original value is returned.

The first version of **precision( )** returns the current value.

Related functions are **width( )** and **fill( )**.

put

```
#include <iostream.h>
ostream &put(char ch);
```

The **put( )** function is a member of **ostream**.

The **put( )** function writes *ch* to the associated output stream. It returns a reference to the stream.

Related functions are **write( )** and **get( )**.

putback

```
#include <iostream.h>
istream &putback(char ch);
```

The **putback( )** function is a member of **istream**.

The **putback( )** function returns *ch* to the associated input stream.

NOTE: *ch* must be the last character read from that stream.

A related function is **peek( )**.

rdstate

```
#include <iostream.h>
int rdstate() const;
```

The **rdstate( )** function is a member of **ios**.

The **rdstate( )** function returns the status of the associated stream. The C++ I/O system maintains status information about the outcome of each I/O operation relative to each active stream. The current state of the I/O system is held in an integer, in which the following flags are encoded:

Name	Meaning
ios::goodbit	No errors occurred.
ios::eofbit	End of file is encountered.
ios::failbit	A nonfatal I/O error has occurred.
ios::badbit	A fatal I/O error has occurred.

These flags are enumerated inside **ios**.

rdstate( ) returns zero (**ios::goodbit**) when no error has occurred; otherwise, an error bit has been set.

Related functions are **eof( )**, **good( )**, **bad( )**, **clear( )**, and **fail( )**.

read

```
#include <iostream.h>
istream &read(char *buf, int num);
```

The **read( )** function is a member of **istream**.

The **read( )** function reads num bytes from the associated input stream and puts them in the buffer pointed to by buf (note that buf may also be of type **unsigned char *** or **signed char ***). If the end of the file is reached before num characters have been read, **read( )** simply stops, and the buffer contains as many characters as were available. (See **gcount( )**.) **read( )** returns a reference to the stream.

Related functions are **gcount( )**, **get( )**, **getline( )**, and **write( )**.

seekg and seekp

14

```
#include <iostream.h>
istream &seekg(streamoff offset, ios::seek_dir origin);
```

```
istream &seekg(streampos position);

ostream &seekp(streamoff offset, ios::seek_dir origin);
ostream &seekp(streampos position);
```

The **seekg( )** function is a member of **istream**, and the **seekp( )** function is a member of **ostream**.

In C++'s I/O system, you perform random access using the **seekg( )** and **seekp( )** functions. To this end, the C++ I/O system manages two pointers associated with a file. One is the *get pointer*, which specifies where in the file the next input operation will occur. The other is the *put pointer*, which specifies where in the file the next output operation will occur. Each time an input or an output operation takes place, the appropriate pointer is automatically sequentially advanced. However, using the **seekg( )** and **seekp( )** functions, it is possible to access the file in a nonsequential fashion.

The two-parameter version of **seekg( )** moves the get pointer *offset* number of bytes from the location specified by *origin*. The two-parameter version of **seekp( )** moves the put pointer *offset* number of bytes from the location specified by *origin*. The *offset* parameter is of type **streamoff**, which is defined in **iostream.h**. A **streamoff** object is capable of containing the largest valid value that *offset* can have.

The *origin* parameter is of type **ios::seek_dir** and is an enumeration that has these values:

ios::beg	Seek from beginning
ios::cur	Seek from current position
ios::end	Seek from end

The single-parameter versions of **seekg( )** and **seekp( )** move the file pointers to the location specified by *position*. This value must have been previously obtained using a call to either **tellg( )** or **tellp( )**, respectively. **streampos** is a type defined in **iostream.h** that is capable of containing the largest valid value that *position* can have. These functions return a reference to the associated stream.

Related functions are **tellg( )** and **tellp( )**.

setf

```
#include <iostream.h>
long setf(long flags);
long setf(long flags1, long flags2);
```

The **setf( )** function is a member of **ios**.

The first version of **setf( )** turns on the format flags specified by *flags*. (All other flags are unaffected.) For example, to turn on the **showpos** flag, you can use this statement:

```
stream.setf(ios::showpos);
```

Here, *stream* is the stream you wish to affect.

It is important to understand that a call to **setf( )** is done relative to a specific stream. There is no concept of calling **setf( )** by itself. Put differently, there is no concept in C++ of global format status. Each stream maintains its own format status information individually.

When you want to set more than one flag, you can OR together the values of the flags you want set.

The second version of **setf( )** affects only the flags that are set in *flags2*. The corresponding flags are first reset and then set according to the flags specified by *flags1*. It is important to understand that even if *flags1* contains other set flags, only those specified by *flags2* will be affected.

Both versions of **setf( )** return the previous settings of the format flags associated with the stream.

Related functions are **unsetf( )** and **flags( )**.

setmode

```
#include <fstream.h>
int setmode(int mode = filebuf::text);
```

14

The **setmode( )** function is a member of **ofstream** and **ifstream**.

The **setmode( )** function sets the mode of the associated stream to either binary or text. (Text is the default.) The valid values for *mode* are **filebuf::text** and **filebuf::binary**.

The function returns the previous mode setting or –1 if an error occurs.

A related function is **open( )**.

str

```
#include <strstrea.h>
char *str();
```

The **str( )** function is a member of **strstream**.

The **str( )** function "freezes" a dynamically allocated input array and returns a pointer to it. Once a dynamic array is frozen, it may not be used for output again. Therefore, you will not want to freeze the array until you are through outputting characters to it.

NOTE: This function is for use with array-based I/O.

Related functions are **strstream( )**, **istrstream( )**, and **ostrstream( )**.

strstream, istrstream, and ostrstream

```
#include <strstrea.h>
strstream();
strstream(char *buf, int size, int mode);

istrstream(const char *buf);
istrstream(const char *buf, int size);

ostrstream();
ostrstream(char *buf, int size, int mode=ios::out)
```

The **strstream** constructor is a member of **strstream**, the **istrstream( )** constructor is a member of **istrstream**, and the **ostrstream( )** constructor is a member of **ostrstream**.

These constructors are used to create array-based streams that support C++'s array-based I/O functions.

For **ostrstream( )**, *buf* is a pointer to the array that collects characters written to the stream. The size of the array is passed in the *size* parameter. By default, the stream is opened for normal output, but you can specify a different mode using the *mode* parameter. The legal values for *mode* are the same as those used with **open( )**. For most purposes, *mode* will be allowed to default. If you use the parameterless version of **ostrstream( )**, a dynamic array is automatically allocated.

For the single-parameter version of **istrstream( )**, *buf* is a pointer to the array that will be used as a source of characters each time input is performed on the stream. The contents of the array pointed to by *buf* must be null terminated. However, the null terminator is never read from the array.

If you wish only part of a string to be used for input, use the two-parameter form of the **istrstream** constructor. Here, only the first *size* elements of the array pointed to by *buf* will be used. This string need not be null terminated, since it is the value of *size* that determines the size of the string.

To create an array-based stream capable of input and output, use **strstream( )**. In the parameterized version, *buf* points to the string that will be used for I/O operations. The value of *size* specifies the size of the array. The value of *mode* determines how the stream operates. For normal input/output operations, *mode* will be **ios::in | ios::out**. For input, the array must be null terminated.

If you use the parameterless version of **strstream( )**, the buffer used for I/O will be dynamically allocated, and the mode is set for read/write operations.

Related functions are **str( )** and **open( )**.

sync_with_stdio

```
#include <iostream.h>
static void sync_with_stdio();
```

14

The **sync_with_stdio( )** function is a member of **ios**.

Calling **sync_with_stdio( )** allows the standard C-like I/O system to be safely used concurrently with the C++ class-based I/O system.

tellg and tellp

```
#include <iostream.h>
streampos tellg();
streampos tellp():
```

The **tellg( )** function is a member of **istream**, and **tellp( )** is a member of **ostream**.

The C++ I/O system manages two pointers associated with a file. One is the *get pointer*, which specifies where in the file the next input operation will occur. The other is the *put pointer*, which specifies where in the file the next output operation will occur. Each time an input or an output operation takes place, the appropriate pointer is automatically sequentially advanced. You can determine the current position of the get pointer using **tellg( )** and of the put pointer using **tellp( )**.

streampos is a type defined in **iostream.h** that is capable of holding the largest value that either function can return.

The values returned by **tellg( )** and **tellp( )** can be used as parameters to **seekg( )** and **seekp( )**, respectively.

Related functions are **seekg( )** and **seekp( )**.

unsetf

```
#include <iostream.h>
long unsetf(long flags);
```

The **unsetf( )** function is a member of **ios**.

The **unsetf( )** function is used to clear one or more format flags.

The flags specified by *flags* are cleared. (All other flags are unaffected.) The previous flag settings are returned.

Related functions are **setf( )** and **flags( )**.

width

```
#include <iostream.h>
int width() const;
int width(int w);
```

The **width( )** function is a member of **ios**.

To obtain the current field width, use the first form of **width( )**. This version returns the current field width.

To set the field width, use the second form. Here, *w* becomes the field width, and the previous field width is returned.

Related functions are **precision( )** and **fill( )**.

write

```
#include <iostream.h>
ostream &write(const char *buf, int num);
```

The **write( )** function is a member of **ostream**.

The **write( )** function writes *num* bytes to the associated output stream from the buffer pointed to by *buf*. (Note that *buf* may also be of type **unsigned char *** or **signed char ***.) It returns a reference to the stream.

Related functions are **read( )** and **put( )**.

14

Chapter 15
The ANSI/ISO Standard
C++ I/O Classes

As explained in Chapter 14, there are two versions of C++'s iostream library: the old style defined by early versions of C++, and the modern approach as defined by the ANSI/ISO Standard for C++ (Standard C++). The old-style library was described in the preceding section. The Standard C++ iostream library is described here.

Using the Standard C++
Iostream Library

There are two fundamental differences between the old-style and the Standard C++ iostream libraries. First, the old-style library was defined in the global namespace. The Standard C++ iostream library is contained in the **std** namespace. Second, the old-style library uses C-like **.h** header files. The Standard C++ library uses C++ headers (which don't use the **.h**).

To use the Standard C++ iostream library, include the header **<iostream>** in your program. After doing that, you will usually want to bring the library into your current namespace using a statement like this:

```
using namespace std;
```

After the **using** statement, both the old-style and modern libraries work in much the same way.

It is not necessary to use the **using** statement just described. Instead, you can include an explicit namespace qualifier each time you refer to a member of the I/O classes. For example, the following explicitly refers to **cout**:

```
std::cout << "This is a test";
```

Of course, if you will be making extensive use of the iostream library, then including the **using** statement makes things less tedious.

15

The Standard C++ I/O Classes

The Standard C++ I/O system is constructed from a rather complex system of template classes. These classes are shown here:

Class	Purpose
basic_ios	Provides general-purpose I/O operations
basic_streambuf	Low-level support for I/O
basic_istream	Support for input operations
basic_ostream	Support for output operations
basic_iostream	Support for input/output operations
basic_filebuf	Low-level support for file I/O
basic_ifstream	Support for file input
basic_ofstream	Support for file output
basic_fstream	Support for file input/output
basic_stringbuf	Low-level support for string-based I/O
basic_istringstream	Support for string-based input
basic_ostringstream	Support for string-based output
basic_stringstream	Support for string-based input/output

Also part of the I/O class hierarchy is the nontemplate class **ios_base.** It provides definitions for various elements of the I/O system.

The C++ I/O system is built upon two related, but different, template class hierarchies. The first is derived from the low-level I/O class called **basic_streambuf.** This class supplies the basic, low-level input and output operations, and provides the underlying support for the entire C++ I/O system. The classes **basic_filebuf** and **basic_stringbuf** are derived from **basic_streambuf.** Unless you are doing advanced I/O programming, you will not need to use **basic_streambuf** or its subclasses directly.

The class hierarchy that you will most commonly be working with is derived from **basic_ios.** This is a high-level I/O class that provides formatting, error checking, and status information related to stream I/O. **basic_ios** is used as a base for several derived classes, including **basic_istream**, **basic_ostream**, and **basic_iostream**. These classes are used to create streams capable of input, output, and input/output, respectively. Specifically, from **basic_istream** are derived the classes **basic_ifstream** and **basic_istringstream**, from **basic_ostream** are derived **basic_ofstream** and **basic_ostringstream**, and from **basic_iostream** are derived **basic_fstream** and **basic_stringstream**. A base class for **basic_ios** is **ios_base**. Thus, any class derived from **basic_ios** has access to the members of **ios_base**.

The I/O classes are parameterized for the type of characters that they act upon and for the traits associated with those characters. For example, here is the template specification for **basic_ios**:

```
template <class CharType, class Attr = char_traits<CharType> >
class basic_ios: public ios_base
```

Here, **CharType** specifies the type of character (such as **char** or **wchar_t**) and **Attr** specifies a type that describes its attributes. The generic type **char_traits** is a utility class that defines the attributes associated with a character.

The I/O library creates two specializations of the template class hierarchies just described: one for 8-bit characters and one for wide characters. Here is a complete list of the mapping of template class names to their character and wide-character versions:

Template Class	Character-Based Class	Wide-Character-Based Class
basic_ios	ios	wios
basic_istream	istream	wistream
basic_ostream	ostream	wostream
basic_iostream	iostream	wiostream
basic_ifstream	ifstream	wifstream
basic_ofstream	ofstream	wofstream
basic_fstream	fstream	wfstream
basic_istringstream	istringstream	wistringstream

15

Template Class	Character-Based Class	Wide-Character-Based Class
basic_ostringstream	ostringstream	wostringstream
basic_stringstream	stringstream	wstringstream
basic_streambuf	streambuf	wstreambuf
basic_filebuf	filebuf	wfilebuf
basic_stringbuf	stringbuf	wstringbuf

Since the vast majority of programmers will be using character-based I/O, those are the names used by this chapter. Thus, when referring to the I/O classes, we will simply use their character-based names rather then their internal, template names. For instance, this chapter will use the name **ios** rather than **basic_ios**, **istream** rather than **basic_istream**, and **fstream** rather than **basic_fstream**. Remember, parallel functions exist for wide-character streams and they work in the same way as those described here.

C++'s Predefined Streams

The Standard C++ iostream library automatically opens the following streams:

Stream	Meaning
cin	Standard input
cout	Standard output
cerr	Standard error output
clog	Buffered version of cerr
wcin	Wide-character version of cin
wcout	Wide-character version of cout
wcerr	Wide-character version of cerr
wclog	Wide-character version of clog

By default, the standard streams are used to communicate with the console. However, in environments that support I/O redirection (such as DOS, UNIX, and Windows), the standard streams can be redirected to other devices or files.

The I/O Headers

The Standard C++ I/O system relies upon several headers. They are shown here:

Header	For
<fstream>	File I/O
<iomanip>	Parameterized I/O manipulators
<ios>	Basic I/O support
<iosfwd>	Forward declarations used by the I/O system
<iostream>	General I/O
<istream>	Basic input support
<ostream>	Basic output support
<sstream>	String-based streams
<streambuf>	Low-level I/O support

Several of these headers are used internally by the I/O system. In general, your program will only include **<iostream>**, **<fstream>**, **<sstream>**, or **<iomanip>**.

The Format Flags

Each stream has associated with it a set of format flags that control the way information is formatted. The **ios_base** class declares a bitmask enumeration called **fmtflags** in which the following values are defined:

adjustfield	basefield	boolalpha	dec
fixed	floatfield	hex	internal
left	oct	right	scientific
showbase	showpoint	showpos	skipws
unitbuf	uppercase		

These values are used to set or clear the format flags, using functions such as **setf( )** and **unsetf( )**.

15

When the **skipws** flag is set, leading whitespace characters (spaces, tabs, and newlines) are discarded when performing input on a stream. When **skipws** is cleared, whitespace characters are not discarded.

When the **left** flag is set, output is left-justified. When **right** is set, output is right-justified. When the **internal** flag is set, a numeric value is padded to fill a field by inserting spaces between any sign or base character. If none of these flags is set, output is right-justified by default.

By default, numeric values are output in decimal. However, it is possible to change the number base. Setting the **oct** flag causes output to be displayed in octal. Setting the **hex** flag causes output to be displayed in hexadecimal. To return output to decimal, set the **dec** flag.

Setting **showbase** causes the base of numeric values to be shown. For example, if the conversion base is hexadecimal, the value 1F will be displayed as 0x1F.

By default, when scientific notation is displayed, the **e** is in lowercase. Also, when a hexadecimal value is displayed, the **x** is in lowercase. When **uppercase** is set, these characters are displayed in uppercase.

Setting **showpos** causes a leading plus sign to be displayed before positive values.

Setting **showpoint** causes a decimal point and trailing zeros to be displayed for all floating-point output—whether needed or not.

By setting the **scientific** flag, floating-point numeric values are displayed using scientific notation. When **fixed** is set, floating-point values are displayed using normal notation. When neither flag is set, the compiler chooses an appropriate method.

When **unitbuf** is set, the buffer is flushed after each insertion operation.

When **boolalpha** is set, Booleans can be input or output using the keywords **true** and **false**.

Since it is common to refer to the **oct**, **dec**, and **hex** fields, they can be collectively referred to as **basefield**. Similarly, the **left**, **right**, and **internal** fields can be referred to as **adjustfield**. Finally, the **scientific** and **fixed** fields can be referenced as **floatfield**.

The I/O Manipulators

In addition to setting or clearing the format flags directly, you can alter the format parameters of a stream through the use of special functions called *manipulators*, which can be included in an I/O expression. The standard manipulators are shown in the following table:

Manipulator	Purpose	Input/Output
boolalpha	Turns on **boolapha** flag	Input/Output
dec	Turns on **dec** flag	Input/Ouput
endl	Output a newline character and flush the stream	Output
ends	Output a null	Output
fixed	Turns on **fixed** flag	Output
flush	Flush a stream	Output
hex	Turns on **hex** flag	Input/Output
internal	Turns on **internal** flag	Output
left	Turns on **left** flag	Output
nobooalpha	Turns off **boolalpha** flag	Input/Output
noshowbase	Turns off **showbase** flag	Output
noshowpoint	Turns off **showpoint** flag	Output
noshowpos	Turns off **showpos** flag	Output
noskipws	Turns off **skipws** flag	Input
nounitbuf	Turns off **unitbuf** flag	Output
nouppercase	Turns off **uppercase** flag	Output
oct	Turns on **oct** flag	Input/Output
resetiosflags(fmtflags *f*)	Turn off the flags specified in *f*	Input/Output
right	Turns on **right** flag	Output
scientific	Turns on **scientific** flag	Output
setbase(int *base*)	Set the number base to *base*	Input/Output
setfill(int *ch*)	Set the fill character to *ch*	Output
setiosflags(fmtflags *f*)	Turn on the flags specified in *f*	Input/Output
setprecision (int *p*)	Set the number of digits of precision	Output
setw(int *w*)	Set the field width to *w*	Output

15

Manipulator	Purpose	Input/Output
showbase	Turns on **showbase** flag	Output
showpoint	Turns on **showpoint** flag	Output
showpos	Turns on **showpos** flag	Output
skipws	Turns on **skipws** flag	Input
unitbuf	Turns on **unitbuf** flag	Output
uppercase	Turns on **uppercase** flag	Output
ws	Skip leading whitespace	Input

To use a manipulator that takes a parameter, you must include **<iomanip>**.

➤ Programming Tip

One of the most interesting format flags found in the modern iostream library is **boolalpha**. This flag can be set either directly or by using the manipulators **boolalpha( )** or **noboolalpha( )**. What makes **boolalpha** so interesting is that setting it allows you to input and output Boolean values using the keywords **true** and **false**. Normally, you must enter 1 for true and zero for false. For example, consider the following program:

```
// Demonstrate boolalpha format flag.
#include <iostream>
using namespace std;

int main()
{
  bool b;

  cout << "Before setting boolalpha flag: ";
  b = true;
  cout << b << " ";
  b = false;
  cout << b << endl;

  cout << "After setting boolalpha flag: ";
  b = true;
```

```
    cout << boolalpha << b << " ";
    b = false;
    cout << b << endl;

    cout << "Enter a Boolean value: ";
    cin >> boolalpha >> b;
    cout << "You entered " << b;

    return 0;
}
```

Here is a sample run:

```
Before setting boolalpha flag: 1 0
After setting boolalpha flag: true false
Enter a Boolean value: true
You entered true
```

Once the **boolalpha** flag has been set, Boolean values are input and output using the words **true** or **false**. As the program shows, you must set the **boolalpha** flag for **cin** and **cout** separately. Like all format flags, setting **boolalpha** for one stream does not imply that it is also set for another.

Several Data Types

In addition to the **fmtflags** type just described, the Standard C++ I/O system defines several other types

The streamsize and streamoff Types

An object of type **streamsize** is capable of holding the largest number of bytes that will be transferred in any one I/O operation. It is typically some form of integer. An object of type **streamoff** is capable of holding a value that indicates an offset position within a stream. It is typically some form of integer. These types are defined in the header **<ios>**, which is automatically included by the I/O system.

15

The streampos and wstreampos Types

An object of type **streampos** is capable of holding a value that represents a position within a **char** stream. The **wstreampos** type is capable of holding a value that represents a position within a **wchar_t** stream. These are defined by in **<iosfwd>**, which is automatically included by the I/O system.

The pos_type and off_type Types

The types **pos_type** and **off_type** create objects (typically integers) that are capable of holding a value that represents the position and an offset, respectively, within a stream. These types are defined by **ios** (and other classes) and are essentially the same as **streamoff** and **streampos** (or their wide-character equivalents).

The openmode Type

The type **openmode** is defined by **ios_base** and describes how a file will be opened. It will be one or more of these values:

app	Append to end of file
ate	Seek to end of file on creation
binary	Open file for binary operations
in	Open file for input
out	Open file for output
trunc	Erase previously existing file

You can combine two or more of these values by ORing them together.

The iostate Type

The current status of an I/O stream is described by an object of type **iostate**, which is an enumeration defined by **ios_base** that includes these members:

Name	Meaning
goodbit	No errors occurred
eofbit	End of file is encountered

Name	Meaning
failbit	A nonfatal I/O error has occurred
badbit	A fatal I/O error has occurred

The seekdir type

The **seekdir** type describes how a random-access file operation will take place. It is defined within **ios_base**. Its valid values are shown here:

beg	Beginning of file
cur	Current location
end	End of file

The failure Class

In **ios_base** is defined the exception type **failure**. It serves as a base class for the types of exceptions that can be thrown by the I/O system. It inherits **exception** (the standard exception class). The **failure** class has the following constructor:

explicit failure(const string &*str*);

Here, *str* is a message that describes the error. This message can be obtained from a **failure** object by calling its **what( )** function, shown here:

virtual const char *what( ) const throw( );

Overloaded << and >> Operators

The following classes overload the << and/or >> operators relative to all of the built-in data types:

basic_istream
basic_ostream
basic_iostream

15

Any classes derived from these classes inherit these operators.

The ANSI/ISO Standard I/O Functions

The remainder of this chapter describes the general-purpose I/O functions defined by ANSI/ISO Standard C++. As explained, the Standard C++ I/O system is built upon an intricate hierarchy of template classes. Many of the members of the low-level classes are not used for application programming. Thus, they are not described here.

bad

```
#include <iostream>
bool bad() const;
```

The **bad( )** function is a member of **ios**.

The **bad( )** function returns **true** if a fatal I/O error has occurred in the associated stream; otherwise, **false** is returned.

A related function is **good( )**.

clear

```
#include <iostream>
void clear(iostate flags = goodbit);
```

The **clear( )** function is a member of **ios**.

The **clear( )** function clears the status flags associated with a stream. If *flags* is **goodbit** (as it is by default), then all error flags are cleared (reset to zero). Otherwise, the status flags will be set to whatever value is specified in *flags*.

A related function is **rdstate( )**.

eof

```
#include <iostream>
bool eof() const;
```

The **eof( )** function is a member of **ios**.

The **eof( )** function returns **true** when the end of the associated input file has been encountered; otherwise, it returns **false**.

Related functions are **bad( )**, **fail( )**, **good( )**, **rdstate( )**, and **clear( )**.

exceptions

```
#include <iostream>
iostate exceptions() const;
void exceptions(iostate flags);
```

The **exceptions( )** function is a member of **ios**.

The first form returns an **iostate** object that indicates which flags cause an exception. The second form sets these values.

A related function is **rdstate( )**.

fail

```
#include <iostream>
bool fail() const;
```

The **fail( )** function is a member of **ios**.

The **fail( )** function returns **true** if an I/O error has occurred in the associated stream. Otherwise, it returns **false**.

Related functions are **good( )**, **eof( )**, **bad( )**, **clear( )**, and **rdstate( )**.

15

fill

```
#include <iostream>
char fill() const;
char fill(char ch);
```

The **fill( )** function is a member of **ios**.

By default, when a field needs to be filled, it is filled with spaces. However, you can specify the fill character using the **fill( )** function and specifying the new fill character in *ch*. The old fill character is returned.

To obtain the current fill character, use the first form of **fill( )**, which returns the current fill character.

Related functions are **precision( )** and **width( )**.

flags

```
#include <iostream>
fmtflags flags() const;
fmtflags flags(fmtflags f);
```

The **flags( )** function is a member of **ios** (inherited from **ios_base**).

The first form of **flags( )** simply returns the current format flags settings of the associated stream.

The second form of **flags( )** sets all format flags associated with a stream as specified by *f*. When you use this version, the bit pattern found in *f* is copied into the format flags associated with the stream. This version also returns the previous settings.

Related functions are **unsetf( )** and **setf( )**.

flush

```
#include <iostream>
ostream &flush();
```

The **flush( )** function is a member of **ostream**.

The **flush( )** function causes the buffer connected to the associated output stream to be physically written to the device. The function returns a reference to its associated stream.

Related functions are **put( )** and **write( )**.

fstream, ifstream, and ofstream

```
#include <fstream>
fstream();
explicit fstream(const char *filename,
                 ios::openmode mode = ios::in | ios::out);

ifstream();
explicit ifstream(const char *filename,
                  ios::openmode mode=ios::in);

ofstream();
explicit ofstream(const char *filename,
                  ios::openmode mode=ios::out | ios::trunc);
```

The **fstream( )**, **ifstream( )**, and **ofstream( )** functions are the constructors of the **fstream**, **ifstream**, and **ofstream** classes, respectively.

The versions of **fstream( )**, **ifstream( )**, and **ofstream( )** that take no parameters create a stream that is not associated with any file. This stream can then be linked to a file using **open( )**.

The versions of **fstream( )**, **ifstream( )**, and **ofstream( )** that take a filename for their first parameters are the most commonly used in application programs. Although it is entirely proper to open a file using the **open( )** function, most of the time you will not do so because these **ifstream**, **ofstream**, and **fstream** constructor functions automatically open the file when the stream is created. The constructor functions have the same parameters and defaults as the **open( )** function. (See **open** for details.) For instance, this is most common way you will see a file opened:

```
ifstream mystream("myfile");
```

If for some reason the file cannot be opened, the value of the associated stream variable will be **false**. Therefore, whether you use a constructor function to open the file or an explicit call to **open( )**, you will want to confirm that the file has actually been opened by testing the value of the stream.

15

Related functions are **close( )** and **open( )**.

➤ Programming Tip

In the old-style iostream library, the **fstream** constructor did not contain a default for the *mode* parameter. That is, it did not automatically open a stream for input and output operations. Thus, when using the old iostream library to open a stream for input and output, both **ios::in** and **ios::out** must be specified explicitly. Keep this in mind if backward compatibility with the old iostream library is a concern.

---

gcount

```
#include <iostream>
streamsize gcount() const;
```

The **gcount( )** function is a member of **istream**.

The **gcount( )** function returns the number of characters read by the last input operation.

Related functions are **get( )**, **getline( )**, and **read( )**.

get

```
#include <iostream>
int get();
istream &get(char &ch):
istream &get(char *buf, streamsize num);
istream &get(char *buf, streamsize num, char delim );
istream &get(streambuf &buf);
istream &get(streambuf &buf, char delim);
```

The **get( )** function is a member of **istream**.

In general, **get( )** reads characters from an input stream. The parameterless form of **get( )** reads a single character from the associated stream and returns that value.

get(char &*ch***)** reads a character from the associated stream and puts that value in *ch*. It returns a reference to the stream.

get(char **buf***, streamsize *num*)** reads characters into the array pointed to by *buf* until either *num*–1 characters have been read, a newline is found, or the end of the file has been encountered. The array pointed to by *buf* will be null terminated by **get( )**. If the newline character is encountered in the input stream, it is not extracted. This function returns a reference to the stream.

get(char **buf***, streamsize *num*, char *delim*)** reads characters into the array pointed to by *buf* until either *num*–1 characters have been read, the character specified by *delim* has been found, or the end of the file has been encountered. The array pointed to by *buf* will be null terminated by **get( )**. If the delimiter character is encountered in the input stream, it is not extracted. This function returns a reference to the stream.

get(streambuf &*buf***)** reads characters from the input stream into the **streambuf** object. Characters are read until a newline is found or the end of the file is encountered. It returns a reference to the stream. If the newline character is encountered in the input stream, it is not extracted.

get(streambuf &*buf***, char *delim*)** reads characters from the input stream into the **streambuf** object. Characters are read until the character specified by *delim* is found or the end of the file is encountered. It returns a reference to the stream. If the delimiter character is encountered in the input stream, it is not extracted.

Related functions are **put( )**, **read( )**, and **getline( )**.

getline

```
#include <iostream>
istream &getline(char *buf, streamsize num);
istream &getline(char *buf, streamsize num, char delim);
```

The **getline( )** function is a member of **istream**.

getline(char **buf***, streamsize *num)*** reads characters into the array pointed to by *buf* until either *num*–1 characters have been read, a newline character has been found, or the end of the file has been encountered. The array pointed to by *buf* will be null terminated by

15

getline( ). If the newline character is encountered in the input stream, it is extracted but is not put into *buf*. This function returns a reference to the stream.

getline(char *buf, streamsize num, char delim) reads characters into the array pointed to by *buf* until either *num*–1 characters have been read, the character specified by *delim* has been found, or the end of the file has been encountered. The array pointed to by *buf* will be null terminated by **getline( )**. If the delimiter character is encountered in the input stream, it is extracted but is not put into *buf*. This function returns a reference to the stream.

Related functions are **get( )** and **read( )**.

---

good

```
#include <iostream>
bool good() const;
```

The **good( )** function is a member of **ios**.

The **good( )** function returns **true** if no I/O errors have occurred in the associated stream; otherwise, it returns **false**.

Related functions are **bad( )**, **fail( )**, **eof( )**, **clear( )**, and **rdstate( )**.

---

ignore

```
#include <iostream>
istream &ignore(streamsize num = 1, int delim = EOF);
```

The **ignore( )** function is a member of **istream**.

You can use the **ignore( )** member function to read and discard characters from the input stream. It reads and discards characters until either *num* characters have been ignored (1 by default) or until the character specified by *delim* is encountered (**EOF** by default). If the delimiting character is encountered, it is removed from the input stream. The function returns a reference to the stream.

Related functions are **get( )** and **getline( )**.

open

```
#include <fstream>
void fstream::open(const char *filename,
                   ios::openmode mode = ios::in | ios:: out);
void ifstream::open(const char *filename,
                    ios::openmode mode = ios::in);
void ofstream::open(const char *filename,
                    ios::openmode mode = ios:: out | ios::trunc);
```

The **open( )** function is a member of **fstream, ifstream,** and **ofstream.**

A file is associated with a stream by using the **open( )** function. Here, *filename* is the name of the file, which may include a path specifier. The value of *mode* determines how the file is opened. It must be one (or more) of these values:

> ios::app
> ios::ate
> ios::binary
> ios::in
> ios::out
> ios::trunc

You can combine two or more of these values by ORing them together.

Including **ios::app** causes all output to that file to be appended to the end. This value can be used only with files capable of output. Including **ios::ate** causes a seek to the end of the file to occur when the file is opened. Although **ios::ate** causes a seek to the end of file, I/O operations can still occur anywhere within the file.

The **ios::binary** value causes the file to be opened for binary I/O operations. By default, files are opened in text mode.

The **ios::in** value specifies that the file is capable of input. The **ios::out** value specifies that the file is capable of output. However, creating an **ifstream** stream implies input, creating an **ofstream** stream implies output, and opening a file using **fstream** implies both input and output.

The **ios::trunc** value causes the contents of a preexisting file by the same name to be destroyed and the file is truncated to zero length.

15

In all cases, if **open( )** fails, the stream will be **false**. Therefore, before using a file, you should test to make sure that the open operation succeeded.

Related functions are **close( )**, **fstream( )**, **ifstream( )**, and **ofstream( )**.

peek

```
#include <iostream>
int peek();
```

The **peek( )** function is a member of **istream**.

The **peek( )** function returns the next character in the stream or **EOF** if the end of the file is encountered. It does not, under any circumstances, remove the character from the stream.

A related function is **get( )**.

precision

```
#include <iostream>
streamsize precision() const;
streamsize precision(streamsize p);
```

The **precision( )** function is a member of **ios** (inherited from **ios_base**).

By default, six digits of precision are displayed when floating-point values are output. However, using the second form of **precision( )**, you can set this number to the value specified in *p*. The original value is returned.

The first version of **precision( )** returns the current value.

Related functions are **width( )** and **fill( )**.

➤ Programming Tip

There are two flavors of manipulators: those without parameters and those with parameters. While the creation of parameterized manipulators is beyond the scope of this book, it is quite easy to create your own parameterless manipulators.

All parameterless output manipulators have this skeleton:

```
ostream &manip-name(ostream &stream)
{
  // your code here
  return stream;
}
```

Here, *manip-name* is the name of the manipulator. Notice that a reference to a stream of type **ostream** is returned. This is necessary if a manipulator is to be used as part of a larger I/O expression. It is important to understand that even though the manipulator has as its single argument a reference to the stream upon which it is operating, no argument is used when the manipulator is inserted in an output operation.

All parameterless input manipulators have this skeleton:

```
istream &manip-name(istream &stream)
{
  // your code here
  return stream;
}
```

An input manipulator receives a reference to the stream for which it was invoked. This stream must be returned by the manipulator.

Here is an example of a simple output manipulator called
setup( ). It turns on left-justification, sets the field width
to 10, and specifies the dollar sign as the fill character.

```
#include <iostream>
#include <iomanip>
using namespace std;

ostream &setup(ostream &stream)
{
  stream.setf(ios::left);
  stream << setw(10) << setfill('$');
  return stream;
}

int main()
{
  cout << 10 << " " << setup << 10;

  return 0;
}
```

Remember: Your manipulator must return *stream*. If it
doesn't, the manipulator cannot be used in a series of input
or output operations.

put

```
#include <iostream>
ostream &put(char ch);
```

The **put( )** function is a member of **ostream**.

The **put( )** function writes *ch* to the associated output stream. It
returns a reference to the stream.

Related functions are **write( )** and **get( )**.

putback

```
#include <iostream>
istream &putback(char ch);
```

The **putback( )** function is a member of **istream**.

The **putback( )** function returns *ch* to the associated input stream.

A related function is **peek( )**.

rdstate

```
#include <iostream>
iostate rdstate() const;
```

The **rdstate( )** function is a member of **ios**.

The **rdstate( )** function returns the status of the associated stream. The C++ I/O system maintains status information about the outcome of each I/O operation relative to each active stream. The current state of a stream is held in an object of type **iostate**, in which the following flags are defined:

Name	Meaning
goodbit	No errors occurred
eofbit	End of file is encountered
failbit	A nonfatal I/O error has occurred
badbit	A fatal I/O error has occurred

These flags are enumerated inside **ios** (via **ios_base**).

rdstate( ) returns **goodbit** when no error has occurred; otherwise, an error bit has been set.

Related functions are **eof( )**, **good( )**, **bad( )**, **clear( )**, **setstate( )**, and **fail( )**.

15

read

```
#include <iostream>
istream &read(char *buf, streamsize num);
```

The **read( )** function is a member of **istream**.

The **read( )** function reads *num* bytes from the associated input stream and puts them in the buffer pointed to by *buf*. If the end of the file is reached before *num* characters have been read, **read( )** simply stops, sets **failbit**, and the buffer contains as many characters as were available. (See **gcount( )**.) **read( )** returns a reference to the stream.

Related functions are **gcount( )**, **readsome( )**, **get( )**, **getline( )**, and **write( )**.

readsome

```
#include <iostream>
streamsize readsome(char *buf, streamsize num);
```

The **readsome( )** function is a member of **istream**.

The **readsome( )** function reads *num* bytes from the associated input stream and puts them in the buffer pointed to by *buf*. If the stream contains less than *num* characters, that number of characters are read. **readsome( )** returns the number of characters read. The difference between **read( )** and **readsome( )** is that **readsome( )** does not set the **failbit** if there are less than *num* characters available.

Related functions are **gcount( )**, **read( )**, and **write( )**.

seekg and seekp

```
#include <iostream>
istream &seekg(off_type offset, ios::seekdir origin)
istream &seekg(pos_type position);
```

```
ostream &seekp(off_type offset, ios::seekdir origin);
ostream &seekp(pos_type position);
```

The **seekg( )** function is a member of **istream**, and the **seekp( )** function is a member of **ostream**.

In C++'s I/O system, you perform random access using the **seekg( )** and **seekp( )** functions. To this end, the I/O system manages two pointers associated with a file. One is the *get pointer*, which specifies where in the file the next input operation will occur. The other is the *put pointer*, which specifies where in the file the next output operation will occur. Each time an input or an output operation takes place, the appropriate pointer is automatically sequentially advanced. However, using the **seekg( )** and **seekp( )** functions, it is possible to access the file in a nonsequential fashion.

The two-parameter version of **seekg( )** moves the get pointer *offset* number of bytes from the location specified by *origin*. The two-parameter version of **seekp( )** moves the put pointer *offset* number of bytes from the location specified by *origin*. The *offset* parameter is of type **off_type**, which is capable of containing the largest valid value that *offset* can have.

The *origin* parameter is of type **seekdir** and is an enumeration that has these values:

ios::beg	Seek from beginning
ios::cur	Seek from current position
ios::end	Seek from end

The single-parameter versions of **seekg( )** and **seekp( )** move the file pointers to the location specified by *position*. This value must have been previously obtained using a call to either **tellg( )** or **tellp( )**, respectively. **pos_type** is a type that is capable of containing the largest valid value that *position* can have. These functions return a reference to the associated stream.

Related functions are **tellg( )** and **tellp( )**.

setf

```
#include <iostream>
fmtflags setf(fmtflags flags);
fmtflags setf(fmtflags flags1, fmtflags flags2);
```

15

The **setf( )** function is a member of **ios** (inherited from **ios_base**).

The **setf( )** function sets the format flags associated with a stream. See the discussion of format flags earlier in this chapter.

The first version of **setf( )** turns on the format flags specified by *flags*. (All other flags are unaffected.) For example, to turn on the **showpos** flag for **cout**, you can use this statement:

```
cout.setf(ios::showpos);
```

When you want to set more than one flag, you can OR together the values of the flags you want set.

It is important to understand that a call to **setf( )** is done relative to a specific stream. There is no concept of calling **setf( )** by itself. Put differently, there is no concept in C++ of global format status. Each stream maintains its own format status information individually.

The second version of **setf( )** affects only the flags that are set in *flags2*. The corresponding flags are first reset and then set according to the flags specified by *flags1*. Even if *flags1* contains other set flags, only those specified by *flags2* will be affected.

Both versions of **setf( )** return the previous settings of the format flags associated with the stream.

Related functions are **unsetf( )** and **flags( )**.

setstate

```
#include <iostream>
void setstate(iostate flags) const;
```

The **setstate( )** function is a member of **ios**.

The **setstate( )** function sets the status of the associated stream as described by *flags*. See **rdstate( )** for further details.

Related functions are **clear( )** and **rdstate( )**.

str

```
#include <sstream>
string str() const;
void str(string &s)
```

The **str( )** function is a member of **stringstream**, **istringstream**, and **ostringstream**.

The first form of **str( )** function returns a **string** object that contains the current contents of the string-based stream.

The second form frees the string currently contained in the string stream and substitutes the string referred to by *s*.

Related functions are **get( )** and **put( )**.

stringstream, istringstream, and ostringstream

```
#include <sstream>
explicit stringstream(ios::openmode mode = ios::in | ios::out);
explicit stringstream(const string &str,
                      ios::openmode mode = ios::in | ios::out);

explicit istringstream(ios::openmode mode=ios::in);
explicit istringstream(const string str, ios::openmode
                      mode =ios::in);

explicit ostringstream(ios::openmode mode=ios::out);
explicit ostringstream(const string str, ios::openmode
                      mode =ios::out);
```

The **stringstream( )**, **istringstream( )**, and **ostringstream( )** functions are the constructors of the **stringstream**, **istringstream**, and **ostringstream** classes, respectively. These construct streams that are tied to strings.

The versions of **stringstream( )**, **istringstream( )**, and **ostringstream( )** that specify only the **openmode** parameter create empty streams. The versions that take a **string** parameter initialize the string stream.

A related function is **str( )**.

sync_with_stdio

```
#include <iostream>
bool sync_with_stdio(bool sync = true);
```

The **sync_with_stdio( )** function is a member of **ios** (inherited from **ios_base**).

Calling **sync_with_stdio( )** allows the C-like I/O system to be safely used concurrently with the C++ class-based I/O system. To turn off synchronization, pass **false** to **sync_with_stdio( )**. The previous setting is returned: **true** for synchronized; **false** for no synchronization. By default, the standard streams are synchronized. This function is reliable only if called prior to any other I/O operations.

tellg and tellp

```
#include <iostream>
pos_type tellg();
pos_type tellp():
```

The **tellg( )** function is a member of **istream**, and **tellp( )** is a member of **ostream**.

The C++ I/O system manages two pointers associated with a file. One is the *get pointer*, which specifies where in the file the next input operation will occur. The other is the *put pointer*, which specifies where in the file the next output operation will occur. Each time an input or an output operation takes place, the appropriate pointer is automatically sequentially advanced. You can determine the current position of the get pointer using **tellg( )** and of the put pointer using **tellp( )**.

pos_type is a type that is capable of holding the largest value that either function can return.

The values returned by **tellg( )** and **tellp( )** can be used as parameters to **seekg( )** and **seekp( )**, respectively.

Related functions are **seekg( )** and **seekp( )**.

unsetf

```
#include <iostream>
void unsetf(fmtflags flags);
```

The **unsetf( )** function is a member of **ios** (inherited from **ios_base**).

The **unsetf( )** function is used to clear one or more format flags.

The flags specified by *flags* are cleared. (All other flags are unaffected.)

Related functions are **setf( )** and **flags( )**.

width

```
#include <iostream>
streamsize width() const;
streamsize width(streamsize w);
```

The **width( )** function is a member of **ios** (inherited from **ios_base**).

To obtain the current field width, use the first form of **width( )**. It returns the current field width. To set the field width, use the second form. Here, *w* becomes the field width, and the previous field width is returned.

Related functions are **precision( )** and **fill( )**.

write

15

```
#include <iostream>
ostream &write(const char *buf, streamsize num);
```

The **write( )** function is a member of **ostream**.

The **write( )** function writes *num* bytes to the associated output stream from the buffer pointed to by *buf*. It returns a reference to the stream.

Related functions are **read( )** and **put( )**.

Chapter 16
The C++ Standard Template Library

A significant subset of the C++ class library is formed by the *standard template library*, or *STL*. The STL provides general-purpose templatized classes and functions that implement many popular and commonly used algorithms and data structures. For example, it includes support for vectors, lists, queues, and stacks. It also defines various routines that access them. Because the STL is constructed from template classes, the algorithms and data structures can be applied to nearly any type of data.

The STL is a large library, and not all of its features can be fully described in this book. Also, the version of the STL described here is the one specified by ANSI/ISO C++ Standard. Older compilers may present a slightly different version of the STL.

An Overview of the STL

At the core of the Standard Template Library are three foundational items: *containers*, *algorithms*, and *iterators*. These items work in conjunction with one another to provide off-the-shelf solutions to a variety of programming problems.

Containers

Containers are objects that hold other objects. There are several different types of containers. For example, the **vector** class defines a dynamic array, **deque** creates a double-ended queue, and **list** provides a linear list. These containers are called *sequence containers* because in STL terminology, a sequence is a linear list. In addition to the basic containers, the STL also defines *associative containers*, which allow efficient retrieval of values based on keys. For example, a **map** provides access to values with unique keys. Thus, a **map** stores a key/value pair and allows a value to be retrieved given its key.

Each container class defines a set of functions that can be applied to the container. For example, a list container includes functions that insert, delete, and merge elements. A stack includes functions that push and pop values.

Algorithms

Algorithms act on containers. They provide the means by which you will manipulate the contents of containers. Their capabilities include initialization, sorting, searching, and transforming the contents of containers. Many algorithms operate on a *range* of elements within a container.

Iterators

Iterators are objects that are, more or less, pointers. They give you the ability to cycle through the contents of a container in much the same way that you would use a pointer to cycle through an array. There are five types of iterators:

Iterator	Access Allowed
Random Access	Store and retrieve values. Elements may be accessed randomly.
Bidirectional	Store and retrieve values. Forward and backward moving.
Forward	Store and retrieve values. Forward moving only.
Input	Retrieve, but not store, values. Forward moving only.
Output	Store, but not retrieve values. Forward moving only.

In general, an iterator that has greater access capabilities can be used in place of one that has lesser capabilities. For example, a forward iterator can be used in place of an input iterator.

Iterators are handled just like pointers. You can increment and decrement them. You can apply the * operator to them. Iterators are declared using the **iterator** type defined by the various containers.

The STL also supports *reverse iterators*. Reverse iterators are either bidirectional or random access iterators that move through a sequence in the reverse direction. Thus, if a reverse iterator points to the end of a sequence, incrementing that iterator will cause it to point one element before the end.

When referring to the various iterator types in template descriptions, this section will use the following terms:

Term	Represents
BiIter	Bidirectional iterator
ForIter	Forward iterator
InIter	Input iterator
OutIter	Output iterator
RandIter	Random access iterator

Other STL Elements

In addition to containers, algorithms, and iterators, the STL relies upon several other standard components for support. Chief among these are allocators, predicates, comparison functions, and function objects.

Each container has defined for it an *allocator*. Allocators manage memory allocation for a container. The default allocator is an object of class **allocator**, but you can define your own allocators if needed by specialized applications. For most uses, the default allocator is sufficient.

Several of the algorithms and containers use a special type of function called a *predicate*. There are two variations of predicates: unary and binary. A unary predicate takes one argument. A binary predicate has two arguments. These functions return true/false results, but the precise conditions that make them return true or false are defined by you. For the rest of this chapter, when a unary predicate function is required, it will be notated using the type **UnPred**. When a binary predicate is required, the type **BinPred** will be used. In a binary predicate, the arguments are always in the order of *first,second*. For both unary and binary predicates, the arguments will contain values of the type of objects being stored by the container.

Some algorithms and classes use a special type of binary predicate that compares two elements. Comparison functions return true if their first argument is less than their second. Comparison functions will be notated using the type **Comp**.

In addition to the headers required by the various STL classes, the C++ standard library includes the **<utility>** and **<functional>** headers that provide support for the STL. For example, in **<utility>** is defined the template class **pair**, which can hold a pair of values.

The templates in **<functional>** help you to construct objects that define **operator( )**. These are called *function objects*, and they can be used in place of function pointers in many places. There are several predefined function objects declared within **<functional>**. They are shown here:

plus	minus	multiplies	divides	modulus
negate	equal_to	not_equal_to	greater	greater_equal
less	less_equal	logical_and	logical_or	logical_not

Perhaps the most widely used function object is **less,** which determines when one object is less than another. Function objects can be used in place of actual function pointers in the STL algorithms described later. Using function objects rather than function pointers allows the STL to generate more efficient code.

Two other entities that populate the STL are *binders* and *negators*. A binder binds an argument to a function object. A negator returns the complement of a predicate.

One final term to know is *adaptor*. In STL terms, an adaptor transforms one thing into another. For example, the container **queue** (which creates a standard queue) is an adaptor for the **deque** container.

➤ Programming Tip

Containers, algorithms, and iterators work together. The best way to understand how is to see an example. The following program demonstrates the **vector** container. A **vector** is similar to an array. However, it has the advantage that it automatically handles its own storage requirements, growing if necessary. A **vector** provides methods so that you can determine its size and add or remove elements.

The following program illustrates the use of a **vector** class:

```cpp
// A short example that demonstrates vector.

#include <iostream>
#include <vector>
using namespace std;

int main()
{
  vector<int> v; // create zero-length vector
  int i;

  // display original size of v
  cout << "size = " << v.size() << endl;

  /* put values onto end of vector —
     vector will grow as needed. */
  for(i=0; i<10; i++) v.push_back(i);

  // display current size of v
  cout << "size now = " << v.size() << endl;

  // can access vector contents using subscripting
  for(i=0; i<10; i++) cout << v[i] << " ";
  cout << endl;

  // can access vector's first and last element
  cout << "front = " << v.front() << endl;
  cout << "back = " << v.back() << endl;

  // access via iterator
  vector<int>::iterator p = v.begin();
  while(p != v.end()) {
    cout << *p << " ";
    p++;
  }

  return 0;
}
```

The output from this program is

```
size = 0
size now = 10
0 1 2 3 4 5 6 7 8 9
front = 0
back = 9
0 1 2 3 4 5 6 7 8 9
```

In this program, the vector is initially created with zero length. The **push_back( )** member function puts values onto the end of the vector, expanding its size as needed. The **size( )** function displays the size of the vector. The vector can be indexed like a normal array. It can also be accessed using an iterator. The function **begin( )** returns an iterator to the start of the vector. The function **end( )** returns an iterator to the end of the vector.

One other point: notice how the iterator **p** was declared. The type **iterator** is defined by several of the container classes.

The Container Classes

The containers defined by the STL are shown here:

Container	Description	Required Header
bitset	A set of bits	<bitset>
deque	A double-ended queue	<deque>
list	A linear list	<list>
map	Stores key/value pairs in which each key is associated with only one value	<map>
multimap	Stores key/value pairs in which one key may be associated with two or more values	<map>
multiset	A set in which each element is not necessarily unique	<set>
priority_queue	A priority queue	<queue>
queue	A queue	<queue>
set	A set in which each element is unique	<set>
stack	A stack.	<stack>
vector	A dynamic array	<vector>

Each of the containers is summarized in the following sections. Since the containers are implemented using template classes, various placeholder data types are used. In the descriptions, the generic type **T** represents the type of data stored by a container.

16

Since the names of the placeholder types in a template class are arbitrary, the container classes declare **typedef**ed versions of these types. This makes the type names concrete. Here are the **typedef** names used by the container classes:

size_type	Some integral type roughly equivalent to **size_t**
reference	A reference to an element
const_reference	A **const** reference to an element
difference_type	Can represent the difference between two addresses
iterator	An iterator
const_iterator	A **const** iterator
reverse_iterator	A reverse iterator
const_reverse_iterator	A **const** reverse iterator
value_type	The type of a value stored in a container (same as the generic type T)
allocator_type	The type of the allocator
key_type	The type of a key
key_compare	The type of a function that compares two keys
mapped_type	The type of value stored in a map (same as the generic type T)
value_compare	The type of a function that compares two values
value_type	The type of the values being operated upon (same as the generic type T)
pointer	The type of a pointer
const_pointer	The type of a **const** pointer
container_type	The type of a container

bitset

The **bitset** class supports operations on a set of bits. Its template specification is

```
template <size_t N> class bitset;
```

Here, *N* specifies the length of the bitset, in bits. It has the following constructors:

bitset( );
bitset(unsigned long *bits*);
explicit bitset(const string &*s*, size_t *i* = 0, size_t *num* = npos);

The first form constructs an empty bitset. The second form constructs a bitset that has its bits set according to those specified in *bits*. The third form constructs a bitset using the string *s*, beginning at *i*. The string must contain only 1's and 0's. Only *num* or *s*.**size( )–i** values are used, whichever is less. The constant **npos** is a value that is sufficiently large to describe the maximum length of *s*.

The output operators << and >> are defined for **bitset**.

bitset contains the following member functions:

Member	Description
bool any( ) const;	Returns true if any bit in the invoking bitset is 1. It returns false otherwise.
size_type count( ) const;	Returns the number of 1 bits.
bitset<N> &flip( );	Reverses the state of all bits in the invoking bitset and returns ***this**.
bitset<N> &flip(size_t *i*);	Reverses the bit in position *i* in the invoking bitset and returns ***this**.
bool none( ) const;	Returns true if no bits are set in the invoking bitset.
bool operator !=(const bitset<N> &*op2*) const;	Returns true if the invoking bitset differs from the one specified by right-hand operator, *op2*.
bool operator ==(const bitset<N> &*op2*) const;	Returns true if the invoking bitset is the same as the one specified by right-hand operator, *op2*.
bitset<N> &operator &=(const bitset<N> &*op2*);	ANDs each bit in the invoking bitset with the corresponding bit in *op2* and leaves the result in the invoking bitset. It returns ***this**.
bitset<N> &operator ^=(const bitset<N> &*op2*);	XORs each bit in the invoking bitset with the corresponding bit in *op2* and leaves the result in the invoking bitset. It returns ***this**.
bitset<N> &operator |=(const bitset<N> &*op2*);	ORs each bit in the invoking bitset with the corresponding bit in *op2* and leaves the result in the invoking bitset. It returns ***this**.

Member	Description
bitset<N> &operator ~=( ) const;	Reverses the state of all bits in the invoking bitset and returns the result.
bitset<N> &operator <<=(size_t *num*);	Left-shifts each bit in the invoking bitset *num* positions and leaves the result in the invoking bitset. It returns ***this**.
bitset<N> &operator >>=(size_t *num*);	Right-shifts each bit in the invoking bitset *num* positions and leaves the result in the invoking bitset. It returns ***this**.
reference operator [ ](size_type *i*);	Returns a reference to bit *i* in the invoking bitset.
bitset<N> &reset( );	Clears all bits in the invoking bitset and returns ***this**.
bitset<N> &reset(size_t *i*);	Clears the bit in position *i* in the invoking bitset and returns ***this**.
bitset<N> &set( );	Sets all bits in the invoking bitset and returns ***this**.
bitset<N> &set(size_t *i*, int *val* = 1);	Sets the bit in position *i* to the value specified by *val* in the invoking bitset and returns ***this**. Any nonzero value for *val* is assumed to be 1.
size_t size( ) const;	Returns the number of bits that the bitset can hold.
bool test(size_t *i*) const;	Returns the state of the bit in position *i*.
string to_string( ) const;	Returns a string that contains a representation of the bit pattern in the invoking bitset.
unsigned long to_ulong( ) const;	Converts the invoking bitset into an unsigned long integer.

16

deque

The **deque** class supports a double-ended queue. Its template specification is

```
template <class T, class Allocator = allocator<T> > class deque
```

Here, **T** is the type of data stored in the **deque**. It has the following constructors:

```
explicit deque(const Allocator &a = Allocator( ) );
explicit deque(size_type num, const T &val = T ( ),
      const Allocator &a = Allocator( ));
deque(const deque<T, Allocator> &ob);
template <class InIter> deque(InIter start, InIter end,
      const Allocator &a = Allocator( ));
```

The first form constructs an empty deque. The second form constructs a deque that has *num* elements with the value *val*. The third form constructs a deque that contains the same elements as *ob*. The fourth form constructs a queue that contains the elements in the range specified by *start* and *end*.

The following comparison operators are defined for **deque**:

```
==, <, <=, !=, >, >=
```

deque contains the following member functions:

Member	Description
template <class InIter> void assign(InIter start, InIter end);	Assigns the deque the sequence defined by *start* and *end*.
void assign(size_type num, const T &val);	Assigns the deque *num* elements of value *val*.
reference at(size_type i); const_reference at(size_type i) const;	Returns a reference to the element specified by *i*.
reference back( ); const_reference back( ) const;	Returns a reference to the last element in the deque.
iterator begin( ); const_iterator begin( ) const;	Returns an iterator to the first element in the deque.
void clear( );	Removes all elements from the deque.
bool empty( ) const;	Returns true if the invoking deque is empty and false otherwise.
const_iterator end( ) const; iterator end( );	Returns an iterator to the end of the deque.
iterator erase(iterator i);	Removes the element pointed to by *i*. Returns an iterator to the element after the one removed.

Member	Description
iterator erase(iterator *start*, iterator *end*);	Removes the elements in the range *start* to *end*. Returns an iterator to the element after the last element removed.
reference front( ); const_reference front( ) const;	Returns a reference to the first element in the deque.
allocator_type get_allocator( ) const;	Returns deque's allocator.
iterator insert(iterator *i*, const T &*val*);	Inserts *val* immediately before the element specified by *i*. An iterator to the element is returned.
void insert(iterator *i*, size_type *num*, const T &*val*)	Inserts *num* copies of *val* immediately before the element specified by *i*.

template <class InIter>
  void insert(iterator *i*,
      InIter *start*, InIter *end*);
	Inserts the sequence defined by *start* and *end* immediately before the element specified by *i*.

size_type max_size( ) const;	Returns the maximum number of elements that the deque can hold.
reference operator[ ](size_type *i*); const_reference operator[ ](size_type *i*) const;	Returns a reference to the *i*th element.
void pop_back( );	Removes the last element in the deque.
void pop_front( );	Removes the first element in the deque.
void push_back(const T &*val*);	Adds an element with the value specified by *val* to the end of the deque.
void push_front(const T &*val*);	Adds an element with the value specified by *val* to the front of the deque.
reverse_iterator rbegin( ); const_reverse_iterator rbegin( ) const;	Returns a reverse iterator to the end of the deque.
reverse_iterator rend( ); const_reverse_iterator rend( ) const;	Returns a reverse iterator to the start of the deque.
void resize(size_type *num*, T *val* = T ( ));	Changes the size of the deque to that specified by *num*. If the deque must be lengthened, those elements with the value specified by *val* are added to the end.
size_type size( ) const;	Returns the number of elements currently in the deque.
void swap(deque<T, Allocator> &*ob*)	Exchanges the elements stored in the invoking deque with those in *ob*.

16

> ## list

The **list** class supports a list. Its template specification is

  template <class T, class Allocator = allocator<T> > class list

Here, **T** is the type of data stored in the list. It has the following constructors:

  explicit list(const Allocator &a = Allocator( ));
  explicit list(size_type *num*, const T &*val* = T ( ),
          const Allocator &a = Allocator( ));
  list(const list<T, Allocator> &*ob*);
  template <class InIter>list(InIter *start*, InIter *end*,
          const Allocator &a = Allocator( ));

The first form constructs an empty list. The second form constructs a list that has *num* elements with the value *val*. The third form constructs a list that contains the same elements as *ob*. The fourth form constructs a list that contains the elements in the range specified by *start* and *end*.

The following comparison operators are defined for **list**:

  ==, <, <=, !=, >, >=

list contains the following member functions:

Member	Description
template <class InIter> void assign(InIter *start*, InIter *end*);	Assigns the list the sequence defined by *start* and *end*.
void assign(size_type *num*, const T &*val*);	Assigns the list *num* elements of value *val*.
reference back( ); const_reference back( ) const;	Returns a reference to the last element in the list.
iterator begin( ); const_iterator begin( ) const;	Returns an iterator to the first element in the list.
void clear( );	Removes all elements from the list.
bool empty( ) const;	Returns true if the invoking list is empty and false otherwise.

Member	Description
iterator end( ); const_iterator end( ) const;	Returns an iterator to the end of the list.
iterator erase(iterator *i*);	Removes the element pointed to by *i*. Returns an iterator to the element after the one removed.
iterator erase(iterator *start*, iterator *end*);	Removes the elements in the range *start* to *end*. Returns an iterator to the element after the last element removed.
reference front( ); const_reference front( ) const;	Returns a reference to the first element in the list.
allocator_type get_allocator( ) const;	Returns list's allocator.
iterator insert(iterator *i*, const T &*val* = T( ));	Inserts *val* immediately before the element specified by *i*. An iterator to the element is returned.
void insert(iterator *i*, size_type *num*, const T & *val*)	Inserts *num* copies of *val* immediately before the element specified by *i*.
template <class InIter> void insert(iterator *i*, InIter *start*, InIter *end*);	Inserts the sequence defined by *start* and *end* immediately before the element specified by *i*.
size_type max_size( ) const;	Returns the maximum number of elements that the list can hold.
void merge(list<T, Allocator> &*ob*); template <class Comp> void merge(<list<T, Allocator> &*ob*, Comp *cmpfn*);	Merges the ordered list contained in *ob* with the ordered invoking list. The result is ordered. After the merge, the list contained in *ob* is empty. In the second form, a comparison function can be specified that determines when one element is less than another.
void pop_back( );	Removes the last element in the list.
void pop_front( );	Removes the first element in the list.
void push_back(const T &*val*);	Adds an element with the value specified by *val* to the end of the list.
void push_front(const T &*val*);	Adds an element with the value specified by *val* to the front of the list.
reverse_iterator rbegin( ); const_reverse_iterator rbegin( ) const;	Returns a reverse iterator to the end of the list.
void remove(const T &*val*);	Removes elements with the value *val* from the list.
template <class UnPred> void Remove_if(UnPred *pr*);	Removes elements for which the unary predicate *pr* is true.

Member	Description
reverse_iterator rend( ); const_reverse_iterator rend( ) const;	Returns a reverse iterator to the start of the list.
void resize(size_type *num*, T *val* = T ( ));	Changes the size of the list to that specified by *num*. If the list must be lengthened, those elements with the value specified by *val* are added to the end.
void reverse( );	Reverses the invoking list.
size_type size( ) const;	Returns the number of elements currently in the list.

void sort( );
template <class Comp>
  void sort(Comp *cmpfn*);
	Sorts the list. The second form sorts the list using the comparison function *cmpfn* to determine when one element is less than another.

void splice(iterator *i*, list<T, Allocator> &*ob*);	The contents of *ob* are inserted into the invoking list at the location pointed to by *i*. After the operation, *ob* is empty.
void splice(iterator *i*, list<T, Allocator> &*ob*, iterator *el*);	The element pointed to by *el* is removed from the list *ob* and stored in the invoking list at the location pointed to by *i*.
void splice(iterator *i*, list<T, Allocator> &ob, iterator *start*, iterator *end*);	The range defined by *start* and *end* is removed from *ob* and stored in the invoking list beginning at the location pointed to by *i*.
void swap(list<T, Allocator> &*ob*)	Exchanges the elements stored in the invoking list with those in *ob*.

void unique( );
template <class BinPred>
  void unique(BinPred *pr*);
	Removes duplicate elements from the invoking list. The second form uses *pr* to determine uniqueness.

map

The **map** class supports an associative container in which
unique keys are mapped with values. Its template specification
is shown here:

```
template <class Key, class T, class Comp = less<Key>,
        class Allocator = allocator<pair<const Key, T> > >
        class map
```

map **307**

16

Here, **Key** is the data type of the keys, **T** is the data type of the values being stored (mapped), and **Comp** is a function that compares two keys. It has the following constructors:

```
explicit map(const Comp &cmpfn = Comp( ),
        const Allocator &a = Allocator( ) );
map(const map<Key, T, Comp, Allocator> &ob);
template <class InIter> map(InIter start, InIter end,
        const Comp &cmpfn = Comp( ),
        const Allocator &a = Allocator( ));
```

The first form constructs an empty map. The second form constructs a map that contains the same elements as *ob*. The third form constructs a map that contains the elements in the range specified by *start* and *end*. The function specified by *cmpfn*, if present, determines the ordering of the map.

The following comparison operators are defined for **map**:

```
==, <, <=, !=, >, >=
```

The member functions contained by **map** are shown here. In the descriptions, **key_type** is the type of the key, and **value_type** represents **pair<Key, T>**.

Member	Description
iterator begin( ); const_iterator begin( ) const;	Returns an iterator to the first element in the map.
void clear( );	Removes all elements from the map.
size_type count(const key_type &k) const;	Returns the number of times *k* occurs in the map (1 or 0).
bool empty( ) const;	Returns true if the invoking map is empty and false otherwise.
iterator end( ); const_iterator end( ) const;	Returns an iterator to the end of the map.

pair<iterator, iterator>
  equal_range(const key_type &k);
pair<const_iterator, const_iterator>
  equal_range(const key_type &k) const;
	Returns a pair of iterators that point to the first and last elements in the map that contain the specified key.

void erase(iterator *i*);	Removes the element pointed to by *i*.
void erase(iterator *start*, iterator *end*);	Removes the elements in the range *start* to *end*.

Member	Description
size_type erase(const key_type &k)	Removes from the map elements that have keys with the value k.
iterator find(const key_type &k); const_iterator find(const key_type &k) const;	Returns an iterator to the specified key. If the key is not found, then an iterator to the end of the map is returned.
allocator_type get_allocator( ) const;	Returns map's allocator.
iterator insert(iterator i, const value_type &val);	Inserts val at or after the element specified by i. An iterator to the element is returned.
template <class InIter> void insert(InIter start, InIter end)	Inserts a range of elements.
pair<iterator, bool> insert(const value_type &val);	Inserts val into the invoking map. An iterator to the element is returned. The element is inserted only if it does not already exist. If the element was inserted, **pair<iterator, true>** is returned. Otherwise, **pair<iterator, false>** is returned.
key_compare key_comp( ) const;	Returns the function object that compares keys.

iterator lower_bound(const key_type &k);
const_iterator
   lower_bound(const key_type &k) const;
	Returns an iterator to the first element in the map with the key equal to or greater than k.

size_type max_size( ) const;	Returns the maximum number of elements that the map can hold.
reference operator[ ](const key_type &i)	Returns a reference to the element specified by i. If this element does not exist, it is inserted.
reverse_iterator rbegin( ); const_reverse_iterator rbegin( ) const;	Returns a reverse iterator to the end of the map.
reverse_iterator rend( ); const_reverse_iterator rend( ) const;	Returns a reverse iterator to the start of the map.
size_type size( ) const;	Returns the number of elements currently in the map.
void swap(map<Key, T, Comp, Allocator> &ob)	Exchanges the elements stored in the invoking map with those in ob.

iterator upper_bound(const key_type &k);
const_iterator
   upper_bound(const key_type &k) const;
	Returns an iterator to the first element in the map with the key greater than k.

value_compare value_comp( ) const;	Returns the function object that compares values.

multimap

The **multimap** class supports an associative container in which possibly nonunique keys are mapped with values. Its template specification is shown here:

> template <class Key, class T, class Comp = less<Key>,
>   class Allocator = allocator<pair<const Key, T> > >
>   class multimap

Here, **Key** is the data of the keys, **T** is the data type of the values being stored (mapped), and **Comp** is a function that compares two keys. It has the following constructors:

> explicit multimap(const Comp &*cmpfn* = Comp( ),
>   const Allocator &*a* = Allocator( ));
> multimap(const multimap<Key, T, Comp, Allocator> &*ob*);
> template <class InIter> multimap(InIter *start*, InIter *end*,
>   const Comp &*cmpfn* = Comp( ),
>   const Allocator &*a* = Allocator( ));

The first form constructs an empty multimap. The second form constructs a multimap that contains the same elements as *ob*. The third form constructs a multimap that contains the elements in the range specified by *start* and *end*. The function specified by *cmpfn*, if present, determines the ordering of the multimap.

The following comparison operators are defined by **multimap**:

> ==, <, <=, !=, >, >=

The member functions contained by **multimap** are shown here. In the descriptions, **key_type** is the type of the key, **T** is the value, and **value_type** represents **pair<Key, T>**.

Member	Description
iterator begin( ); const_iterator begin( ) const;	Returns an iterator to the first element in the multimap.
void clear( );	Removes all elements from the multimap.

Member	Description
size_type count(const key_type &k) const;	Returns the number of times k occurs in the multimap.
bool empty( ) const;	Returns true if the invoking multimap is empty and false otherwise.
iterator end( ); const_iterator end( ) const;	Returns an iterator to the end of the list.

pair<iterator, iterator>
  equal_range(const key_type &k);
pair<const_iterator, const_iterator>
  equal_range(const key_type &k) const;
	Returns a pair of iterators that point to the first and last elements in the multimap that contain the specified key.

void erase(iterator i);	Removes the element pointed to by i.
void erase(iterator start, iterator end);	Removes the elements in the range start to end.
size_type erase(const key_type &k)	Removes from the multimap elements that have keys with the value k.
iterator find(const key_type &k); const_iterator find(const key_type &k) const;	Returns an iterator to the specified key. If the key is not found, then an iterator to the end of the multimap is returned.
allocator_type get_allocator( ) const;	Returns multimap's allocator.
iterator insert(iterator i, const value_type &val);	Inserts val at or after the element specified by i. An iterator to the element is returned.
template <class InIter> void insert(InIter start, InIter end)	Inserts a range of elements.
iterator insert(const value_type &val);	Inserts val into the invoking multimap.
key_compare key_comp( ) const;	Returns the function object that compares keys.

iterator lower_bound(const key_type &k);
const_iterator
  lower_bound(const key_type &k) const;
	Returns an iterator to the first element in the multimap with the key equal to or greater than k.

size_type max_size( ) const;	Returns the maximum number of elements that the multimap can hold.
reverse_iterator rbegin( ); const_reverse_iterator rbegin( ) const;	Returns a reverse iterator to the end of the multimap.
reverse_iterator rend( ); const_reverse_iterator rend( ) const;	Returns a reverse iterator to the start of the multimap.
size_type size( ) const;	Returns the number of elements currently in the multimap.

Member	Description
void swap(multimap<Key, T, Comp, Allocator> &ob)	Exchanges the elements stored in the invoking multimap with those in ob.
iterator upper_bound(const key_type &k); const_iterator upper_bound(const key_type &k) const;	Returns an iterator to the first element in the multimap with the key greater than k.
value_compare value_comp( ) const;	Returns the function object that compares values.

16

multiset

The **multiset** class supports a set in which possibly nonunique keys are mapped with values. Its template specification is shown here:

```
template <class Key, class Comp = less<Key>,
        class Allocator = allocator<Key> > class multiset
```

Here, **Key** is the data of the keys and **Comp** is a function that compares two keys. It has the following constructors:

```
explicit multiset(const Comp &cmpfn = Comp( ),
        const Allocator &a = Allocator( ) );
multiset(const multiset<Key, Comp, Allocator> &ob);
template <class InIter> multiset(InIter start, InIter end,
        const Comp &cmpfn = Comp( ),
        const Allocator &a = Allocator( ));
```

The first form constructs an empty multiset. The second form constructs a multiset that contains the same elements as ob. The third form constructs a multiset that contains the elements in the range specified by start and end. The function specified by cmpfn, if present, determines the ordering of the set.

The following comparison operators are defined for **multiset**:

```
==, <, <=, !=, >, >=
```

The member functions contained by **multiset** are shown here. In the descriptions, both **key_type** and **value_type** are **typedefs** for **Key**.

Member	Description
iterator begin( ); const_iterator begin( ) const;	Returns an iterator to the first element in the multiset.
void clear( );	Removes all elements from the multiset.
size_type count(const key_type &k) const;	Returns the number of times k occurs in the multiset.
bool empty( ) const;	Returns true if the invoking multiset is empty and false otherwise.
iterator end( ); const_iterator end( ) const;	Returns an iterator to the end of the list.
pair<iterator, iterator> equal_range(const key_type &k) const;	Returns a pair of iterators that point to the first and last elements in the multiset that contain the specified key.
void erase(iterator i);	Removes the element pointed to by i.
void erase(iterator start, iterator end);	Removes the elements in the range start to end.
size_type erase(const key_type &k)	Removes from the multiset elements that have keys with the value k.
iterator find(const key_type &k) const;	Returns an iterator to the specified key. If the key is not found, then an iterator to the end of the multiset is returned.
allocator_type get_allocator( ) const;	Returns multiset's allocator.
iterator insert(iterator i, const value_type &val);	Inserts val at or after the element specified by i. An iterator to the element is returned.
template <class InIter> void insert(InIter start, InIter end)	Inserts a range of elements.
iterator insert(const value_type &val);	Inserts val into the invoking multiset. An iterator to the element is returned.
key_compare key_comp( ) const;	Returns the function object that compares keys.
iterator lower_bound(const key_type &k) const;	Returns an iterator to the first element in the multiset with the key equal to or greater than k.
size_type max_size( ) const;	Returns the maximum number of elements that the multiset can hold.
reverse_iterator rbegin( ); const_reverse_iterator rbegin( ) const;	Returns a reverse iterator to the end of the multiset.

Member	Description
reverse_iterator rend( ); const_reverse_iterator rend( ) const;	Returns a reverse iterator to the start of the multiset.
size_type size( ) const;	Returns the number of elements currently in the multiset.
void swap(multiset<Key, Comp, Allocator> &*ob*)	Exchanges the elements stored in the invoking multiset with those in *ob*.
iterator upper_bound(const key_type &*k*) const;	Returns an iterator to the first element in the multiset with the key greater than *k*.
value_compare value_comp( ) const;	Returns the function object that compares values.

queue

The **queue** class supports a single-ended queue. Its template specification is shown here:

> template <class T, class Container = deque<T> > class queue

Here, **T** is the type of data being stored and **Container** is the type of container used to hold the queue. It has the following constructor:

> explicit queue(const Container &*cnt* = Container( ));

The **queue( )** constructor creates an empty queue. By default, it uses a **deque** as a container, but a **queue** can only be accessed in a first-in, first-out manner. You can also use a **list** as a container for a queue. The container is held in a protected object called **c** of type **Container**.

The following comparison operators are defined for **queue**:

> ==, <, <=, !=, >, >=

queue contains the following member functions:

Member	Description
value_type &back( ); const value_type &back( ) const;	Returns a reference to the last element in the queue
bool empty( ) const;	Returns true if the invoking queue is empty and false otherwise
value_type &front( ); const value_type &front( ) const;	Returns a reference to the first element in the queue
void pop( );	Removes the first element in the queue
void push(const T &val);	Adds an element with the value specified by val to the end of the queue
size_type size( ) const;	Returns the number of elements currently in the queue

priority_queue

The **priority_queue** class supports a single-ended priority queue. Its template specification is shown here:

```
template <class T, class Container = vector<T>,
          class Comp = less<Container::value_type> >
    class priority_queue
```

Here, **T** is the type of data being stored. **Container** is the type of container used to hold the queue, and **Comp** specifies the comparison function that determines when one member for the priority queue is lower in priority than another. It has the following constructors:

```
explicit priority_queue(const Comp &cmpfn = Comp( ),
          Container &cnt = Container( ));
template <class InIter> priority_queue(InIter start, InIter end,
          const Comp &cmpfn = Comp( ),
          Container &cnt = Container( ));
```

The first **priority_queue( )** constructor creates an empty priority queue. The second creates a priority queue that contains the elements specified by the range *start* and *end*. By default, it uses a **vector** as a container. You can also use a **deque** as a container for a priority queue. The container is held in a protected object called **c** of type **Container**.

priority_queue contains the following member functions:

Member	Description
bool empty( ) const;	Returns true if the invoking priority queue is empty and false otherwise.
void pop( );	Removes the first element in the priority queue.
void push(const T &*val*);	Adds an element to the priority queue.
size_type size( ) const;	Returns the number of elements currently in the priority queue.
const value_type &top( ) const;	Returns a reference to the element with the highest priority. The element is not removed.

set

The **set** class supports a set in which possibly unique keys are mapped with values. Its template specification is shown here:

template <class Key, class Comp = less<Key>,
        class Allocator = allocator<Key> > class set

Here, **Key** is the data of the keys and **Comp** is a function that compares two keys. It has the following constructors:

explicit set(const Comp &*cmpfn* = Comp( ),
        const Allocator &*a* = Allocator( ));
set(const set<Key, Comp, Allocator> &*ob*);
template <class InIter> set(InIter *start*, InIter *end*,
        const Comp &*cmpfn* = Comp( ),
        const Allocator &*a* = Allocator( ));

The first form constructs an empty set. The second form constructs a set that contains the same elements as *ob*. The third form constructs a set that contains the elements in the range specified by *start* and *end*. The function specified by *cmpfn*, if present, determines the ordering of the set.

The following comparison operators are defined for **set**:

==, <, <=, !=, >, >=

The member functions contained by **set** are shown here:

Member	Description
iterator begin( ); const_iterator begin( ) const;	Returns an iterator to the first element in the set.
void clear( );	Removes all elements from the set.
size_type count(const key_type &*k*) const;	Returns the number of times *k* occurs in the set.
bool empty( ) const;	Returns true if the invoking set is empty and false otherwise.
const_iterator end( ) const; iterator end( );	Returns an iterator to the end of the set.
pair<iterator, iterator> equal_range(const key_type &*k*) const;	Returns a pair of iterators that point to the first and last elements in the set that contain the specified key.
void erase(iterator *i*);	Removes the element pointed to by *i*.
void erase(iterator *start*, iterator *end*);	Removes the elements in the range *start* to *end*.
size_type erase(const key_type &*k*)	Removes from the set elements that have keys with the value *k*. The number of elements removed is returned.
iterator find(const key_type &*k*) const;	Returns an iterator to the specified key. If the key is not found, then an iterator to the end of the set is returned.
allocator_type get_allocator( ) const;	Returns set's allocator.
iterator insert(iterator *i*, const value_type &*val*);	Inserts *val* at or after the element specified by *i*. Duplicate elements are not inserted. An iterator to the element is returned.

Member	Description
template <class InIter> void insert(InIter *start*, InIter *end*);	Inserts a range of elements. Duplicate elements are not inserted.
pair<iterator, bool> insert(const value_type &*val*);	Inserts *val* into the invoking set. An iterator to the element is returned. The element is inserted only if it does not already exist. If the element was inserted, **pair<iterator, true>** is returned. Otherwise, **pair<iterator, false>** is returned.
iterator lower_bound(const key_type &*k*) const;	Returns an iterator to the first element in the set with the key equal to or greater than *k*.
key_compare key_comp( ) const;	Returns the function object that compares keys.
size_type max_size( ) const;	Returns the maximum number of elements that the set can hold.
reverse_iterator rbegin( ); const_reverse_iterator rbegin( ) const;	Returns a reverse iterator to the end of the set.
reverse_iterator rend( ); const_reverse_iterator rend( ) const;	Returns a reverse iterator to the start of the set.
size_type size( ) const;	Returns the number of elements currently in the set.
void swap(set<Key, Comp,Allocator> &*ob*);	Exchanges the elements stored in the invoking set with those in *ob*.
iterator upper_bound(const key_type &*k*) const;	Returns an iterator to the first element in the set with the key greater than *k*.
value_compare value_comp( ) const;	Returns the function object that compares values.

stack

The **stack** class supports a stack. Its template specification is shown here:

```
template <class T, class Container = deque<T> > class stack
```

Here, **T** is the type of data being stored and **Container** is the type of container used to hold the queue. It has the following constructor:

explicit stack(const Container &*cnt* = Container( ));

The **stack( )** constructor creates an empty stack. By default, it uses a **deque** as a container, but a **stack** can be accessed only in a last-in, first-out manner. You may also use a **vector** or **list** as a container for a stack. The container is held in a protected member called **c** of type **Container**.

The following comparison operators are defined for **stack**:

==, <, <=, !=, >, >=

stack contains the following member functions:

Member	Description
bool empty( ) const;	Returns true if the invoking stack is empty and false otherwise.
void pop( );	Removes the top of the stack, which is technically the last element in the container.
void push(const T &*val*);	Pushes an element onto the end of the stack. The last element in the container represents the top of the stack.
size_type size( ) const;	Returns the number of elements currently in the stack.
value_type &top( ); cont value_type &top( ) const;	Returns a reference to the top of the stack, which is the last element in the container. The element is not removed.

vector

The **vector** class supports a dynamic array. Its template specification is shown here:

template <class T, class Allocator = allocator<T> > class vector

Here, **T** is the type of data being stored and **Allocator** specifies the allocator. It has the following constructors:

```
explicit vector(const Allocator &a = Allocator( ));
explicit vector(size_type num, const T &val = T ( ),
        const Allocator &a = Allocator( ));
vector(const vector<T, Allocator> &ob);
template <class InIter> vector(InIter start, InIter end,
        const Allocator &a = Allocator( ));
```

The first form constructs an empty vector. The second form constructs a vector that has *num* elements with the value *val*. The third form constructs a vector that contains the same elements as *ob*. The fourth form constructs a vector that contains the elements in the range specified by *start* and *end*.

The following comparison operators are defined for **vector**:

```
==, <, <=, !=, >, >=
```

vector contains the following member functions:

Member	Description
template <class InIter> void assign(InIter *start*, InIter *end*);	Assigns the vector the sequence defined by *start* and *end*.
void assign(size_type *num*, const T &*val*);	Assigns the vector *num* elements of value *val*.
reference at(size_type *i*); const_reference at(size_type *i*) const;	Returns a reference to an element specified by *i*.
reference back( ); const_reference back( ) const;	Returns a reference to the last element in the vector.
iterator begin( ); const_iterator begin( ) const;	Returns an iterator to the first element in the vector.
size_type capacity( ) const;	Returns the current capacity of the vector. This is the number of elements it can hold before it will need to allocate more memory.
void clear( );	Removes all elements from the vector.
bool empty( ) const;	Returns true if the invoking vector is empty and false otherwise.
iterator end( ); const_iterator end( ) const;	Returns an iterator to the end of the vector.

Member	Description
iterator erase(iterator *i*);	Removes the element pointed to by *i*. Returns an iterator to the element after the one removed.
iterator erase(iterator *start*, iterator *end*);	Removes the elements in the range *start* to *end*. Returns an iterator to the element after the last element removed.
reference front( ); const_reference front( ) const;	Returns a reference to the first element in the vector.
allocator_type get_allocator( ) const;	Returns vector's allocator.
iterator insert(iterator *i*, const T &*val*);	Inserts *val* immediately before the element specified by *i*. An iterator to the element is returned.
void insert(iterator *i*, size_type *num*, const T & *val*)	Inserts *num* copies of *val* immediately before the element specified by *i*.
template <class InIter> void insert(iterator *i*, InIter *start*, InIter *end*);	Inserts the sequence defined by *start* and *end* immediately before the element specified by *i*.
size_type max_size( ) const;	Returns the maximum number of elements that the vector can hold.
reference operator[ ](size_type *i*) const; const_reference operator[ ](size_type *i*) const;	Returns a reference to the element specified by *i*.
void pop_back( );	Removes the last element in the vector.
void push_back(const T &*val*);	Adds an element with the value specified by *val* to the end of the vector.
reverse_iterator rbegin( ); const_reverse_iterator rbegin( ) const;	Returns a reverse iterator to the end of the vector.
reverse_iterator rend( ); const_reverse_iterator rend( ) const;	Returns a reverse iterator to the start of the vector.
void reserve(size_type *num*);	Sets the capacity of the vector so that it is equal to at least *num*.
void resize(size_type *num*, T val = T ( ));	Changes the size of the vector to that specified by *num*. If the vector must be lengthened, then elements with the value specified by *val* are added to the end.
size_type size( ) const;	Returns the number of elements currently in the vector.
void swap(vector<T, Allocator> &*ob*)	Exchanges the elements stored in the invoking vector with those in *ob*.

The STL also contains a specialization of **vector** for Boolean values. It includes all of the functionality of **vector** and adds these two members:

void flip( );	Reverses all bits in the vector
static void swap(reference *i*, reference *j*);	Exchanges the bits specified by *i* and *j*

The STL Algorithms

The algorithms defined by the Standard Template Library are described here. These algorithms operate on containers through iterators. All of the algorithms are template functions. Here are descriptions of the generic type names used by the algorithms:

Generic Name	Represents
BiIter	Bidirectional iterator
ForIter	Forward iterator
InIter	Input iterator
OutIter	Output iterator
RandIter	Random access iterator
T	Some type of data
Size	Some type of integer
Func	Some type of function
Generator	A function that generates objects
BinPred	Binary predicate
UnPred	Unary predicate
Comp	Comparison function

adjacent_find

```
template <class ForIter>
    ForIter adjacent_find(ForIter start, ForIter end);
template <class ForIter, class BinPred>
    ForIter adjacent_find(ForIter start, ForIter end,
                          BinPred pfn);
```

The **adjacent_find( )** algorithm searches for adjacent matching elements within a sequence specified by *start* and *end* and returns an iterator to the first element. If no adjacent pair is found, *end* is returned. The first version looks for equivalent elements. The second version lets you specify your own method for determining matching elements.

binary_search

```
template <class ForIter, class T>
    bool binary_search(ForIter start, ForIter end, const T &val);
template <class ForIter, class T, class Comp>
    bool binary_search(ForIter start, ForIter end, const T &val,
                       Comp cmpfn);
```

The **binary_search( )** algorithm performs a binary search on an ordered sequence beginning at *start* and ending with *end* for the value specified by *val*. It returns true if the *val* is found and false otherwise. The first version compares the elements in the specified sequence for equality. The second version allows you to specify your own comparison function.

copy

```
template <class InIter, class OutIter>
    OutIter copy(InIter start, InIter end, OutIter result);
```

The **copy( )** algorithm copies a sequence beginning at *start* and ending with *end*, putting the result into the sequence pointed to by *result*. It returns a pointer to the end of the resulting sequence. The range to be copied must not overlap with *result*.

copy_backward

```
template <class BiIter1, class BiIter2>
    BiIter2 copy_backward(BiIter1 start, BiIter1 end, BiIter2 result);
```

The **copy_backward( )** algorithm is the same as **copy( )** except that it moves the elements from the end of the sequence first.

count

```
template <class InIter, class T>
    size_t count(InIter start, InIter end, const T &val);
```

The **count( )** algorithm returns the number of elements in the sequence beginning at *start* and ending at *end* that match *val*.

count_if

```
template <class InIter, class UnPred>
    size_t count(InIter start, InIter end, UnPred pfn);
```

The **count_if( )** algorithm returns the number of elements in the sequence beginning at *start* and ending at *end* for which the unary predicate *pfn* returns true.

equal

```
template <class InIter1, class InIter2>
    bool equal(InIter1 start1, InIter1 end1, InIter2 start2);
template <class InIter1, class InIter2, class BinPred>
    bool equal(InIter1 start1, InIter1 end1, InIter2 start2,
               BinPred pfn);
```

The **equal( )** algorithm determines if two ranges are the same. The range determined by *start1* and *end1* is tested against the sequence pointed to by *start2*. If the ranges are the same, true is returned. Otherwise, false is returned.

The second form allows you to specify a binary predicate that determines when two elements are equal.

equal_range

```
template <class ForIter, class T>
    pair<ForIter, ForIter> equal_range(ForIter start,
                                        ForIter end, const T &val);
template <class ForIter, class T, class Comp>
    pair<ForIter, ForIter> equal_range(ForIter start, ForIter end,
                                       const T &val, Comp cmpfn);
```

The **equal_range( )** algorithm returns a range in which an element can be inserted into a sequence without disrupting the ordering of the sequence. The region in which to search for such a range is specified by *start* and *end*. The value is passed in *val*. To specify your own search criteria, specify the comparison function *cmpfn*.

The template class **pair** is a utility class that can hold a pair of objects in its **first** and **second** members.

fill and fill_n

```
template <class ForIter, class T>
    void fill(ForIter start, ForIter end, const T &val);
template <class ForIter, class Size, class T>
    void fill_n(ForIter start, Size num, const T &val);
```

The **fill( )** and **fill_n( )** algorithms fill a range with the value specified by *val*. For **fill( )**, the range is specified by *start* and *end*. For **fill_n( )**, the range begins at *start* and runs for *num* elements.

find

```
template <class InIter, class T>
    InIter find(InIter start, InIter end, const T &val);
```

The **find( )** algorithm searches the range *start* to *end* for the value specified by *val*. It returns an iterator to the first occurrence of the element or to *end* if the value is not in the sequence.

find_end

```
template <class ForIter1, class ForIter2>
    FwdIter1 find_end(ForIter1 start1, ForIter1 end1,
                      ForIter2 start2, ForIter2 end2);
template <class ForIter1, class ForIter2, class BinPred>
    FwdIter1 find_end(ForIter1 start1, ForIter1 end1,
                      ForIter2 start2, ForIter2 end2, BinPred pfn);
```

The **find_end( )** algorithm finds the last iterator of the subsequence defined by *start2* and *end2* within the range *start1* and *end1*. If the sequence is found, an iterator to the last element in the sequence is returned. Otherwise, the iterator *end1* is returned.

The second form allows you to specify a binary predicate that determines when elements match.

find_first_of

```
template <class ForIter1, class ForIter2>
    FwdIter1 find_first_of(ForIter1 start1, ForIter1 end1,
                           ForIter2 start2, ForIter2 end2);
template <class ForIter1, class ForIter2, class BinPred>
    FwdIter1 find_first_of(ForIter1 start1, ForIter1 end1,
                           ForIter2 start2, ForIter2 end2,
                           BinPred pfn);
```

The **find_first_of( )** algorithm finds the first element within the sequence defined by *start1* and *end1* that matches an element within the range *start2* and *end2*. If no matching element is found, the iterator *end1* is returned.

The second form allows you to specify a binary predicate that determines when elements match.

find_if

```
template <class InIter, class UnPred>
    InIter find_if(InIter start, InIter end, UnPred pfn);
```

The **find_if( )** algorithm searches the range *start* to *end* for an element for which the unary predicate *pfn* returns true. It returns an iterator to the first occurrence of the element or to *end* if the value is not in the sequence.

for_each

```
template<class InIter, class Func>
    Func for_each(InIter start, InIter end, Func fn);
```

The **for_each( )** algorithm applies the function *fn* to the range of elements specified by *start* and *end*. It returns *fn*.

generate and generate_n

```
template <class ForIter, class Generator>
    void generate(ForIter start, ForIter end, Generator fngen);
template <class ForIter, class Size, class Generator>
    void generate_n(OutIter start, Size num, Generator fngen);
```

The algorithms **generate( )** and **generate_n( )** assign elements in a range of values returned by a generator function. For **generate( )**, the range being assigned is specified by *start* and *end*. For **generate_n( )**, the range begins at *start* and runs for *num* elements. The generator function is passed in *fngen*. It has no parameters.

includes

```
template <class InIter1, class InIter2>
    bool includes(InIter1 start1, InIter1 end1,
```

```
                InIter2 start2, InIter2 end2);
template <class InIter1, class InIter2, class Comp>
    bool includes(InIter1 start1, InIter1 end1,
                  InIter2 start2, InIter2 end2, Comp cmpfn);
```

The **includes( )** algorithm determines if the sequence defined by *start1* and *end1* includes all of the elements in the sequence defined by *start2* and *end2*. It returns true if the elements are all found and false otherwise.

The second form allows you to specify a comparison function that determines when one element is less than another.

inplace_merge

```
template <class BiIter>
    void inplace_merge(BiIter start, BiIter mid, BiIter end);
template <class BiIter, class Comp>
    void inplace_merge(BiIter start, BiIter mid, BiIter end,
                       Comp cmpfn);
```

Within a single sequence, the **inplace_merge( )** algorithm merges the range defined by *start* and *mid* with the range defined by *mid* and *end*. Both ranges must be sorted in increasing order. After executing, the resulting sequence is sorted in increasing order.

The second form allows you to specify a comparison function that determines when one element is less than another.

iter_swap

```
template <class ForIter1, class ForIter2>
    void iter_swap(ForIter1 i, ForIter2 j)
```

The **iter_swap( )** algorithm exchanges the values pointed to by its two iterator arguments.

lexicographical_compare

```
template <class InIter1, class InIter2>
    bool lexicographical_compare(InIter1 start1, InIter1 end1,
                                 InIter2 start2, InIter2 end2);
template <class InIter1, class InIter2, class Comp>
    bool lexicographical_compare(InIter1 start1, InIter1 end1,
                                 InIter2 start2, InIter2 end2,
                                 Comp cmpfn);
```

The **lexicographical_compare( )** algorithm alphabetically compares
the sequence defined by *start1* and *end1* with the sequence
defined by *start2* and *end2*. It returns true if the first sequence is
lexicographically less than the second (that is, if the first sequence
would come before the second using dictionary order).

The second form allows you to specify a comparison function that
determines when one element is less than another.

lower_bound

```
template <class ForIter, class T>
    ForIter lower_bound(ForIter start, ForIter end, const T &val);
template <class ForIter, class T, class Comp>
    ForIter lower_bound(ForIter start, ForIter end, const T &val,
                        Comp cmpfn);
```

The **lower_bound( )** algorithm finds the first point in the sequence
defined by *start* and *end* that is not less than *val*. It returns an
iterator to this point.

The second form allows you to specify a comparison function that
determines when one element is less than another.

make_heap

```
template <class RandIter>
    void make_heap(RandIter start, RandIter end);
```

```
template <class RandIter, class Comp>
    void make_heap(RandIter start, RandIter end, Comp cmpfn);
```

16

The **make_heap( )** algorithm constructs a heap from the sequence
defined by *start* and *end*.

The second form allows you to specify a comparison function that
determines when one element is less than another.

max

```
template <class T>
    const T &max(const T &i, const T &j);
template <class T, class Comp>
    const T &max(const T &i, const T &j, Comp cmpfn);
```

The **max( )** algorithm returns the maximum of two values.

The second form allows you to specify a comparison function that
determines when one element is less than another.

max_element

```
template <class ForIter>
    ForIter max_element(ForIter start, ForIter last);
template <class ForIter, class Comp>
    ForIter max_element(ForIter start, ForIter last, Comp cmpfn);
```

The **max_element( )** algorithm returns an iterator to the maximum
element within the range *start* and *last*.

The second form allows you to specify a comparison function that
determines when one element is less than another.

merge

```
template <class InIter1, class InIter2, class OutIter>
    OutIter merge(InIter1 start1, InIter1 end1,
                  InIter2 start2, InIter2 end2,
```

```
                OutIter result);
template <class InIter1, class InIter2, class OutIter, class Comp>
    OutIter merge(InIter1 start1, InIter1 end1,
                  InIter2 start2, InIter2 end2,
                  OutIter result, Comp cmpfn);
```

The **merge( )** algorithm merges two ordered sequences, placing the result into a third sequence. The sequences to be merged are defined by *start1*, *end1* and *start2*, *end2*. The result is put into the sequence pointed to by *result*. An iterator to the end of the resulting sequence is returned.

The second form allows you to specify a comparison function that determines when one element is less than another.

min

```
template <class T>
    const T &min(const T &i, const T &j);
template <class T, class Comp>
    const T &min(const T &i, const T &j, Comp cmpfn);
```

The **min( )** algorithm returns the minimum of two values.

The second form allows you to specify a comparison function that determines when one element is less than another.

min_element

```
template <class ForIter>
    ForIter min_element(ForIter start, ForIter last);
template <class ForIter, class Comp>
    ForIter min_element(ForIter start, ForIter last, Comp cmpfn);
```

The **min_element( )** algorithm returns an iterator to the minimum element within the range *start* and *last*.

The second form allows you to specify a comparison function that determines when one element is less than another.

mismatch

```
template <class InIter1, class InIter2>
    pair<InIter1, InIter2> mismatch(InIter1 start1, InIter1 end1,
                                    InIter2 start2);
template <class InIter1, class InIter2, class BinPred>
    pair<InIter1, InIter2> mismatch(InIter1 start1, InIter1 end1,
                                    InIter2 start2, BinPred pfn);
```

The **mismatch( )** algorithm finds the first mismatch between the elements in two sequences. Iterators to the two elements are returned. If no mismatch is found, then the iterators *last1* and *first2* + (*last1* − *first1*) are returned.

The second form allows you to specify a binary predicate that determines when one element is equal to another.

The **pair** template class contains two data members called **first** and **second**, which hold the pair of values.

next_permutation

```
template <class BiIter>
    bool next_permutation(BiIter start, BiIter end);
template <class BiIter, class Comp>
    bool next_permutation(BiIter start, BiIter end, Comp cmfn);
```

The **next_permutation( )** algorithm constructs the next permutation of a sequence. The permutations are generated assuming that a sorted sequence, from low to high, represents the first permutation. If the next permutation does not exist, **next_permutation( )** sorts the sequence as its first permutation and returns false. Otherwise, it returns true.

The second form allows you to specify a comparison function that determines when one element is less than another.

nth_element

```
template <class RandIter>
    void nth_element(RandIter start, RandIter element, RandIter end);
template <class RandIter, class Comp>
    void nth_element(RandIter start, RandIter element, RandIter end,
                     Comp cmpfn);
```

The **nth_element( )** algorithm arranges the sequence specified by
start and *end* such that all elements less than *element* come before
that element and all elements greater than *element* come after it.

The second form allows you to specify a comparison function that
determines when one element is greater than another.

partial_sort

```
template <class RandIter>
    void partial_sort(RandIter start, RandIter mid, RandIter end);
template <class RandIter, class Comp>
    void partial_sort(RandIter start, RandIter mid,
                      RandIter end, Comp cmpfn);
```

The **partial_sort( )** algorithm sorts the range *start* to *end*. However,
after execution, only elements in the range *start* to *mid* will be in
sorted order.

The second form allows you to specify a comparison function that
determines when one element is less than another.

partial_sort_copy

```
template <class InIter, class RandIter>
    RandIter partial_sort_copy(InIter start, InIter end,
                               RandIter res_start, RandIter res_end);
template <class InIter, class RandIter, class Comp>
```

```
RandIter partial_sort_copy(InIter start, InIter end,
                           RandIter res_start, RandIter res_end,
                           Comp cmpfn);
```

The **partial_sort_copy( )** algorithm sorts the range *start* to *end* and then copies as many elements as will fit into the result sequence defined by *res_start* and *res_end*. It returns an iterator to the last element copied into the result sequence.

The second form allows you to specify a comparison function that determines when one element is less than another.

partition

```
template <class BiIter, class UnPred>
    BiIter partition(BiIter start, BiIter end, UnPred pfn);
```

The **partition( )** algorithm arranges the sequence defined by *start* and *end* such that all elements for which the predicate specified by *pfn* returns true come before those for which the predicate returns false. It returns an iterator to the beginning of the elements for which the predicate is false.

pop_heap

```
template <class RandIter>
    void pop_heap(RandIter start, RandIter end);
template <class RandIter, class Comp>
    void pop_heap(RandIter start, RandIter end, Comp cmpfn);
```

The **pop_heap( )** exchanges the *first* and *last*–1 elements and then rebuilds the heap using the range *first* through *last*–1. Thus, the first element of the original heap is removed and a new heap is constructed that consists of the remaining elements. Although the element is removed from the heap, it is still present in the container.

The second form allows you to specify a comparison function that determines when one element is less than another.

prev_permutation

```
template <class BiIter>
    bool prev_permutation(BiIter start, BiIter end);
template <class BiIter, class Comp>
    bool prev_permutation(BiIter start, BiIter end, Comp cmpfn);
```

The **prev_permutation( )** algorithm constructs the previous permutation of a sequence. The permutations are generated assuming that a sorted sequence, from low to high, represents the first permutation. If the next permutation does not exist, **prev_permutation( )** sorts the sequence as its final permutation and returns false. Otherwise, it returns true.

The second form allows you to specify a comparison function that determines when one element is less than another.

push_heap

```
template <class RandIter>
    void push_heap(RandIter start, RandIter end);
template <class RandIter, class Comp>
    void push_heap(RandIter start, RandIter end, Comp cmpfn);
```

The **push_heap( )** algorithm pushes the element at *end*–1 onto the heap defined by *start* through *end*–1. The range specified by *start* and *end*–1 is assumed to represent a valid heap.

The second form allows you to specify a comparison function that determines when one element is less than another.

random_shuffle

```
template <class RandIter>
    void random_shuffle(RandIter start, RandIter end);
template <class RandIter, class Generator>
    void random_shuffle(RandIter start, RandIter end,
                        Generator rand_gen);
```

The **random_shuffle( )** algorithm randomizes the sequence defined by *start* and *end*.

The second form specifies a custom random number generator. This function must have the following general form:

rand_gen(*num*);

It must return a random number between zero and *num*.

remove, remove_if, remove_copy, and remove_copy_if

```
template <class ForIter, class T>
    ForIter remove(ForIter start, ForIter end, const T &val);
template <class ForIter, class UnPred>
    ForIter remove_if(ForIter start, ForIter end,   UnPred pfn);
template <class ForIter, class OutIter, class T>
    OutIter remove_copy(InIter start, InIter end,
                        OutIter result, const T &val);
template <class ForIter, class OutIter, class UnPred>
    OutIter remove_copy_it(InIter start, InIter end,
                        OutIter result, UnPred pfn);
```

The **remove( )** algorithm removes elements from the specified range that are equal to *val*. It returns an iterator to the end of the remaining elements.

The **remove_if( )** algorithm removes elements from the specified range for which the predicate *pfn* is true. It returns an iterator to the end of the remaining elements.

The **remove_copy( )** algorithm copies elements from the specified range that are equal to *val* and puts the result into the sequence pointed to by *result*. It returns an iterator to the end of the result.

The **remove_copy_if( )** algorithm copies elements from the specified range for which the predicate *pfn* is true and puts the result into the sequence pointed to by *result*. It returns an iterator to the end of the result.

replace, replace_copy, replace_if, and replace_copy_if

```
template <class ForIter, class T>
    void replace(ForIter start, ForIter end,
                 const T &old, Const T &new);
template <class ForIter, class UnPred, class T>
    void replace_if(ForIter start, ForIter end,
                    UnPred pfn, Const T &new);
template <class ForIter, class OutIter, class T>
    OutIter replace_copy(InIter start, InIter end, OutIter result,
                         const T &old, Const T &new);
template <class ForIter, class OutIter, class UnPred, class T>
    OutIter replace_copy_if(InIter start, InIter end, OutIter result,
                            UnPred pfn, Const T &new);
```

Within the specified range, the **replace( )** algorithm replaces elements with the value *old* with elements that have the value *new*.

Within the specified range, the **replace_if( )** algorithm replaces those elements for which the predicate *pfn* is true with elements that have the value *new*.

Within the specified range, the **replace_copy( )** algorithm copies elements to *result*. In the process, it replaces elements that have the value *old* with elements that have the value *new*. The original range is unchanged. An iterator to the end of *result* is returned.

Within the specified range, the **replace_copy_if( )** algorithm copies elements to *result*. In the process, it replaces elements for which the predicate *pfn* returns true with elements that have the value *new*. The original range is unchanged. An iterator to the end of *result* is returned.

reverse and reverse_copy

```
template <class BiIter>
    void reverse(BiIter start, BiIter end);
template <class BiIter, class OutIter>
    OutIter reverse_copy(BiIter first, BiIter last, OutIter result);
```

The **reverse( )** algorithm reverses the order of the range specified by *start* and *end*.

The **reverse_copy( )** algorithm copies in reverse order the range specified by *start* and *end* and stores the result in *result*. It returns an iterator to the end of *result*.

rotate and rotate_copy

```
template <class ForIter>
  void rotate(ForIter start, ForIter mid, ForIter end);
template <class ForIter, class OutIter>
    OutIter rotate_copy(ForIter start, ForIter mid,
                        ForIter end, OutIter result);
```

The **rotate( )** algorithm left-rotates the elements in the range specified by *start* and *end* so that the element specified by *mid* becomes the new first element.

The **rotate_copy( )** algorithm copies the range specified by *start* and *end*, storing the result in *result*. In the process, it left-rotates the elements so that the element specified by *mid* becomes the new first element. It returns an iterator to the end of *result*.

search

```
template <class ForIter1, class ForIter2>
    ForIter1 search(ForIter1 start1, ForIter1 end1,
                    ForIter2 start2, ForIter2 end2);
template <class ForIter1, class ForIter2, class BinPred>
    ForIter1 search(ForIter1 start1, ForIter1 end1,
                    ForIter2 start2, ForIter2 end2, BinPred pfn);
```

The **search( )** algorithm searches for a subsequence within a sequence. The sequence being searched is defined by *start1* and *end1*. The subsequence being sought is specified by *start2* and *end2*. If the subsequence is found, an iterator to its beginning is returned. Otherwise, *end1* is returned.

The second form allows you to specify a binary predicate that determines when one element is equal to another.

search_n

```
template <class ForIter, class Size, class T>
   ForIter search_n(ForIter start, ForIter end,
                    Size num, const T &val);
template <class ForIter, class Size, class T, class BinPred>
   ForIter search_n(ForIter start, ForIter end,
                    Size num, const T &val, BinPred pfn);
```

The **search_n( )** algorithm searches for a sequence of *num* similar elements within a sequence. The sequence being searched is defined by *start* and *end*. If the subsequence is found, an iterator to its beginning is returned. Otherwise, *end* is returned.

The second form allows you to specify a binary predicate that determines when one element is equal to another.

set_difference

```
template <class InIter1, class InIter2, class OutIter>
   OutIter set_difference(InIter1 start1, InIter1 end1,
                    InIter2 start2, InIter2 end2, OutIter result);
template <class InIter1, class InIter2, class OutIter, class Comp>
   OutIter set_difference(InIter1 start1, InIter1 end1,
                    InIter2 start2, InIter2 end2,
                    OutIter result, Comp cmpfn);
```

The **set_difference( )** algorithm produces a sequence that contains the difference between the two ordered sets defined by *start1*, *end1* and *start2*, *end2*. That is, the set defined by *start2*, *end2* is subtracted from the set defined by *start1*, *end1*. The result is ordered and put into *result*. It returns an iterator to the end of the result.

The second form allows you to specify a comparison function that determines when one element is less than another.

set_intersection

```
template <class InIter1, class InIter2, class OutIter>
    OutIter set_intersection(InIter1 start1, InIter1 end1,
                InIter2 start2, InIter2 end2, OutIter result);
template <class InIter1, class InIter2, class OutIter, class Comp>
    OutIter set_intersection(InIter1 start1, InIter1 end1,
                InIter2 start2, InIter2 end2,
                OutIter result, Comp cmpfn);
```

The **set_intersection( )** algorithm produces a sequence that contains the intersection of the two ordered sets defined by *start1*, *end1* and *start2*, *end2*. These are the elements found in both the sets. The result is ordered and put into *result*. It returns an iterator to the end of the result.

The second form allows you to specify a comparison function that determines when one element is less than another.

set_symmetric_difference

```
template <class InIter1, class InIter2, class OutIter>
    OutIter set_symmetric_difference(InIter1 start1, InIter1 end1,
                InIter2 start2, InIter2 end2, OutIter result);
template <class InIter1, class InIter2, class OutIter, class Comp>
    OutIter set_symmetric_difference(InIter1 start1, InIter1 end1,
                InIter2 start2, InIter2 end2, OutIter result,
                Comp cmpfn);
```

The **set_symmetric_difference( )** algorithm produces a sequence that contains the symmetric difference between the two ordered sets defined by *start1*, *end1* and *start2*, *end2*. That is, the resultant set contains only those elements that are not common to both sets. The result is ordered and put into *result*. It returns an iterator to the end of the result.

The second form allows you to specify a comparison function that determines when one element is less than another.

set_union

```
template <class InIter1, class InIter2, class OutIter>
    OutIter set_union(InIter1 start1, InIter1 end1,
                InIter2 start2, InIter2 end2, OutIter result);
template <class InIter1, class InIter2, class OutIter, class Comp>
    OutIter set_union(InIter1 start1, InIter1 end1,
                InIter2 start2, InIter2 end2, OutIter result,
                Comp cmpfn);
```

The **set_union( )** algorithm produces a sequence that contains the union of the two ordered sets defined by *start1*, *end1* and *start2*, *end2*. Thus, the resultant set contains those elements that are in both sets. The result is ordered and put into *result*. It returns an iterator to the end of the result.

The second form allows you to specify a comparison function that determines when one element is less than another.

sort

```
template <class RandIter>
    void sort(RandIter start, RandIter end);
template <class RandIter, class Comp>
    void sort(RandIter start, RandIter end, Comp cmpfn);
```

The **sort( )** algorithm sorts the range specified by *start* and *end*.

The second form allows you to specify a comparison function that determines when one element is less than another.

sort_heap

```
template <class RandIter>
    void sort_heap(RandIter start, RandIter end);
template <class RandIter, class Comp>
    void sort_heap(RandIter start, RandIter end, Comp cmpfn);
```

The **sort_heap( )** algorithm sorts a heap within the range specified by *start* and *end*.

The second form allows you to specify a comparison function that determines when one element is less than another.

stable_partition

```
template <class BiIter, class UnPred>
    BiIter stable_partition(BiIter start, BiIter end, UnPred pfn);
```

The **stable_partition( )** algorithm arranges the sequence defined by *start* and *end* such that all elements for which the predicate specified by *pfn* returns true come before those for which the predicate returns false. The partitioning is stable. This means that the relative ordering of the sequence is preserved. It returns an iterator to the beginning of the elements for which the predicate is false.

stable_sort

```
template <class RandIter>
    void stable_sort(RandIter start, RandIter end);
template <class RandIter, class Comp>
    void stable_sort(RandIter start, RandIter end, Comp cmpfn);
```

The **sort( )** algorithm sorts the range specified by *start* and *end*. The sort is stable. This means that equal elements are not rearranged.

The second form allows you to specify a comparison function that determines when one element is less than another.

swap

```
template <class T>
    void swap(T &i, T &j);
```

The **swap( )** algorithm exchanges the values referred to by *i* and *j*.

swap_ranges

```
template <class ForIter1, class ForIter2>
    ForIter2 swap_ranges(ForIter1 start1, ForIter1 end1,
                         ForIter2 start2);
```

The **swap_ranges( )** algorithm exchanges elements in the range specified by *start1* and *end1* with elements in the sequence beginning at *start2*. It returns a pointer to the end of the sequence specified by *start2*.

transform

```
template <class InIter, class OutIter, class Func>
    OutIter transform(InIter start, InIter end,
                      OutIter result, Func unaryfunc);
template <class InIter1, class InIter2, class OutIter, class Func>
    OutIter transform(InIter1 start1, InIter1 end1,
                      InIter2 start2, OutIter result,
                      Func binaryfunc);
```

The **transform( )** algorithm applies a function to a range of elements and stores the outcome in *result*. In the first form, the range is specified by *start* and *end*. The function to be applied is specified by *unaryfunc*. This function receives the value of an element in its parameter, and it must return its transformation.

In the second form, the transformation is applied using a binary operator function that receives the value of an element from the sequence to be transformed in its first parameter and an element from the second sequence as its second parameter.

Both versions return an iterator to the end of the resulting sequence.

➤ Programming Tip

One of the more interesting algorithms is **transform( )** because it modifies each element in range according to a function that you provide. For example, the following program uses a simple transformation function called **xform( )** to square the contents of a list. Notice that the resulting sequence is stored in the same list that provided the original sequence.

```
// An example of the transform algorithm.
#include <iostream>
#include <list>
#include <algorithm>
using namespace std;

// A simple transformation function.
int xform(int i) {
  return i * i; // square original value
}

int main()
{
  list<int> xl;
  int i;

  // put values into list
  for(i=0; i<10; i++) xl.push_back(i);

  cout << "Original contents of xl: ";
  list<int>::iterator p = xl.begin();
  while(p != xl.end()) {
    cout << *p << " ";
    p++;
  }

  cout << endl;

  // transform xl
```

```
   p = transform(xl.begin(), xl.end(), xl.begin(), xform);

   cout << "Transformed contents of xl: ";
   p = xl.begin();
   while(p != xl.end()) {
     cout << *p << " ";
     p++;
   }

   return 0;
}
```

The output produced by the program is shown here:

```
Original contents of xl: 0 1 2 3 4 5 6 7 8 9
Transformed contents of xl: 0 1 4 9 16 25 36 49 64 81
```

As you can see, each element in **xl** has been squared.

unique and unique_copy

```
template <class ForIter>
    ForIter unique(ForIter start, ForIter end);
template <class ForIter, class BinPred>
    ForIter unique(ForIter start, ForIter end, BinPred pfn);
template <class ForIter, class OutIter>
    OutIter unique_copy(ForIter start, ForIter end, OutIter result);
template <class ForIter, class OutIter, class BinPred>
    OutIter unique_copy(ForIter start, ForIter end, OutIter result,
                        BinPred pfn);
```

The **unique( )** algorithm eliminates consecutive, duplicate elements from the specified range. The second form allows you to specify a binary predicate that determines when one element is equal to another. **unique( )** returns an iterator to the end of the range.

The **unique_copy( )** algorithm copies the range specified by *start* and *end*, eliminating consecutive duplicate elements in the process. The outcome is put into *result*. The second form allows you to specify a binary predicate that determines when one

element is equal to another. **unique_copy( )** returns an iterator to
the end of the range.

upper_bound

```
template <class ForIter, class T>
    ForIter upper_bound(ForIter start, ForIter end, const T &val);
template <class ForIter, class T, class Comp>
    ForIter upper_bound(ForIter start, ForIter end, const T &val,
                        Comp cmpfn);
```

The **upper_bound( )** algorithm finds the last point in the sequence
defined by *start* and *end* that is not greater than *val*. It returns an
iterator to this point.

The second form allows you to specify a comparison function that
determines when one element is less than another.

Chapter 17
The C++ String, Exception, and Complex Classes

In addition to the iostream library and the STL, the C++ standard library defines several other classes. While many of these are special-purpose classes, three are widely used, supporting strings, exceptions, and complex arithmetic. They are described here.

Strings

C++ supports character strings two ways. The first is as a null-terminated character array. This is sometimes referred to as a *C string*. The second way is as a class object of type **basic_string**. There are two specializations of **basic_string**: **string**, which supports **char** strings, and **wstring**, which supports **wchar_t** (wide character) strings. Most often, you will use string objects of type **string**. To use the C++ string classes, you must include **<string>**.

The **basic_string** class is essentially a container. This means that iterators and the STL algorithms can operate on strings. However, strings have additional capabilities.

A class used by **basic_string** is **char_traits**, which defines several attributes of the characters that comprise a string. It is important to understand that while the most common strings are made up of either **char** or **wchar_t** characters, **basic_string** can operate on any object that can be used to represent a text character.

The template specification for **basic_string** is

```
template <class CharType, class Attr = char_traits<CharType>,
          class Allocator = allocator<T> > class basic_string
```

Here, **CharType** is the type of character being used, **Attr** is the class that describes the character's traits, and **Allocator** specifies the allocator. **basic_string** has the following constructors:

```
explicit basic_string(const Allocator &a = Allocator( ));
basic_string(size_type len, CharType ch,
        const Allocator &a = Allocator( ))
basic_string(const CharType *str; const Allocator &a = Allocator( ));
basic_string(const CharType *str; size_type len,
        const Allocator &a = Allocator( ));
basic_string(const basic_string &str, size_type indx = 0,
        size_type len=npos, const Allocator &a = Allocator( ));
template <class InIter> basic_string(InIter start, InIter end,
        const Allocator &a = Allocator( ));
```

The first form constructs an empty string. The second form constructs a string that has *len* characters of value *ch*. The third form constructs a string that contains the same elements as *str*. The fourth form constructs a string that contains a substring of *str* that begins at zero and is *len* characters long. The fifth form constructs a string from another **basic_string** using the substring that begins at *indx* that is *len* characters long. The sixth form constructs a *string* that contains the elements in the range specified by *start* and *end*.

The following comparison operators are defined for **basic_string**:

==, <, <=, !=, >, >=

Also defined is the + operator, which yields the result of concatenating one string with another and the I/O operators << and >>, which can be used to input and output strings.

The + operator can be used to concatenate a string object with another string object or a string object with a C-style string. That is, the following variations are supported:

string + string
string + C-string
C-string + string

The + operator can also be used to concatenate a character onto the end of a string.

The **basic_string** class defines the constant **npos**, which is usually –1. This constant represents the length of the longest possible string.

In the descriptions, the generic type **CharType** represents the type of character stored by a string. Since the names of the placeholder types in a template class are arbitrary, **basic_string** declares **typedef**ed versions of these types. This makes the type names concrete. The types defined by **basic_string** are shown here:

17

size_type	Some integral type loosely equivalent to **size_t**
reference	A reference to a character within a string
const_reference	A **const** reference to a character within a string
iterator	An iterator
const_iterator	A **const** iterator
reverse_iterator	A reverse iterator
const_reverse_iterator	A **const** reverse iterator
value_type	The type of character stored in a string
allocator_type	The type of the allocator
pointer	A pointer to a character within a string
const_pointer	A **const** pointer to a character within a string
traits_type	A **typedef** for **char_traits<CharType>**
difference_type	A type that can store the difference between two addresses

The member functions defined by **basic_string** are shown in the following table. Since the vast majority of programmers will be using **char** strings (and to keep the descriptions easy to understand), the table uses the type **string**, but the functions also apply to objects of type **wstring** (or any other type of **basic_string**).

Member	Description
string &append(const string &*str*);	Appends *str* onto the end of the invoking string. Returns ***this**.
string &append(const string &*str*, size_type *indx*, size_type *len*);	Appends a substring of *str* onto the end of the invoking string. The substring being appended begins at *indx* and runs for *len* characters. Returns ***this**.
string &append(const CharType **str*);	Appends *str* onto the end of the invoking string. Returns ***this**.

Member	Description
string &append(const CharType *str, size_type num);	Appends the first num characters from str onto the end of the invoking string. Returns *this.
string &append(size_type len, CharType ch);	Appends len characters specified by ch to the end of the invoking string. Returns *this.
template<class InIter> string &append(InIter start, InIter end);	Appends the sequence specified by start and end onto the end of the invoking string. *this is returned.
string &assign(const string &str);	Assigns str to the invoking string. Returns *this.
string &assign(const string &str, size_type indx, size_type len);	Assigns a substring of str to the invoking string. The substring being assigned begins at indx and runs for len characters. Returns *this.
string &assign(const CharType *str);	Assigns str to the invoking string. Returns * this.
string &assign(const CharType *str, size_type len);	Assigns the first len character from str to the invoking string. Returns *this.
string &assign(size_type len, CharType ch);	Assigns len characters specified by ch to the end of the invoking string. Returns *this.
template<class InIter> string &assign(InIter start, InIter end);	Assigns the sequence specified by start and end to the invoking string. *this is returned.
reference at(size_type indx); const_reference at(size_type indx) const;	Returns a reference to the character specified by indx.
iterator begin( ); const_iterator begin( ) const;	Returns an iterator to the first element in the string.
const CharType *c_str( ) const;	Returns a pointer to a C-style (i.e., null-terminated) version of the invoking string.

Member	Description
size_type capacity( ) const;	Returns the current capacity of the string. This is the number of characters it can hold before it will need to allocate more memory.
int compare(const string &str) const;	Compares str to the invoking string. It returns one of the following: Less than zero if **this** < str Zero if **this** == str Greater than zero if **this** > str
int compare(size_type indx, size_type len, const string &str) const;	Compares str to a substring within the invoking string. The substring begins at indx and is len characters long. It returns one of the following: Less than zero if **this** < str Zero if **this** == str Greater than zero if **this** > str
int compare(size_type indx, size_type len, const string &str, size_type indx2, size_type len2) const;	Compares a substring of str to a substring within the invoking string. The substring in the invoking string begins at indx and is len characters long. The substring in str begins at indx2 and is len2 characters long. It returns one of the following: Less than zero if **this** < str Zero if **this** == str Greater than zero if **this** > str
int compare(const CharType *str) const;	Compares str to the invoking string. It returns one of the following: Less than zero if **this** < str Zero if **this** == str Greater than zero if **this** > str

17

Member	Description
int compare(size_type *indx*, size_type *len*, const CharType **str*, size_type *len2* = npos) const;	Compares a substring of *str* to a substring within the invoking string. The substring in the invoking string begins at *indx* and is *len* characters long. The substring in *str* begins at zero and is *len2* characters long. It returns one of the following: Less than zero if ***this** < *str* Zero if ***this** == *str* Greater than zero if ***this** > *str*
size_type copy(CharType **str*, size_type *len*, size_type *indx* = 0) const;	Beginning at *indx*, copies *len* characters from the invoking string into the character array pointed to by *str*. Returns the number of characters copied.
const CharType *data( ) const;	Returns a pointer to the first character in the invoking string.
bool empty( ) const;	Returns **true** if the invoking string is empty and **false** otherwise.
iterator end( ); const_iterator end( ) const;	Returns an iterator to the end of the string.
iterator erase(iterator *i*);	Removes character pointed to by *i*. Returns an iterator to the character after the one removed.
iterator erase(iterator *start*, iterator *end*);	Removes characters in the range *start* to *end*. Returns an iterator to the character after the last character removed.
string &erase(size_type *indx* = 0, size_type *len* = npos);	Beginning at *indx*, removes *len* characters from the invoking string. Returns ***this**.
size_type find(const string &*str*, size_type *indx* = 0) const;	Returns the index of the first occurrence of *str* within the invoking string. The search begins at index *indx*. **npos** is returned if no match is found.

Member	Description
size_type find(const CharType *str, size_type indx = 0) const;	Returns the index of the first occurrence of str within the invoking string. The search begins at index indx. **npos** is returned if no match is found.

size_type find(const CharType *str,
        size_type indx,
        size_type len) const;
	Returns the index of the first occurrence of the first len characters of str within the invoking string. The search begins at index indx. **npos** is returned if no match is found.

size_type find(CharType ch, size_type indx = 0) const;	Returns the index of the first occurrence of ch within the invoking string. The search begins at index indx. **npos** is returned if no match is found.
size_type find_first_of(const string &str, size_type indx = 0) const;	Returns the index of the first character within the invoking string that matches any character in str. The search begins at index indx. **npos** is returned if no match is found.
size_type find_first_of(const CharType *str, size_type indx = 0) const;	Returns the index of the first character within the invoking string that matches any character in str. The search begins at index indx. **npos** is returned if no match is found.

size_type find_first_of(const CharType *str,
        size_type indx,
        size_type len) const;
	Returns the index of the first character within the invoking string that matches any character in the first len characters of str. The search begins at index indx. **npos** is returned if no match is found.

size_type find_first_of(CharType ch, size_type indx = 0) const;	Returns the index of the first occurrence of ch within the invoking string. The search begins at index indx. **npos** is returned if no match is found.

17

Member	Description

size_type find_first_not_of(
  const string &*str*,
  size_type *indx* = 0) const;
	Returns the index of the first character within the invoking string that does not match any character in *str*. The search begins at index *indx*. **npos** is returned if no mismatch is found.

size_type find_first_not_of(
  const CharType *str*,
  size_type *indx* = 0) const;
	Returns the index of the first character within the invoking string that does not match any character in *str*. The search begins at index *indx*. **npos** is returned if no mismatch is found.

size_type find_first_not_of(
  const CharType *str*,
  size_type *indx*,
  size_type *len*) const;
	Returns the index of the first character within the invoking string that does not match any character in the first *len* characters of *str*. The search begins at index *indx*. **npos** is returned if no mismatch is found.

size_type find_first_not_of(
  CharType *ch*,
  size_type *indx* = 0) const;
	Returns the index of the first character within the invoking string that does not match *ch*. The search begins at index *indx*. **npos** is returned if no mismatch is found.

size_type find_last_of(const string &*str*, size_type *indx* = npos) const;	Returns the index of the last character within the invoking string that matches any character in *str*. The search begins at index *indx*. **npos** is returned if no match is found.
size_type find_last_of(const CharType *str*, size_type *indx* = npos) const;	Returns the index of the last character within the invoking string that matches any character in *str*. The search begins at index *indx*. **npos** is returned if no match is found.

Member	Description
size_type find_last_of(const CharType *str, size_type indx, size_type len) const;	Returns the index of the last character within the invoking string that matches any character in the first len characters of str. The search begins at index indx. **npos** is returned if no match is found.
size_type find_last_of(CharType ch, size_type indx = npos) const;	Returns the index of the last occurrence of ch within the invoking string. The search begins at index indx. **npos** is returned if no match is found.
size_type find_last_not_of(const string &str, size_type indx = npos) const;	Returns the index of the last character within the invoking string that does not match any character in str. The search begins at index indx. **npos** is returned if no mismatch is found.
size_type find_last_not_of(const CharType *str, size_type indx = npos) const;	Returns the index of the last character within the invoking string that does not match any character in str. The search begins at index indx. **npos** is returned if no mismatch is found.
size_type find_last_not_of(const CharType *str, size_type indx, size_type len) const;	Returns the index of the last character within the invoking string that does not match any character in the first len characters of str. The search begins at index indx. **npos** is returned if no mismatch is found.
size_type find_last_not_of(CharType ch, size_type indx = npos) const;	Returns the index of the last character within the invoking string that does not match ch. The search begins at index indx. **npos** is returned if no mismatch is found.

17

Member	Description
allocator_type get_allocator( ) const;	Returns the string's allocator.
iterator insert(iterator *i*, const CharType &*ch*);	Inserts *ch* immediately before the character specified by *indx*. An iterator to the character is returned.
string &insert(size_type *indx*, const string &*str*);	Inserts *str* into the invoking string at the index specified by *indx*. Returns ***this**.

string &insert(size_type *indx1*,
        const string &*str*,
        size_type *indx2*,
        size_type *len*);
	Inserts a substring of *str* into the invoking string at the index specified by *indx1*. The substring begins at *indx2* and is *len* characters long. Returns ***this**.

string &insert(size_type *indx*, const CharType **str*);	Inserts *str* into the invoking string at the index specified by *indx*. Returns ***this**.

string &insert(size_type *indx*,
        const CharType **str*,
        size_type *len*);
	Inserts the first *len* characters of *str* into the invoking string at the index specified by *indx*. Returns ***this**.

string &insert(size_type *indx*,
        size_type *len*,
        CharType *ch*);
	Inserts *len* characters of value *ch* into the invoking string at the index specified by *indx*. Returns ***this**.

void insert(iterator *i*, size_type *len*, const CharType &*ch*)	Inserts *len* copies of *ch* immediately before the element specified by *i*.

template <class InIter>
  void insert(iterator *i*, InIter *start*,
        InIter *end*);
	Inserts the sequence defined by *start* and *end* immediately before the element specified by *i*.

size_type length( ) const;	Returns the number of characters in the string.
size_type max_size( ) const;	Returns the maximum number of characters that the string can hold.
reference operator[ ](size_type *indx*) const; const_reference operator[ ](size_type *indx*) const;	Returns a reference to the character specified by *indx*.

string &operator=(const string &*str*);
string &operator=(const CharType **str*);
string &operator=(CharType *ch*);
	Assigns the specified string or character to the invoking string. Returns ***this**.

Member	Description

string &operator+=(const string &*str*);
string &operator+=(const CharType *str*);
string &operator+=(CharType *ch*);
	Appends the specified string or character onto the end of the invoking string. Returns ***this**.

reverse_iterator rbegin( ); const_reverse_iterator rbegin( ) const;	Returns a reverse iterator to the end of the string.
reverse_iterator rend( ); const_reverse_iterator rend( ) const;	Returns a reverse iterator to the start of the string.

string &replace(size_type *indx*,
        size_type *len*,
        const string &*str*);
	Replaces up to *len* characters in the invoking string, beginning at *indx* with the string in *str*. Returns ***this**.

string &replace(size_type *indx1*,
        size_type *len1*,
        const string &*str*,
        size_type *indx2*,
        size_type *len2*);
	Replaces up to *len1* characters in the invoking string beginning at *indx1* with the *len2* characters from the string in *str* that begin at *indx2*. Returns ***this**.

string &replace(size_type *indx*,
        size_type *len*,
        const CharType *str*);
	Replaces up to *len* characters in the invoking string, beginning at *indx* with the string in *str*. Returns ***this**.

string &replace(size_type *indx1*,
        size_type *len1*,
        const CharType *str*,
        size_type *len2*);
	Replaces up to *len1* characters in the invoking string beginning at *indx1* with the *len2* characters from the string in *str*. Returns ***this**.

string &replace(size_type *indx*,
        size_type *len1*,
        size_type *len2*,
        CharType *ch*);
	Replaces up to *len1* characters in the invoking string beginning at *indx* with *len2* characters specified by *ch*. Returns ***this**.

string &replace(iterator *start*,
        iterator *end*,
        const string &*str*);
	Replaces the range specified by *start* and *end* with *str*. Returns ***this**.

string &replace(iterator *start*,
        iterator *end*,
        const CharType *str*);
	Replaces the range specified by *start* and *end* with *str*. Returns ***this**.

17

Member	Description
string &replace(iterator *start*, iterator *end*, const CharType *str*, size_type *len*);	Replaces the range specified by *start* and *end* with the first *len* characters from *str*. Returns ***this**.
string &replace(iterator *start*, iterator *end*, size_type *len*, CharType *ch*);	Replaces the range specified by *start* and *end* with *len* characters specified by *ch*. Returns ***this**.
template <class InIter> string &replace(iterator *start1*, iterator *end1*, InIter *start2*, InIter *end2*);	Replaces the range specified by *start1* and *end1* with the characters specified by *start2* and *end2*. Returns ***this**.
void reserve(size_type *num* = 0);	Sets the capacity of the string so that it is equal to at least *num*.
void resize(size_type *num*) void resize(size_type *num*, CharType *ch*);	Changes the size of the string to that specified by *num*. If the string must be lengthened, then elements with the value specified by *ch* are added to the end.
size_type rfind(const string &*str*, size_type *indx* = npos) const;	Returns the index of the last occurrence of *str* within the invoking string. The search begins at index *indx*. **npos** is returned if no match is found.
size_type rfind(const CharType *str*, size_type *indx* = npos) const;	Returns the index of the last occurrence of *str* within the invoking string. The search begins at index *indx*. **npos** is returned if no match is found.
size_type rfind(const CharType *str*, size_type *indx*, size_type *len*) const;	Returns the index of the last occurrence of the first *len* characters of *str* within the invoking string. The search begins at index *indx*. **npos** is returned if no match is found.
size_type rfind(CharType *ch*, size_type *indx* = npos) const;	Returns the index of the last occurrence of *ch* within the invoking string. The search begins at index *indx*. **npos** is returned if no match is found.

Member	Description
size_type size( ) const;	Returns the number of characters currently in the string.
string substr(size_type *indx* = 0, size_type *len* = npos) const;	Returns a substring of *len* characters beginning at *indx* within the invoking string.
void swap(string &*str*)	Exchanges the characters stored in the invoking string with those in *str*.

17

➤ Programming Tip

While the traditional C-style strings have always been simple to use, the C++ string classes make string handling extraordinarily easy. For example, using **string** objects, you can use the assignment operator to assign a quoted string to a **string**, the relational operators to compare strings, and a wide variety of string manipulation functions that make substring operations convenient. For example, consider the following program:

```
// Demonstrate strings.
#include <iostream>
#include <string>
using namespace std;

int main()
{
  string str1 = "abcdefghijklmnopqrstuvwxyz";
  string str2;
  string str3(str1);

  str2 = str1.substr(10, 5);

  cout << "str1: " << str1 << endl;
  cout << "str2: " << str2 << endl;
  cout << "str3: " << str3 << endl;

  str1.replace(5, 10, "");
  cout << "str1.replace(5, 10, \"\"): " << str1 << endl;
```

```
    str1 = "one";
    str2 = "two";
    str3 = "three";

    cout << "str1.compare(str2): ";
    cout << str1.compare(str2) << endl;

    if(str1<str2) cout << "str1 is less than str2\n";

    string str4 = str1 + " " + str2 + " " + str3;
    cout << "str4: " << str4 << endl;

    int i = str4.find("wo");
    cout << "str4.substr(i): " << str4.substr(i);

    return 0;
}
```

The output from the program is shown here:

```
str1: abcdefghijklmnopqrstuvwxyz
str2: klmno
str3: abcdefghijklmnopqrstuvwxyz
str1.replace(5, 10, ""): abcdepqrstuvwxyz
str1.compare(str2): -1
str1 is less than str2
str4: one two three
str4.substr(i): wo three
```

Notice the ease with which the string handling is accomplished. For example, the + concatenates strings and the < compares two strings. To accomplish these operations using C-style, null-terminated strings, less convenient calls to the strcat( ) and strcmp( ) functions would have been required. Because C++ string objects can be freely mixed with C-style null-terminated strings, there is no disadvantage to using them in your program— and there are considerable benefits to be gained.

> # Exceptions

The standard C++ library defines two headers that relate to exceptions: **<exception>** and **<stdexcept>**. Exceptions are used to report error conditions. Each header is examined here.

<exception>

The **<exception>** header defines classes, types, and functions that relate to exception handling. The classes defined by **<exception>** are shown here:

```
class exception {
public:
  exception() throw();
  exception(const bad_exception &ob) throw();
  virtual ~exception() throw();

  exception &operator=(const exception &ob) throw();
  virtual const char *what(() const throw();
};

class bad_exception: public exception {
public:
  bad_exception() throw();
  bad_exception(const bad_exception &ob) throw();
  virtual ~bad_exception() throw();

  bad_exception &operator=(const bad_exception &ob) throw();
  virtual const char *what(() const throw();
};
```

The **exception** class is a base for all exceptions defined by the C++ standard library. The **bad_exception** class is the type of exception thrown by the **unexpected( )** function. In each, the member function **what( )** returns a pointer to a null-terminated string that describes the exception.

Several important classes are derived from **exception**. The first is **bad_alloc**, thrown when the **new** operator fails. Next is **bad_typeid**. It is thrown when an illegal **typeid** expression is executed. Finally, **bad_cast** is thrown when an invalid dynamic cast is attempted. These classes contain the same members as **exception**.

The types defined by **<exception>** are as follows:

Type	Meaning
terminate_handler	typedef void (*terminate_handler) ( );
unexpected_handler	typedef void (*unexpected_handler) ( );

The functions declared in **<exception>** are shown here:

Function	Description
terminate_handler set_terminate(terminate_handler *fn*) throw( );	Sets the function specified by *fn* as the terminate handler. A pointer to the old terminate handler is returned.
unexpected_handler set_unexpected(unexpected_handler *fn*) throw( );	Sets the function specified by *fn* as the unexpected handler. A pointer to the old unexpected handler is returned.
void terminate( );	Calls the terminate handler when a fatal exception is unhandled. Calls **abort( )** by default.
bool uncaught_exception( );	Returns true if an exception is uncaught.
void unexpected( );	Calls the unexpected exception handler when a function throws a disallowed exception. By default, **terminate( )** is called.

<stdexcept>

The header **<stdexcept>** defines several standard exceptions that may be thrown by C++ library functions and/or its runtime system. There are two general types of exceptions defined by **<stdexcept>**: logic errors and runtime errors. Logic errors occur because of mistakes made by the programmer. Runtime errors occur because of mistakes in library functions or the runtime system and are beyond programmer control.

The standard exceptions defined by C++ caused by logic errors are derived from the base class **logic_error**. These exceptions are shown here:

Exception	Meaning
domain_error	Domain error occurred.
invalid_argument	Invalid argument used in function call.
length_error	An attempt was made to create an object that was too large.
out_of_range	An argument to a function was not in the required range.

The following runtime exceptions are derived from the base class **runtime_error**:

Exception	Meaning
overflow_error	Arithmetic overflow occurred.
range_error	An internal range error occurred.
underflow_error	An underflow occurred.

The complex Class

The header **<complex>** defines the **complex** class, which represents complex numbers. It also defines a series of functions and operators that operate on objects of type **complex**.

The template specification for **complex** is shown here:

```
template <class T> class complex
```

Here, **T** specifies the type used to store the components of a complex number. There are three predefined specializations of **complex**:

```
class complex<float>
class complex<double>
class complex<long double>
```

The **complex** class has the following constructors:

    complex(const T &real = T( ), const T = &imaginary = T( ));
    complex(const complex &ob);
    template <class T1> complex(const complex<T1> &ob);

The first constructs a **complex** object with a real component of *real* and an imaginary component of *imaginary*. These values default to zero if not specified. The second creates a copy of *ob*. The third creates a complex object from *ob*.

The following operations are defined for complex objects:

+	–	*	/
–=	+=	/=	*=
=	==	!=	

The nonassignment operators are overloaded three ways: once for operations involving a **complex** object on the left and a scalar object on the right, again for operations involving a scalar on the left and a **complex** object on the right, and finally for operations involving two **complex** objects. For example, the following types of operations are allowed:

    complex_ob + scalar
    scalar + complex_ob
    complex_ob + complex_ob

Operations involving scalar quantities affect only the real component.

Two member functions are defined for **complex**: **real( )** and **imag( )**. They are shown here:

    T real( ) const;
    T imag( ) const;

The **real( )** function returns the real component of the invoking object and **imag( )** returns the imaginary component. The following functions are also defined for **complex** objects:

Function	Description
template <class T> T abs(const complex<T> &ob);	Returns the absolute value of ob
template <class T> T arg(const complex<T> &ob);	Returns the phase angle of ob
template <class T> complex<T> conj(const complex<T> &ob);	Returns the conjugate of ob
template <class T> complex<T> cos(const complex<T> &ob);	Returns the cosine of ob
template <class T> complex<T> cosh(const complex<T> &ob);	Returns the hyperbolic cosine of ob
template <class T> complex<T> exp(const complex<T> &ob);	Returns the e^{ob}
template <class T> T imag(const complex<T> &ob);	Returns the imaginary component of ob
template <class T> complex<T> log(const complex<T> &ob);	Returns the natural logarithm of ob
template <class T> complex<T> log10(const complex<T> &ob);	Returns the base 10 logarithm of ob
template <class T> T norm(const complex<T> &ob);	Returns the magnitude of ob squared
template <class T> complex<T> polar(const T &v, const T &theta=0);	Returns a complex number that has the magnitude specified by v and a phase angle of theta
template <class T> complex<T> pow(const complex<T> &b, int e);	Returns b^e
template <class T> complex<T> pow(const complex<T> &b, const T &e);	Returns b^e
template <class T> complex<T> pow(const complex<T> &b, const complex<T> &e);	Returns b^e
template <class T> complex<T> pow(const T &b, const complex<T> &e);	Returns b^e

Function	Description
template <class T> T real(const complex<T> &ob);	Returns the real component of ob
template <class T> complex<T> sin(const complex<T> &ob);	Returns the sine of ob

template <class T>
  complex<T>
    sinh(const complex<T> &ob);
	Returns the hyperbolic sine of ob

template <class T>
  complex<T>
    sqrt(const complex<T> &ob);
	Returns the square root of ob

template <class T>
  complex<T>
    tan(const complex<T> &ob);
	Returns the tangent of ob

template <class T>
  complex<T>
    tanh(const complex<T> &ob);
	Returns the hyperbolic tangent of ob

Chapter 18
Library Features Added by C99

The C99 Standard added features to the C library two ways. First, it added functions to headers previously defined by C89. For example, significant additions were made to the mathematics library supported by the **<math.h>** header. These additional functions were covered in the preceding chapters. Second, new categories of functions, ranging from support for complex arithmetic to type-generic macros, were created, along with new headers to support them. These new library elements are described in this chapter. Keep in mind that none of the features described here are supported by C++.

The Complex Library

C99 adds complex arithmetic capabilities to C. At the outset, it is important to state that the C99 complex math library differs completely from the complex class library defined by C++. If you will be programming in C++, you will want to use the C++ complex library. The C99 complex library is appropriate only for programmers restricted to the C language.

The C99 complex library is supported by the **<complex.h>** header. The following macros are defined:

Macro	Expands To
complex	_Complex
imaginary	_Imaginary
_Complex_I	(const float _Complex) i
_Imaginary_I	(const float _Imaginary) i
I	_Imaginary_I (or _Complex_I if imaginary types are not supported)

Here, i represents the imaginary value, which is the square root of -1. Support for imaginary types is optional.

_Complex and **_Imaginary**, rather than **complex** and **imaginary**, were specified as a keywords by C99 because many existing C89

367

programs had already defined their own custom complex data types using the names **complex** and **imaginary**. By using the keywords **_Complex** and **_Imaginary**, C99 avoids breaking preexisting code. For new programs, however, it is best to include **<complex.h>** and then use the **complex** and **imaginary** macros.

The complex math functions are shown below. Notice that **float complex**, **double complex**, and **long double complex** versions of each function are defined. The **float complex** version uses the suffix **f**, and the **long double complex** version uses the suffix **l**. Also, angles are in radians.

Function	Description

float cabsf(float complex *arg*);
double cabs(double complex *arg*);
long double cabsl(long double complex *arg*);
	Returns the complex absolute value of *arg*

float complex cacosf(float complex *arg*);
double complex cacos(double complex *arg*);
long double complex cacosl(long double complex *arg*);
	Returns the complex arc cosine of *arg*

float complex cacoshf(float complex *arg*);
double complex cacosh(double complex *arg*);
long double complex cacoshl(long double complex *arg*);
	Returns the complex arc hyperbolic cosine of *arg*

float cargf(float complex *arg*);
double carg(double complex *arg*);
long double cargl(long double complex *arg*);
	Returns the phase angle of *arg*

float complex casinf(float complex *arg*);
double complex casin(double complex *arg*);
long double complex casinl(long double complex *arg*);
	Returns the complex arc sine of *arg*

float complex casinhf(float complex *arg*);
double complex casinh(double complex *arg*);
long double complex casinhl(long double complex *arg*);
	Returns the complex arc hyperbolic sine of *arg*

float complex catanf(float complex *arg*);
double complex catan(double complex *arg*);
long double complex catanl(long double complex *arg*);
	Returns the complex arc tangent of *arg*

float complex catanhf(float complex *arg*);
double complex catanh(double complex *arg*);
long double complex catanhl(long double complex *arg*);
	Returns the complex arc hyperbolic tangent of *arg*

Function	Description

float complex ccosf(float complex *arg*);
double complex ccos(double complex *arg*);
long double complex ccosl(long double
        complex *arg*);
	Returns the complex
	cosine of *arg*

float complex ccoshf(float complex *arg*);
double complex ccosh(double complex *arg*);
long double complex ccoshl(long double
        complex *arg*);
	Returns the complex
	hyperbolic cosine of
	arg

float complex cexpf(float complex *arg*);
double complex cexp(double complex *arg*);
long double complex cexpl(long double
        complex *arg*);
	Returns the complex
	value e^{arg}, where e
	is the natural
	logarithm base

float cimagf(float complex *arg*);
double cimag(double complex *arg*);
long double cimagl(long double complex *arg*);
	Returns the
	imaginary part of *arg*

float complex clogf(float complex *arg*);
double complex clog(double complex *arg*);
long double complex clogl(long double
        complex *arg*);
	Returns the complex
	natural logarithm
	of *arg*

float complex conjf(float complex *arg*);
double complex conj(double complex *arg*);
long double complex conjl(long double
        complex *arg*);
	Returns the complex
	conjugate of *arg*

float complex cpowf(float complex *a*,
        long double complex *b*);
double complex cpow(double complex *a*,
        double complex *b*);
long double complex cpowl(long double complex *a*,
        long double complex *b*);
	Returns the complex
	value of a^b

float complex cprojf(float complex *arg*);
double complex cproj(double complex *arg*);
long double complex cprojl(long double
        complex *arg*);
	Returns the
	projection of *arg*
	onto the Riemann
	sphere

float crealf(float complex *arg*);
double creal(double complex *arg*);
long double creall(long double complex *arg*);
	Returns the real
	part of *arg*

float complex csinf(float complex *arg*);
double complex csin(double complex *arg*);
long double complex csinl(long double
        complex *arg*);
	Returns the complex
	sine of *arg*

float complex csinhf(float complex *arg*);
double complex csinh(double complex *arg*);
long double complex csinhl(long double
        complex *arg*);
	Returns the complex
	hyperbolic sine of *arg*

18

Function	Description

float complex csqrtf(float complex *arg*);
double complex csqrt(double complex *arg*);
long double complex csqrtl(long double
complex *arg*);
	Returns the complex
	square root of *arg*

float complex ctanf(float complex *arg*);
double complex ctan(double complex *arg*);
long double complex ctanl(long double
complex *arg*);
	Returns the complex
	tangent of *arg*

float complex ctanhf(float complex *arg*);
double complex ctanh(double complex *arg*);
long double complex ctanhl(long double
complex *arg*);
	Returns the complex
	hyperbolic tangent
	of *arg*

The Floating-Point Environment Library

In the header **<fenv.h>**, C99 declares functions that access the floating-point environment. These functions are shown in the following table:

Function	Description
void feclearexcept(int *ex*);	Clears the exceptions specified by *ex*.
void fegetexceptflag(fexcept_t *fptr*, int *ex*);	The state of the floating-point exception flags specified by *ex* are stored in the variable pointed to by *fptr*.
void feraiseexcept(int *ex*);	Raises the exceptions specified by *ex*.
void fesetexceptflag(const fexcept_t *fptr*, int *ex*);	Sets the floating-point status flags specified by *ex* to the state of the flags in the object pointed to by *fptr*.
int fetestexcept(int *ex*);	Bitwise ORs the exceptions specified in *ex* with the current floating-point status flags and returns the result.
int fegetround(void);	Returns a value that indicates the current rounding direction.
int fesetround(int *direction*);	Sets the current rounding direction to that specified by *direction*. A return value of zero indicates success.

Function	Description
void fegetenv(fenv_t *envptr);	The object pointed to by *envptr* receives the floating-point environment.
int feholdexcept(fenv_t *envptr);	Causes nonstop floating-point exception handling to be used. It also stores the floating-point environment in the variable pointed to by *envptr* and clears the status flags. It returns zero if successful.
void fesetenv(const fenv_t *envptr);	Sets the floating-point environment to that pointed to by *envptr*, but does not raise floating-point exceptions. This object must have been obtained by calling either **fegetenv( )** or **feholdexcept( )**.
void feupdateenv(const fenv_t *envptr);	Sets the floating-point environment to that pointed to by *envptr*. It first saves any current exceptions, and raises these exceptions after the environment pointed to by *envptr* has been set. The object pointed to by *envptr* must have been obtained by calling either **fegetenv( )** or **feholdexcept( )**.

The **<fenv.h>** header also defines the types **fenv_t** and **fexcept_t**, which represent the floating-point environment and the floating-point status flags, respectively. The macro **FE_DFL_ENV** specifies a pointer to the default floating-point environment defined at the start of program execution.

The following floating-point exception macros are defined:

FE_DIVBYZERO	**FE_INEXACT**	**FE_INVALID**
FE_OVERFLOW	**FE_UNDERFLOW**	**FE_ALL_EXCEPT**

Any combination of these macros can be stored in an **int** object by ORing them together.

18

The following rounding-direction macros are defined:

FE_DOWNWARD   **FE_TONEAREST**   **FE_TOWARDZERO**   **FE_UPWARD**

These macros indicate the method that is used to round values.

In order for the floating-point environment flags to be tested, the pragma **FENV_ACCESS** will need to be set to the on position. Whether floating-point flag access is on or off by default is implementation-defined.

The <stdint.h> Header

The C99 header **<stdint.h>** does not declare any functions, but it does define a large number of integer types and macros. The integer types are used to declare integers of known sizes or that manifest a specified trait.

Macros of the form **int*N*_t** specify an integer with *N* bits. For example, **int16_t** specifies a 16-bit signed integer. Macros of the form **uint*N*_t** specify an unsigned integer with *N* bits. For example, **uint32_t** specifies a 32-bit unsigned integer. Macros with the values 8, 16, 32, and 64 for *N* will be available in all environments that offer integers in these widths.

Macros of the form **int_least*N*_t** specify an integer with at least *N* bits. Macros of the form **uint_least*N*_t** specify an unsigned integer with at least *N* bits. Macros with the values 8, 16, 32, and 64 for *N* will be available in all environments. For example, **int_least16_t** is a valid type.

Macros of the form **int_fast*N*_t** specify the fastest integer type that has at least *N* bits. Macros of the form **uint_fast*N*_t** specify the fastest unsigned integer type that has at least *N* bits. Macros with the values 8, 16, 32, and 64 for *N* will be available in all environments. For example, **int_fast32_t** is valid in all settings.

The type **intmax_t** specifies a maximum-sized signed integer and the type **uintmax_t** specifies a maximum-sized unsigned integer.

Also defined are the **intptr_t** and **uintptr_t** types. These can be used to create integers that can hold pointers. These types are optional.

<stdint.h> defines several function-like macros that expand into constants of a specified integer type. These macros have the following general forms:

INT*N*_C(*value*)
UINT*N*_C(*value*)

where *N* is the bit width of the desired type. Each macro creates a constant that has at least *N* bits that contains the specified value.

Also defined are the following macros:

INTMAX_C(*value*)
UINTMAX_C(*value*)

These create maximum-width constants of the specified value.

Integer Format Conversion Functions

C99 adds a few specialized integer format conversion functions that allow you to convert to and from greatest-width integers. The header that supports these functions is **<inttypes.h>**, which includes **<stdint.h>**. The **<inttypes.h>** header defines one type: the structure **imaxdiv_t**, which holds the value returned by the **imaxdiv( )** function. The integer conversion functions are shown here:

Function	Description
intmax_t imaxabs(intmax_t *arg*);	Returns the absolute value of *arg*.
imaxdiv_t imaxdiv(intmax_t *numerator*, intmax_t *denominator*);	Returns an **imaxdiv_t** structure that contains the outcome of *numerator/denominator*. The quotient is the **quot** field and the remainder is in the **rem** field. Both **quot** and **rem** are of type **intmax_t**.

Function	Description
intmax_t strtoimax(const char * restrict *start*, char ** restrict *end*, int *base*);	The greatest-width integer version of **strtol( )**.
uintmax_t strtoumax(const char * restrict *start*, char ** restrict *end*, int *base*);	The greatest-width integer version of **strtoul( )**.
intmax_t wcstoimax(const char * restrict *start*, char ** restrict *end*, int *base*);	The greatest-width integer version of **wcstol( )**.
uintmax_t wcstoumax(const char * restrict *start*, char ** restrict *end*, int *base*);	The greatest-width integer version of **wcstoul( )**.

<inttypes.h> also defines many macros that can be used in calls to the **printf( )** and **scanf( )** family of functions to specify various integer conversions. The **printf( )** macros begin with **PRI** and the **scanf( )** macros begin with **SCN**. These prefixes are then followed by a conversion specifier, such as **d** or **u,** and then a type name, such as *N,* **MAX**, **PTR**, **FAST***N*, or **LEAST***N*, where *N* specifies the number of bits. Consult your compiler's documentation for a precise list of conversion macros supported.

Type-Generic Math Macros

C99 defines three versions for most mathematical functions: one for **float**, one for **double**, and one for **long double** parameters. For example, C99 defines these functions for the sine operation:

```
double sin(double arg);
float sinf(float arg);
long double sinl(long double arg);
```

The operation of all three functions is the same, except for the data upon which they operate. In all cases, the **double** version is the original function defined by C89. The **float** and **long double** versions were added by C99. The **float** versions use the **f** suffix, and **long double** versions use the **l** suffix. (Different names are required because C does not support function overloading.) By providing three different functions, C99 enables you to call the one that most precisely fits the circumstances. As described earlier in this chapter, the complex math functions also provide three versions of each function, for the same reason.

As useful as the three versions of the math and complex functions are, they are not particularly convenient. First, you have to remember to specify the proper suffix for the data you are passing. This is both tedious and error-prone. Second, if you change the type of data being passed to one of these functions during project development, you will need to remember to change the suffix as well. Again, tedious and error-prone. To address these (and other) issues, C99 defines a set of *type-generic macros* that can be used in place of the math or complex functions. These macros automatically translate into the proper function based upon the type of the argument. The type-generic macros are defined in **<tgmath.h>**, which automatically includes **<math.h>** and **<complex.h>**.

The type-generic macros use the same names as the double version of the math or complex functions to which they translate. (These are also the same names defined by C89 and C++.) Thus, the type-generic macro for **sin( )**, **sinf( )**, and **sinl( )** is **sin( )**. The type-generic macro of **csin( )**, **csinf( )**, and **csinl( )** is also **sin( )**. As explained, the proper function is called based upon the argument. For example, given

```
long double ldbl;
float complex fcmplx;
```

Then,

```
cos(ldbl)
```

translates into

```
cosl(ldbl)
```

and

```
cos(fcmplx)
```

translates into

```
ccosf(fcmplx)
```

As these examples illustrate, the use of type-generic macros offers the C programmer convenience without loss of performance, precision, or portability.

NOTE: If you are programming in C++, the type-generic macros are not needed because C++ provides overloaded versions of the math and complex functions.

The <stdbool.h> Header

C99 adds the header **<stdbool.h>,** which supports the **_Bool** data type. Although it does not define any functions, it does define these four macros:

Macro	Expands To
bool	_Bool
true	1
false	0
_ _bool_true_false_are_defined	1

The reason that C99 specified **_Bool** rather than **bool** as a keyword is that many existing C programs had already defined their own custom versions of **bool**. By defining the Boolean type as **_Bool,** C99 avoids breaking this preexisting code. The same reasoning goes for **true** and **false**. However, for new programs, it is best to include **<stdbool.h>** and then use the **bool, true**, and **false** macros. One advantage of doing so is that it allows you to create code that is compatible with C++.